IN THE IMAGE AND LIKENESS OF GOD

VLADIMIR LOSSKY

IN THE IMAGE
AND
LIKENESS OF GOD

Edited by
JOHN H. ERICKSON
and
THOMAS E. BIRD

with an Introduction by
JOHN MEYENDORFF

and a Bibliography by
THOMAS E. BIRD

ST VLADIMIR'S SEMINARY PRESS
CRESTWOOD, NEW YORK 10707
1985

First published under the title
*A L'IMAGE ET A LA RESSEMBLANCE
DE DIEU*
by Aubier Montaigne in 1967

Library of Congress Cataloging in Publication Data

Lossky, Vladimir, 1903-1958.
In the image and likeness of God.

Translation of: A l'image et à la ressemblance de Dieu.
Bibliography: p.
1. Orthodox Eastern Church—Doctrines—Addresses,
essays, lectures. 2. Theology—Collected works—20th century.
I. Erickson, John H. II. Bird, Thomas E. III. Title.
BX260.L613   1985   230'.19   85-2150
ISBN 0-913836-13-3

IN THE IMAGE
AND
LIKENESS OF GOD

ISBN 0-913836-13-3

PRINTED IN THE UNITED STATES OF AMERICA
BY
ATHENS PRINTING COMPANY
New York, NY 10018

Table of Contents

Acknowledgement

The present volume represents an English translation of *A l'image et à la ressemblance de Dieu* (Aubier-Montaigne, Paris, 1967), a collection of essays by the late Vladimir Lossky, selected and arranged by him in the present order shortly before his death. All these essays had appeared in print earlier, chiefly in diverse French journals: "L'apophase et la théologie trinitaire," Collège philosophique, Centre de Documentation Universitaire, Paris, n.d. (Chapter 1). " 'Ténèbre' et 'Lumière' dans la connaissance de Dieu," in *Ordre, Désordre, Lumière,* Collège philosophique, Vrin, Paris, 1952 (Chapter 2). "La Théologie de la Lumière chez saint Grégoire de Thessalonique," in *Dieu Vivant* 1, Editions du Seuil, Paris, 1945, pp. 94-118 (Chapter 3). "La Procession du Saint-Esprit dans la doctrine trinitaire orthodoxe," Editions Sétor, Paris, 1948 (Chapter 4). "Rédemption et déification," in *Messager de l'Exarchat du Patriarche russe en Europe occidentale* no. 15 (1953) pp. 161-170 (Chapter 5). "La notion théologique de la Personne humaine," *Messager* ...no. 24 (1955) pp. 227-235 (Chapter 6). "La Théologie de l'Image," *Messager*...no. 30-31 (1959) pp. 123-133 (Chapter 7). "La Tradition et les traditions," *Messager*...no. 30-31 (1959) pp. 101-121 (Chapter 8). "Du Troisième Attribut de l'Eglise," *Dieu Vivant* 10, Editions du Seuil, Paris, 1948, pp. 78-89 (Chapter 9). "La conscience catholique. Implications anthropologiques du dogme de l'Eglise," *Contacts*

42 (1963) pp. 76-88 (Chapter 10). "Panagia," *Messager*...
no. 4 (1950) pp. 40-50 (Chapter 11). "Domination et règne
(étude eschatologique)," *Messager*...no. 17 (1954) pp. 43-
55 (Chapter 12).

A number of these essays also have appeared in English
translations, which have served as a basis for the present
edition: "Darkness and Light in the Knowledge of God,"
trans. Edward Every, *The Eastern Churches Quarterly* 8
(1950) pp. 460-471 (Chapter 2). "The Procession of the
Holy Spirit in the Orthodox Triadology," trans. Edward
Every, *The Eastern Churches Quarterly* 7 (1948) pp. 31-53
(Chapter 4). "Redemption and Deification," trans. Edward
Every, *Sobornost* series 3, no. 2 (Winter 1947) pp. 47-56
(Chapter 5). "The Theology of the Image," trans. Joan Ford,
Sobornost series 3, no. 22 (Winter 1957-58), pp. 510-520
(Chapter 7). "Tradition and traditions," trans. G.E.H. Palmer
and E. Kadloubovsky, in *The Meaning of Icons,* Boston
Book and Art Shop, Boston, 1952, pp. 13-24 (Chapter 8).
"Concerning the Third Mark of the Church: Catholicity,"
trans. Austin Oakley, *The Christian East* 1 (1951) pp. 142-149
(Chapter 9). "Panagia," trans. Edward Every, in *The Mother
of God* (ed. E. L. Mascall), Dacre Press, London, 1949,
pp. 24-37 (Chapter 11). "Dominion and Kingship: An
Eschatological Study," trans. A.M. Allchin, *Sobornost* series 3,
no. 14 (Winter 1953) pp. 67-79 (Chapter 12). The remaining four essays have been translated by Prof. Thomas E.
Bird, Queens College, New York, to whom also is due the
bibliography of Lossky's works.

All these translations—originally made in widely differing circumstances—have been modified to a greater or lesser
degree, partly for the sake of consistency and coherence,
partly to conform more closely to the original French. Further,
since the original essays themselves are hardly homogenous,
a few formal changes also have been made, chiefly in the
citation of sources, paragraph division, *etc.,* in order to bring
of modicum of uniformity to the volume. Hopefully the
unifying theological vision of Lossky will compensate for the
formal inconsistencies which remain.

Foreword

Vladimir Lossky, one of the best Orthodox theologians of our time, died in 1958 at the age of 55, in Paris.

At the time of his death, he had published only one book: *The Mystical Theology of the Eastern Church* (original French edition, Paris, 1944; English translation, London, 1957). It was widely recognized, however, not only as a brilliant introduction to the most essential aspect of Orthodox theology, but also as an Orthodox challenge to the understanding of God-man relations which prevailed in Western Christianity. One of Lossky's most attractive traits was that his theology never reduced itself to a monologue, neither did it suggest that Orthodox truth is to be confessed in self-righteous isolation. He addressed himself to the living Christian faith of his readers, Orthodox and non-Orthodox, whom he always respected and whom, therefore, he approached in total intellectual honesty, winning the admiration even of those who disagreed with him.

Lossky's uncompromising faithfulness to Scriptural and patristic tradition, coupled with his constant concern for an articulate Orthodox witness in the West, make his works indispensable to any contemporary educated Orthodox Christian who wants to take his faith seriously and to be able to speak about it to others. We are all indebted to Lossky's guidance in this respect.

At the time of his death, however, few suspected the

remarkable number of Lossky's writings which had remained unpublished. Through the efforts of his friends and disciples, his lectures on the *Vision of God* appeared in 1961 in French, English, and German, while his monumental doctoral dissertation on Meister Eckhart was published in Paris with a foreword by Etienne Gilson, the greatest living specialist in the philosophy of the Middle Ages. Never before had theological debate between East and West gone so deep and involved such outstanding and knowledgeable people from both sides.

The present volume represents a collection of Lossky's articles, published over the years in various periodicals. Several translators in England and in America worked on translation from the original French. Their selfless dedication to Lossky's memory and to the cause of making true Orthodox theology known in the English-speaking world deserves our praise and our gratitude. Responsible editorial work on these disparate texts was accomplished, on behalf of St. Vladimir's Seminary Press, by Mr. John H. Erickson, Instructor in Canon Law and Church History at the seminary.

Under the general title *In the Image and Likeness of God*, the book contains articles on themes which Lossky also treated elsewhere: the importance of "apophatic" (or "negative") theology, the vision of divine light, and the doctrine of the procession of the Holy Spirit from the Father. As in his other writings, he brilliantly shows that these doctrines are not peripheral to the Christian Gospel, but stand at its very center and reveal the true and living God of Scriptures, always different from and transcendent to all concepts and philosophies. The particularly important point made here by Lossky concerns the relationship between the Orthodox doctrine of the Trinity and the Orthodox understanding of man: like the divine Persons of the Trinity, the human "person"—in the image of God—in its absolute uniqueness, but equally absolute "relatedness" in love to other persons, can only be understood theologically.

Equally important is Lossky's treatment of "Redemption" (Chapter 5). He shows that the Scriptural images which explain the salvation of man in Christ are not to be understood in isolation from each other. Atonement, as "satisfaction of divine justice," for example, is an image which must be contemplated in the context of the Scriptural and patristic notion of "communion" and "deification." Otherwise, understood one-sidedly, it can distort the meaning of Christ's saving work.

Thus, even as a collection of essays written in different circumstances and at different times, Lossky's *In the Image and Likeness of God* is a very consistent doctrinal statement of the Orthodox understanding of man's destiny as communion in love with the Triune God. The growing body of Orthodox theological literature in the English language will be greatly enriched through the publication of this book.

John Meyendorff

1

Apophasis and Trinitarian Theology

The negative way of the knowledge of God is an ascendant undertaking of the mind that progressively eliminates all positive attributes of the object it wishes to attain, in order to culminate finally in a kind of apprehension by supreme ignorance of Him who cannot be an object of knowledge. We can say that it is an intellectual experience of the mind's failure when confronted with something beyond the conceivable. In fact, consciousness of the failure of human understanding constitutes an element common to all that we can call *apophasis,* or negative theology, whether this apophasis remains within the limits of intellection, simply declaring the radical lack of correspondence between our mind and the reality it wishes to attain, or whether it wishes to surpass the limits of understanding, imparting to the ignorance of what God is in His inaccessible nature the value of a mystical knowledge superior to the intellect, ὑπὲρ νοῦν.

The apophatic element, as the consciousness of intellectual failure, is present in various forms in most Christian theologians (exceptions are rare). We can say as well that it is not foreign to sacred art, where failure of artistic means of expression, deliberately conspicuous in the very art of the iconographer, corresponds to the learned ignorance of the theologian. However just as iconographic "antinaturalistic" apophaticism is not iconoclasm, so also the antirationalistic negative way is not gnosimachian: it cannot result in the suppression of theological thought without detriment to the essential fact of Christianity: the incarnation of the Word, the central event of revelation, which makes iconography as well as theology possible.

The apophasis of the Old Testament, which expressed itself in the prohibition of all images, was suppressed by the fact that "the image of the substance of the Father" revealed Himself, having assumed human nature. But at the same time a new negative element entered into the canon of the art of icons, whose sacred schematism is a call to detachment, to purification of the senses, in order to contemplate the divine Person who has come in the flesh. So also for New Testament thought, that which was negative and exclusive in Judaic monotheism vanishes before the necessity of recognizing in Christ a divine Person, consubstantial with the Father. But at the same time, in order for Trinitarian theology to become possible, it was necessary for apophasis to preside at a divesting of the mind—for the mind to raise itself to the notion of a God who transcends all relation with created being, absolutely independent, in what He is, of the existence of creatures.

Despite the undeniable fact that the negative elements of a progressive divesting of the mind among Christian theologians are in general linked, in their elaboration, with the speculative technique of Middle and Neo-Platonism, it would be unfair necessarily to see in Christian apophasis a sign of the Hellenization of Christian thought. The existence of an apophatic attitude—of a going beyond everything that has a connection with created finitude—is implied in the paradox of the Christian revelation: the transcendent God becomes immanent in the world, but in the very immanence of His economy, which leads to the incarnation and to death on the cross, He reveals Himself as transcendent, as ontologically independent of all created being. This is a condition without which one could not imagine the voluntary and absolutely gratuitous character of Christ's redemptive work and, in general, of all that is the divine "economy" beginning with the creation of the world, where the expression *ex nihilo* must indicate precisely the absence of all necessity *ex parte Dei*—a certain divine contingency, if one dares to put it so, in the act of the creative will. Economy is the work of the will, while Trinitarian being belongs to the transcendent nature of God.

This is the basis of the distinction between οἰκονομία and θεολογία, which goes back to the fourth and perhaps even to the third century and which remains common to most of the Greek Fathers and to all of the Byzantine tradition. Θεολογία—which was for Origen a knowledge, a *gnosis* of God in the λόγος—means, in the fourth century, everything which concerns Trinitarian doctrine, everything which can be said of God considered in Himself, outside of His creative and redemptive economy. In order to reach this "theology" properly so-called, one therefore must go beyond the aspect under which we know God as Creator of the universe, in order to be able to extricate the notion of the Trinity from the cosmological implications proper to the "economy." To the economy in which God reveals Himself in creating the world and in becoming incarnate, we must respond by theology, confessing the transcendent nature of the Trinity in an ascent of thought which necessarily has an apophatic thrust.

Now, we cannot know God outside of the economy in which He reveals Himself. The Father reveals Himself through the Son in the Holy Spirit; and this revelation of the Trinity always remains "economic," inasmuch as outside of the grace received in the Holy Spirit, no one could recognize in Christ the Son of God and in this way be elevated to knowledge of the Father. This is the classical *via* of theognosis traced by St. Basil. "The way of knowing God goes from the one Spirit, through the one Son, to the

one Father; and inversely, essential goodness, natural
sanctity, and royal dignity flow from the Father, through
the Only-Begotten, to the Spirit," he says in his *Treatise on
the Holy Spirit.*[1] So also, every act of the divine economy
follows this descending line: from the Father, through the
Son, in the Holy Spirit. Accordingly, the way of the knowledge of God, contrary to that of the manifestation of God,
will be not a katabasis, a descent, but an anabasis, an ascent—
an ascent towards the source of all manifesting energy,
towards the "thearchy," according to the vocabulary of
Pseudo-Dionysius, or towards the monarchy of the Father,
according to the expression of St. Basil and other Greek
Fathers of the fourth century.

But on this level one must abandon the descending line
of revelation of the nature of the Father through the Son
in the Spirit, in order to be able to recognize the consubstantiality of the three hypostases beyond all manifesting
economy. It is an exclusive attachment to the economic
aspect of the Trinity, with stress on the cosmological significance of the Logos, which renders Ante-Nicene Trinitarian
theology suspect of subordinationism. To speak of God in
Himself, outside of any cosmological link, outside of any
engagement in the οίκονομία *vis-a-vis* the created world,
it is necessary for theology—the knowledge which one can
have of the consubstantial Trinity—to be the result of a way
of abstraction, of an apophatic decanting by negation of all
the attributes (Goodness, Wisdom, Life, Love, *etc.*) which
in the plane of economy can be attached to notions of the
divine hypostases[2]—of all the attributes which manifest the
divine nature in creation. What will subsist beyond all
negating or positing, is the notion of the absolute hypostatic
difference and of the equally absolute essential identity of
the Father, the Son, and the Holy Spirit. And at the same
time triadological terms and distinctions—nature, essence,
person, hypostasis—still will remain inaccurate, despite their
mathematical purity (or perhaps because of this purity),
expressing above all the deficiency of language and the

---

[1]P.G. 32, col. 153B.
[2]For example, when we say "The Son is Wisdom" or "The Spirit is Love."

failure of the mind before the mystery of the personal God who reveals Himself as transcending every relation with the created.

Every Trinitarian theology which wishes to be disengaged from cosmological implications in order to be able to ascribe some of its notions to the beyond, to God-in-Himself, ought to have recourse to apophasis. But one could ask by the same token whether all the apophasis which can be found in Christian thinkers necessarily results in a Trinitarian theology. To reply to this question, it would be necessary to examine a number of cases of the use of the negative method in theology, classifying them according to different types of Christian apophasis. I hope to be able to do this one day, but for the moment I must limit myself to two cases of the use of the negative way by Christian theologians: I shall speak here of Clement of Alexandria and of Pseudo-Dionysius.

The former, who died at the beginning of the third century, *ca.* 215 A.D., professed an economic Trinitarian doctrine, despite some efforts which he made to go beyond it. By his philosophical formation he was very close to the intellectual circles of Middle Platonism. As we shall see, the *via remotionis* of Clement remains in the framework of a Trinitarian theology of the Ante-Nicene type.

As to the second theologian—the mysterious author of the "Areopagite writings," who surely lived after Nicaea and after the great Cappadocians (probably toward the end of the fifth or at the beginning of the sixth century)— the question of the Trinitarian result of his apophasis is less clear. In fact, Dionysius' technique of apophasis, borrowed from the Plotinian tradition, seems to be necessarily linked to a conception of the One, transcendent to everything which can be named, and thus transcendent to the Trinitarian notions of Christian theology as well. This is all the more serious because it is precisely the author of the Dionysian *corpus* who, under cover of the authority of St. Paul's disciple, introduces the negative way in its most elaborate form into the theological and mystical tradition of the East and of the West.

The question concerning Dionysius which we shall have to pose, after having taken note of the triadic apophasis of Clement, can be formulated in this way: since apophasis or negative theology ought to prevail, according to Dionysius, over kataphasis or the way of affirmations, the personal characteristics affirmed by Trinitarian theology ought to be denied, just as other affirmations relative to the attributes common to the three hypostases have been. If this is the case, one can ask whether Dionysius' apophasis, which seems to go beyond the Trinity, does not imply an aspect of the divinity which would be superior to the personal God of the Judaeo-Christian tradition. And since apophasis is the common property of religious thought—since one finds it in India as well as among the Greek Neo-Platonists or later in Islamic mysticism—one would have a right to see in the Dionysian negative method the sanction of a primacy of natural mysticism over revealed theology. A mystical syncretism would then superimpose itself upon the faith of the Church, and the pagan altar of the Θεὸς ἄγνωστος would remain superior to the Christian altar of a revealed God, of Him who was preached by St. Paul on the Areopagus. Would the self-styled disciple of the apostle of the Gentiles reverse things in this way, Hellenizing the God of Christian theology? Before approaching this troubling question, let us say a few words about the use of apophasis by Clement of Alexandria.

2

As the author of the *Areopagitica* does later, Clement reserves the negative way for those who have been initiated into the Christian mysteries. It is a contemplation of God which one reaches by way of intellectual abstractions—a contemplation which, according to Clement, ought to correspond to the ἐποπτεία, the highest degree of the mysteries of Eleusis. The use of the language of the mysteries and the effort to establish parallels between the stages of Christian gnosis and those of the Hellenic mysteries are explained by Clement of Alexandria's attitude toward Greek wisdom: it profited in large measure by the revelation given to Israel, whether by simply plagiarizing Moses and the prophets or by receiving a partial revelation through the deceit of an angel, similar to the deceit of Prometheus, who stole the fire of Olympus in order to communicate it to mortals. This being said, one understands the ease with which Clement established a concordance between the Holy Scriptures and the philosophers, and especially with Plato, "the friend of Truth."

As for apophasis, it is thus implied, as we have said, in the Christian ἐποπτεία, which is the "fourth part"—the "theological" part—of Moses' "philosophy." Therefore it follows the part which Clement calls "natural contemplation" (φυσικὴ θεορία) and corresponds to what Plato himself also would class among the "great mysteries of true being" (τῶν μεγάλων ὄντως εἶναι μυστηρίων), to what Aristotle calls μετὰ τὰ φυσικὰ (*Stromata* I, 28).

The negative way by which one sets out toward contemplation is described in the fifth book of the *Stromata*. It is presented at first as a "geometric analysis." Beginning with a body, by abstraction one eliminates volume, surface and length, in order to obtain a punctual unity. Eliminating next the situation of the point in space—its τόπος—one reaches the notion of an intelligible monad, which one will strip of everything which can be attributed to intelligible beings in order to approach a certain notion of God.

The first movement of apophasis, which Clement calls analysis, is found under the same name among the representatives of Middle Platonism, in the second century. Celsus, that adversary of the Christians, in the *True Discourse* (Ἀληθὴς λόγος), which we know only by Origen's citations, places analysis, or the way of successive abstractions, among the three rational ways of the knowledge of God. Albinus spoke of it before him in the *Didaskalikos*. But the Platonizing philosophers combined the negative way ("analysis") with the positive way ("synthesis," or knowledge of the first Cause in its effects), thus obtaining a third way, that of "analogy" or eminence, in order to render "intelligible," as Celsus says, "in a certain inexpressible quality, the God who is beyond everything" (Origen, *Contra Celsum* VII, 44-45). On the other hand, Clement of Alexandria holds to analysis and keeps for the negative way its independent value. But the analysis which leads to the notion of an intelligible monad cannot suffice for him. As he says elsewhere, in the *Pedagogus* (I, 8), "God is One and beyond the One, and superior to the monad itself" (ἓν δὲ ὁ Θεός, καὶ ἐπέκεινα τοῦ ἑνὸς καὶ ὑπὲρ αὐτὴν μονάδα). Let us note that well before Clement, Philo—who had seen in the monad the Logos, the perfect image of God—declared that God is beyond the monad (*Legum allegoriae* II, 3; *De vita cont.* I, 2). For the Jewish philosopher and for the Christian theologian, the living God of Scripture transcended the intelligible monad, and the apophatic search had to pursue what lies beyond, in the dark of Sinai. This Biblical image is common to Philo and to Clement.

Here begins the second apophatic movement and, at the same time, a Trinitarian theognosis, which Clement sketches briefly in this way: "We fling ourselves (ἀπορρίψομεν) upon the majesty (μέγεθος) of Christ. If we then advance through Holiness towards the Abyss (βάθος), we shall have a kind of knowledge of God-who-contains-everything (παντοκράτωρ), knowing not what He is, but what He is not" (οὐχ ὁ ἐστιν, ὁ δὲ μὴ ἐστιν γνωρίσαντες, —*Stromata* V, 11). Nonetheless, it seems that Clement remains on the level of speculation when he proposes to know God in what He is not. His apophasis has nothing ecstatic about it. It is not a way of mystical union.

Reaching the summit of things intelligible—ἐπὶ τὴν κορυφὴν τῶν νοητῶν—one notices with Plato that, if it is difficult to find God, it is impossible to express Him (*Timaeus* 28 c). Having been informed of Moses' ascent of Sinai, Plato knew that "holy theory" had permitted the legislator of the Jews to reach the intelligible summits which are the "region of God" (χῶρα τοῦ Θεοῦ), difficult to find. Plato also calls it the "region of the Ideas" (plagiarizing a little from Moses, according to Clement), having learned from Moses that God is a region, because he contains every-

thing (ὡς τῶν ἁπάντων καὶ τῶν ὅλων πεφιεκτικόν).
Evidently this is a Plato somewhat Aristotelianized, the
Plato of Middle Platonism. As with Albinus, the ideas are
the thoughts of God and do not subsist outside of Him,
even though they constitute, so to speak, the divine "second
principle." For Clement of Alexandria, this second principle
is called the majesty or grandeur of Christ, of Christ-the-
Logos, place of the ideas. It is necessary to surpass it in
order to go "by Sanctity" toward the Abyss of the Father.
Sanctity means, without any doubt, the Holy Spirit; for
further on Clement makes it clear that the Father cannot be
recognized except by divine grace and by the Word who is
near to Him (V, 12), and that all intellectual investigation
remains "formless and blind" without the grace of the
knowledge which comes from the Father through the Son.

We would expect Plato to give way to Moses—that the
philosopher, after having spoken of transcendent Good and
of the "region of the Ideas," would be silent at last before
the revelation of the living God, who through the Son confers
the grace of knowledge, the gift of Christian gnosis. Indeed
Plato is silent for a moment and permits St. John to speak.
John, who according to Clement is one of the greatest
gnostics (along with James, Peter and Paul), would say
that no one has ever seen God, except the only Son who is
in the bosom of the Father. It is he who manifests God
to us. Clement would explain that the bosom (κόλπος)
is the Abyss, "the invisible and inexpressible" (τὸ ἀόρατον
καὶ ἄρρητον) which Moses had encountered in the shadow,
beyond the "Majesty of Christ," as that which enveloped
him; for the Father-Pantokrator contains all, He Himself
being contained by nothing. He is therefore inaccessible and
unlimited (ἀνέφικτος καὶ ἀπέραντος). This is the reason
for the transcendence and the unknowability of the Father,
who, in contrast to the Son, is called the "Unbegotten."
Since there is nothing in the order of knowledge which can
be anterior to the notion of the unbegotten God, demon-
strative science which proceeds from anterior and more
evident truths is not of any assistance here and must give

way to the unfruitful and unformed apophasis of a despairing agnosticism.

But here Plato again picks up the conversation in order to help the Christian theologian out of a difficulty, by reminding him discreetly that, if it is impossible to know God through our own powers, there is always the resource of grace, that "God-given virtue" of which he had spoken in the *Meno*—virtue which is sent by divine fate, by the Θεία μοῖρα. Grace, for Clement, is above all a new aptitude for knowing, a ἕξις γνωστική which obtains for the perfect Christian, for the gnostic (today one would say for the "spiritual" or "contemplative"), eternal contemplation (ἀΐδιος θεορία), *i.e.* the capacity for seeing God-Pantokrator face to face (V, 11). This is the limit of apophasis for Clement of Alexandria. Its object is the transcendence of the Father. After having conducted the intelligence towards a complete aporia before the transcendent abyss, negative investigation is suppressed by the grace which the Father sends through the Son in "Sanctity."

If Clement's apophasis is triadic, to the extent that it implies the notion of three Persons who are not suppressed by the *via remotionis,* nonetheless it is determined only by the hypostasis of the Father, the only truly transcendent hypostasis in this view of the "economic Trinity," so close to the schemes of Middle Platonism. The notion of the hypostasis of the Father is so close to that of the divine essence that it is almost impossible to dissociate them. The Father is limitless (ἀπέραντος), and the expression "Abyss of the Father" proclaims without a doubt the infinity of essence which belongs to Him, which is of the essence of the "unbegotten God" as opposed to the Logos. For while the Logos becomes the "begotten" Son in identity (ἐν ταὐτότητι—without doubt, in essential identity), He acquires His personal character "by delimitation and not by essence" (κατὰ περιγραφὴν καὶ οὐ κατ' οὐσίαν—*Excerpta ex Theodoto* c. 19). There is a manifest effort here to go beyond the economic aspect in order to express the essential identity of the Son with the transcendent and infinite Father, which without doubt excludes from Clement's thought all Trinitarian subordinationism. But, in the order of theognosis, the opposition between the knowable hypostasis of the Son and the unknowability of the Father always subsists. It is conditioned by the triadological ambiguity which results from opposing the limitless Unbegotten to the "limited" Person of the begotten Son. After its first movement, that of analysis, Clement's apophasis aims solely at the unknowability of the Father: the two other hypostases —the Son and "Holiness" (the Holy Spirit, not distinguished from grace and rather eclipsed)—play the role of mystagogues, suppressing natural ignorance by the gnosis which they give of the transcendent Being of the Father. This apophasis can be called triadic, since it does not go beyond the notion of the personal God in three hypostases, but it is not triadological, for, having as its object the transcendence of the Father-Pantokrator, this negative way does nothing to transpose Trinitarian notions into the beyond. Clement's Trinitarian thought has nothing of θεολογία, in the sense which the Fathers of the fourth century will impart to the term. Rather, all its merits lie in the economic perspective which is its own.

3

The author of *Mystical Theology* belongs to a totally different epoch, subsequent to the great "Trinitarian century." The ambiguities of Clement of Alexandria and even the imprecisions of a St. Athanasius have been ousted from the language of theology by the terminological labors of the three Cappadocians. The "abyss of the Father" has become, in the terminology of Gregory of Nazianzus, "the ocean of undefined and undetermined essence" (*Or.* 38, *In theophania*)—an expression which will be taken up again and propagated by St. John of Damascus, from whom it will later pass into Scholastic Latin (*pelagus essentiae infinitae*) and will be cited by Thomas Aquinas and other theologians. The three hypostases extend to the infinity of essence, and Gregory of Nazianzus himself speaks of "the infinite connaturality of the Infinite Three" (*Or.* 40, *In sanctum baptisma*). Thus infinity, which for Clement of Alexandria was the reason for the transcendence and the unknowability of the Father, becomes an attribute of the common nature of the Three. The three hypostases, decanted, stripped of all economic attribution, maintain only the relative properties of paternity, filiation, and procession, necessary only to make theological discourse possible. But then, in order to be liberated from the logical category of relation, which permits of limitation due to opposition, Trinitarian theology comes to be expressed antinomically. "They are One distinctly and distinct conjointly, somewhat paradoxical as that formula may be," Gregory of Nazianzus says (*Or.* 23, 8, *De pace*); and St. Basil strives to show that the Trinity is not a matter of arithmetic numbers (*De Spiritu Sancto* c. 18). A movement of apophasis therefore accompanies the Trinitarian theology of the Cappadocians and, in the last analysis, deconceptualizes the concepts which are ascribed to the mystery of a personal God in His transcendent nature.

It is time to ask whether Dionysius' apophasis can be considered a supreme θεολογία—whether it transfers beyond the knowable the Trinity of divine Persons—or whether it goes beyond this in its negative rush toward a superessential identity which, at the same time, would be a suprapersonal Unity. If this is the case, the author of *Mystical Theology* was a docile instrument in an offensive return of Platonism, which he introduced in its Plotinian form at the very heart of Christian theology.

Certainly there is much in common between the mystical theology of Dionysius and Plotinian apophasis, such as is described in the sixth *Ennead*. The same progressive stripping away is pursued on the way to mystical union. I am prepared here to recognize the appropriateness of the reproach that has been made against me: that I have somewhat hardened the difference between Plotinus and Dionysius in that which concerns the properly mystical element of their apophasis, *i.e.* the unitive way as such.[3] Certainly the unitive

---

[3]M. de Gandillac, *La Sagesse de Plotin* (Paris, 1952) p. xvii n. 3.

way in Dionysius is dominated by the notion of Unity—of the One who is contrary to all otherness from which one must be liberated in order to enter into union with "Him who is beyond everything" (*De mystica theologia* 1, 1). But one might ask if the notion of Him to whom one is united does not surpass the notion of the Unity to which the mystical ascent of the human subject aspires. It is difficult to dissociate the mystical and unitive aspect of Dionysian apophasis from its dialectical structure. Nevertheless we are going to examine only this last aspect, the properly intellectual side of the *via remotionis*, in order to be able to reply to the question: in what measure does the apophasis of Pseudo-Dionysius remain faithful to the exigencies of a Trinitarian theology?

The Περὶ μυστικῆς θεολογίας is a treatise on the negative way. It also occupies first place in the plan which Dionysius himself gives to the ensemble of his treatises on the knowledge of God. Among these works, he cites two unknown treatises; one may ask whether these have been lost, or whether they are simply a fiction. With the treatise on *Divine Names,* which has come down to us, they ought to form the "kataphatic," or affirmative group of studies. The most voluminous of the three would have been the study of *Symbolic Theology,* which was supposed to have examined the application of sensible images to God and to have interpreted Biblical anthropomorphisms. The treatise on *Divine Names,* which must precede it, is more concise, for it has as its object the intelligible attributions, such as Good, Being, Life, Wisdom, Power of God, *etc.,* which are less numerous than the sensible images. Finally, the briefest of the kataphatic treatises, the first of the three (for the affirmative way descends from superior notions), bears the title *On Hypotyposes* or *Outlines of Theology.* In this treatise, says Dionysius, "We have celebrated the principal affirmations of affirmative theology, showing in what sense the excellent nature of God is called one, in what sense it is called trine, what in it can be called Paternity and Filiation, what theology means when it speaks of the Spirit" (*De myst. theol.,* 5). There is no doubt that the *Theological*

Hypotyposes (if this treatise ever existed) would have had as its object Trinitarian properties, since the following treatises were devoted principally to the study of the attributes of the nature common to the three Persons. The treatise on *Mystical Theology* goes beyond the *Theological Hypotyposes* in its supreme concision and inclines towards the cessation of all speech and all thought, in order to celebrate by silence Him who cannot be known except by unknowing. It seems, therefore, that the bounds of Trinitarian theology ought finally to be swept away by apophasis, rather than be found again in the beyond, towards which the negative way makes us progressively ascend.

In fact, after enumerating—while denying them—the intelligible attributes, the apophatic ascent in Dionysius' mystical theology does not stop at the properties-relations of the divine Persons: transcendent Divinity is neither Filiation nor Paternity nor anything which is accessible to our understanding (*De myst. theol.*, 5). However, one should not rush to draw conclusions about the supratrinitarian consequences of Dionysian apophasis. This would be to misunderstand the dialectic which governs the game of negations and affirmations. One can define it as an intellectual discipline of the non-opposition of opposites—a discipline which is proper for all discourse about true transcendence, the transcendence which remains "unimaginable" for non-Christians (*Ibid.* 1, 5). This is not the way of eminence, whose outlines can be found in Middle Platonism—the way towards which Thomas Aquinas wished to channel the Areopagite's apophasis in order to restore an affirmed signification to God, denying merely the human mode of signifying Him. Dionysius' negations triumph over affirmations; and, if the author of *Divine Names* allows the formation of superlatives in ὑπερ-, these names do not signify the transcendent nature in itself but its processions *ad extra* (πρόοδοι) or "virtues" (δυνάμεις), in the measure that these transcend all created participations and remain united to the "Superessence," from which they are ineffably distinguished. The non-opposition of negative and positive in "theology" properly so-called thus implies, in the doctrine of attributes, the idea of unity of the transcendent nature which prevails over distinctions, over the διακρίσεις of manifesting energies, without suppressing, for all that, their real character. The principle of preeminence of negations over affirmations therefore remains confirmed at the level of *Divine Names*. The transcendent God of θεολογία becomes more and more immanent, so to speak, in his economy, by which "the energies descend to us," according to the expression of the great Cappadocians, Platonized by Dionysius, who speaks of δυνάμεις. But in order to speak of the "Superessence," it is necessary, by means of apophasis, to go beyond economic manifestations and to enter Trinitarian theology, which is the summit of kataphasis according to the plan of Dionysian theognosis.

The few bits of information which one finds in the *corpus* about what Dionysius' triadological treatise [*Theological Hypotyposes*] should be like allows us to affirm that the rule of non-opposition, which presides over utilization of apophasis, excludes every attempt to reduce the Trinity of hypostases to a primordial, transpersonal Unity. In the last chapter of *Divine Names,* devoted to the name of the One, Dionysius declares that "The transcendent Deity is celebrated at the same time both as Unity and as Trinity. In fact, He is not knowable either by us or by any other kind of being, whether as Unity or as Trinity" (*De div. nom.* 13, 3). Denied in their opposition, the two terms must be understood together, in a sort of σύνοψις or simultaneous vision which identifies by distinguishing. And Dionysius continues: "In order to celebrate in all truth that which in it is more than united, as well as the divine fecundity, we attribute by faith the name of Unity and that of Trinity to Him who is above all names and who transcends superessentially all that exists" (*Ibid.*). The principle of "divine fecundity" (τὸ θεογόνον) is upheld at the same level as "super-unity," which suggests the distinction between nature and hypostases without submitting the Trinity to Unity, contrary to what has been said of processions *ad extra,* where the διακρίσεις were submitted to the ἑνώσεις.

At the beginning of this same treatise, after having reproduced almost literally the negative conclusion of the first hypothesis of the *Parmenides* (*De div. nom.* 1, 5; *Parm.* 142a), Dionysius asks himself how one can speak of divine names in the face of this radical unknowability. Then, referring to his triadological treatise (perhaps fictitious), he adds: "As I have already said in my *Hypotyposes,* the Unknowable, the Superessential, the Good-in-itself, He who is—I mean the *triadic Henad* [or Unitrinity]⁴—cannot be attained either in words or in thought" (*De div. nom.* 1, 5). Thus true transcendence, which Christians alone can confess, belongs to the "Unitrinity," and this contradictory term must express the "synopsis" of the One and the Three, the object of *Mystical Theology.*

One could not attain the transcendent Trinity of θεολο-γία through the notion of "opposed relation." Let us not forget that, if the God of the philosophers is not the living God, the God of the theologians is such only by halves, as long as this last step has not been taken. That is why we have seen the terms of Paternity and Filiation denied by the apophasis of *Mystical Theology*—denied by virtue of the principle of non-opposition, which dominates this supreme stage of Dionysian theognosis. How can the two, the Father and the Son, be opposed, when one would need to find an opposition impossible for human logic, the opposition of the Three, in order truly to explain the mystery of a personal God? Since we cannot oppose the Three, absolutely different in their absolute identity, the logic of opposition as well as use of arithmetic numbers must remain on this side of the consubstantial Trinity. Is the Triad not an exclusion of the Dyad, a surpassing of the principle of the opposition of two relative terms? In fact, it suggests to us a distinction more radical than that of two opposites: an *absolute* difference, which can only be personal, proper to the three divine Hypostases, "united by distinction and distinct by Union" (*De div. nom.* 2, 4). The author of the *corpus* here seems to be strictly dependent on the Cappadocians' handling of

---

⁴Τὴν τριαδικὴν ἐνάδα. M. de Gandillac (*op. cit.* p. 73) has translated this term most felicitously as "Unitrinity."

the Trinitarian problem.[5]

The same principle of triadic non-opposition was formulated "hermetically" by Gregory of Nazianzus with the image of the Monad which is set in motion in order to surpass the Dyad and to come to rest at the Triad (*Or.* 23, 8; *Or.* 29, 2). A tributary of the same Trinitarian conceptions, Dionysius finds at the end of his theognosis the principle of personal non-opposition, the root of the unknowability of the transcendent God-Trinity, the object of "theology" properly so-called, which can only be "mystical."

In concluding our study of the negative method and Trinitarian theology, we can state that in the two cases briefly examined here, apophasis has a very different character. Determined by the transcendence of the Father-Pantokrator in Clement of Alexandria, it does not succeed in liberating Trinitarian theology from the cosmological implications of economy. What the Alexandrian *didascalus* was not able to express was later accomplished by "the capable unknown," who, after the Cappadocians, delivers the final blow to the triadic schemes of the Platonic tradition, by identifying the unknowable God of the negative way with the "Unitrinity" of Christian transcendence.

The apophasis of *Mystical Theology* is not determined by the principle of absolute identity of the transcendent One to Being. The dialectic of affirmations and non-opposed negations, applied to Trinitarian dogma, makes it necessary to go beyond the One opposed to the Other. It is not the impersonal Monad, but the "superessential and more-than-divine Triad" that the author of *Mystical Theology* invokes at the beginning of his treatise, in order that It direct "even beyond unknowing" and towards the way of union with triune Divinity, the theologian in search of the God of Christian revelation, who transcends the opposition between the transcendent and the immanent, since He is beyond all affirmation and all negation.

---

[5]This dependance, shown by Fr. Ceslas Péra, gives his article "Denys le Mystique et la Théomachia," *Révue des sciences philosophiques et théologiques* 25 (1936) pp. 47-50, its great worth.

2

Darkness and Light in the Knowledge of God

In dealing with the knowledge of God, it is impossible to talk about darkness without talking about light simultaneously. But in most religions, and also in all philosophical systems animated by a religious spirit, the place attributed to light is so important that it is almost possible to identify knowledge of God with light, though "light" sometimes is to be taken in the sense of a metaphor and sometimes is understood in a real sense as a datum of religious experience. Thus as we consider the question of darkness in relation to knowledge of God in the thought of the patristic age, we shall be dealing with darkness in connection with light; we shall be raising the question as to the sense in which the two contradictory terms, darkness and light, could refer to God in the works of some of the theologians and spiritual writers of the first centuries of Christianity.

First of all, how could a Christian thinker ascribe to God anything that might be "darkness" when all the writers of Holy Scripture agree in opposing all that is "darkness" to

31

God, who is "light"? St. John announces as a revelation received from Christ Himself that "God is Light and in Him is no Darkness at all" (I John 1:5). The world which refuses to receive the divine revelation and is enclosed in its own self-sufficiency is opposed to the light and is seen as "darkness"; and all that will be definitively separated from God is destined for "the outer darkness" (σκότος τὸ ἐξότερον) where no communion with God is possible any longer. If God is known as light, the loss of this knowledge is darkness; and, since eternal life consists in "knowing the Father and His Son Jesus Christ," absence of knowledge of God ends in the darkness of Hell. Light, whether interpreted in an allegorical or in a real sense, will then always accompany communion with God, whereas the dark reality can overrun human consciousness only when human consciousness dwells on the borders of eternal death and final separation from God. Thus the obvious sense of darkness seems to be, above all, pejorative. It is the absence of God (1) in the order of knowledge (ignorance of divine things and atheism), (2) in the moral order (hostility to all that comes from God), and (3) in the ontological order, where darkness is no longer to be taken metaphorically (the condition of all beings in a state of definitive separation from God).

However this may be, it is possible for darkness to be taken in a different sense which, in relation to knowledge of God, is not always pejorative or privative. The word can signify the presence of God as well as His absence. The meaning of darkness as an accompanying condition of the divine presence has its source in the Bible. It is enough here to remember Psalm 17 (18), "He made darkness His covering around Him," and, above all, the nineteenth and twentieth chapters of Exodus, where Moses meets God in the darkness which covered the summit of Mount Sinai. The darkness of Sinai may be variously interpreted, but it is always connected with the knowledge of God, whose allegorical expression, for many Christian exegetes, is the ascent of Moses. But even before specifically Christian exegesis, Philo of Alexandria interpreted the darkness of Exodus in the same sense, as a condition of the knowledge of God.

There is an ambiguity in the idea of darkness in the works of Philo. It seems possible to distinguish two meanings of the term: one is objective, and makes darkness (γνόφος) a sensible symbol for expressing the unknowability of the divine essence, which transcends every creature; the other is subjective, where darkness signifies the "formless and blind search" of the knowing subject, incapable of grasping God.

Both these Philonistic meanings of darkness appear again in the works of Clement of Alexandria, who makes use of the very expressions employed by Philo in order to emphasize the absolute transcendence of God, inaccessible to all intellectual searching. However in the works of Clement, the image of the darkness of Sinai seems to stand less for the unknowability of the transcendent God than for the ignorance about God proper to human reason when left to its own natural resources. Clement's negative way (which corresponds to the ascent of Moses) does not end in the sort of unknowing which would have the value of knowing in relation to the Unknowable. The "way of analysis," as Clement calls it, leads only to the summit of things intelligible, of things which can be understood. This summit is the "region" (χῶρα) of God, which Plato calls "the region of the Ideas"—for, in Clement's mind, there is no doubt that Plato has read the Bible; thus he must have learned from Moses that God is a "region," in that He contains all.[1] It is beyond the summit of Sinai, beyond the summit of intelligible things, that ignorance begins, for Moses enters into the darkness to stand face to face with God. This darkness has a subjective and pejorative meaning: it signifies "the unbelief and ignorance of the multitude that cannot know God." "Among men one cannot learn things concerning God." That is why Moses speaks to God in the darkness of human ignorance, "formless and blind," demanding of God that He should show Himself to him. This is a confession of faith in a personal God, transcending all human knowledge and unable to be known unless He reveals Himself by the power which comes from Him, "by

---

[1] Cf. p. 20 above.

the grace and the word which is with God." All γνῶσις comes from God through His Son (*Strom.* V, 11); it is a grace which He gives. But to attain it, by going beyond the summit of intelligible things, we must make the leap of faith, for, as Clement puts it, "we fling ourselves (ἀπορρίψομεν) upon the majesty of Christ" (*ibid.*). For indeed, St. John teaches us (John 1:18) that "no one has ever seen God; the only Son, who is in the bosom of the Father, He has made Him known." It is through the Son that we are liberated from the dark shadows of human ignorance, to receive the light of gnosis and "to apprehend the unknowable" (τὸ ἄγνωστον νοεῖν—*Strom.* V, 12). But here it appears that the Christian "gnostic," when once liberated from the darkness of his subjective ignorance, comes to a different kind of ignorance, which is not to be taken in a pejorative sense. For it Clement uses another term than "darkness" (γνόφος or σκότος). He calls it the "abyss" (βάθος), a term borrowed from the Valentinian gnostics, which he uses to signify the transcendence of the Father. Clement indeed tells us that, starting from "the majesty of Christ" one proceeds "through holiness" towards the abyss of God-who-contains-all (παντοκράτωρ), "knowing God not in what He is but in what He is not" (*Strom.* V, 11). It is "the bosom of the Father" that contains the Logos, the Father Himself being the unengendered God, all-containing without being contained or circumscribed by any other. Thus even in His revelation by grace and by the Son, God remains unknowable, the abyss that we contemplate face to face, knowing Him in what He is not. Apophasis here appears anew, this time in relation to an abyss which is the Father, in order to make us aware of His radical transcendence.

Here we are dealing with an economic aspect of the Trinity: the Father who reveals Himself through the Son and the Holy Spirit (or rather, to be faithful to Clement's terminology, through the Logos and Grace), remaining throughout transcendent to him who contemplates the invisible. The line of demarcation passes between the abyss of the Father and the Son who reveals Him. Objective

ignorance of God (which other writers call "darkness")
is indicated in the writings of Clement through the character
of "abyss" which he attributes to the essence of the Father.
This implies in gnosis itself—which is the perfection of the
Christian, according to Clement—a negative element, corresponding to a comprehension of God's transcendence. However this aspect of the matter is insufficiently developed by
Clement of Alexandria, and we have to wait until Gregory
of Nyssa to find a notion of ignorance and darkness as a
means of knowing the transcendent God.

In the works of Origen the terminology of night in
relation to the knowledge of God is entirely absent. The
darkness of Sinai plays no vital role: it is mainly a symbol
of the weakness of human intelligence, fettered by the
limiting conditions of bodily life (*Contra Celsum* VI, 17);
it is an imperfection, a natural obstacle that ought to be
overcome in intellectual contemplation. Fr. Daniélou has
rightly said in his book on Origen that the mysticism of
Origen is "a mysticism of light" and that this "is perhaps
his limitation. . . . Origen stops in the realm of gnosis which
Gregory will pass beyond."[2]

The limitations of this mysticism of light are most evident
in Evagrius Ponticus, the monk of Skete, who represents the
Origenist tradition in spirituality. In the writings of this
Post-Nicene author (end of the fourth century) we are
no longer dealing with knowledge of the transcendent Father
through the intermediary of the Logos, as in Clement and
Origen. Evagrius talks about an "essential gnosis" due to an
enlightening act of the Holy Trinity. At the summit of contemplation, in what Evagrius calls "pure prayer," the human
νοῦς sees the light of the Trinity which deifies it. In the
act of contemplating God, the human intelligence compre-
hends itself, it sees itself in seeing Him. This perception
is simultaneous: in knowing God, the νοῦς knows itself as
the place of God's presence, as a receptacle for the light
of the Trinity; it then sees itself as transparent as the sap-

[2]*Origène* (Paris, 1948) pp. 291, 296.

phire and the sky. This is the "naked intellect" (νοῦς γυμνός), the intellect which is "fulfilled in the vision of itself and which has merited participation in the contemplation of the Holy Trinity" (*Cent.* III, 6).

This doctrine, which is not found in the same form in the works of Origen, may be compared to the idea of θεορία in the writings of St. Gregory of Nyssa, where God is contemplated in the mirror of the soul. But in Evagrius this vision of the light of God in the deified νοῦς is the summit, the final end which knows nothing transcending it. As in Origen, there is no going out of oneself "beyond the νοῦς," nor is there any divine darkness or knowing through unknowing. We know only one passage where Evagrius says "Blessed is he that has descended into infinite ignorance" (Μακάριος ὁ φθάσας εἰς τὴν ἀπέραντον ἀγνωσίαν— *Cent.* III, 88). The word "descended" (φθάσας) would be astonishing if the matter in hand were really an ecstatic state superior to that of the contemplation of the light of the Trinity in the soul. In fact, as Fr. Hausherr has shown,[3] Evagrius means by ἀπέραντος ἀγνωσία—"infinite ignorance"—the exclusion from the mind of all knowledge except knowledge of God. In the act of contemplating the Trinity, the "naked intellect" becomes infinitely ignorant of all that is inferior to this divine gnosis. We may recall St. Gregory of Nazianzus, whom Evagrius often calls his teacher. For him also the darkness of Sinai into which Moses went to meet God does not mean a mode of communion with God superior to θεορία: γνόφος, for St. Gregory of Nazianzus, is the ignorance of the multitude about God (*Or.* 28, 15); light is superior to darkness. For Evagrius, the νοῦς need not go out of itself, beyond itself, because by its very nature the νοῦς is a receiver of divine light. When once it has reached its pure state, the νοῦς in seeing itself sees God, who fills it with His light. The receptivity of the νοῦς in the contemplation of the Trinity is part of its nature: the νοῦς is perfectly νοῦς only in the measure in which it contemplates God. Here we find again the basic idea of

---

[3]"Ignorance infinie," *Orientalia Christiana Periodica* 2 (1936) pp. 351-62.

Origen's thought, his Platonistic intellectualism, the close
relationship between the intelligible and the divine, between
the human νοῦς, in God's image, and the Trinity. The
contemplation of the Holy Trinity is uniform: it has no
degrees. Here also the thought of Evagrius differs from
that of St. Gregory of Nyssa, for whom union with God is
an infinite progress of the soul.

In the writings of Gregory of Nyssa, darkness is an
allegorization of the darkness of Exodus in combination
with the image of night in the Song of Songs. It signifies
that "the closer the spirit comes to contemplation, the more
it sees that the divine nature is invisible. The true knowledge
of Him whom it seeks lies in understanding that seeing
consists in not seeing" (*Vita Moys.*). If in Origen and
Evagrius darkness is a hindrance which separates us from
the light of the Trinity, it seems that for Gregory of Nyssa,
the cloud of Sinai represents, on the contrary, a mode of
communion with God which is more perfect and more
advanced than the luminous vision in which God manifested
Himself to Moses at the beginning of his way, in the burning
bush. If God appears first as light and then as darkness,
this means for Gregory that of the divine essence there is
no vision, and that union with God is a way surpassing
vision or ϑεορία, going beyond intelligence to where knowledge vanishes and only love remains—or, rather, to where
gnosis becomes ἀγάπη. Desiring God more and more, the
soul grows without ceasing, going beyond herself and outside herself; and in the measure in which she unites herself
more and more to God, her love becomes more ardent and
insatiable. Thus the Bride of the Song of Songs awaits her
Bridegroom in the awareness that the union will never have
an end, that ascent in God has no limit, that beatitude is
an infinite progress.

Despite the impression that an experience of life is
being described, which we like H.-Ch. Puech have in reading
the passages in Gregory of Nyssa which describe the infinite
nocturnal course through which created being attains con-

sciousness of the infinity of union with God,[4] the question may be raised whether in these passages the notion of darkness represents a concrete religious experience beyond the realm of light, or whether it is not better to see in darkness the metaphorical expression of a dogmatic fact—the fact of the absolute transcendence of the divine nature. In any case the resemblances sometimes traced between the darkness of the patristic tradition and the dark night of the mysticism of John of the Cross seem to be rather artificial, in spite of the' references to "Dionysius" in the works of the great Spanish contemplative. In John of the Cross, the mystic night stands for a passive state, in which the soul finds itself without any luminous communication. In Gregory of Nyssa, on the contrary, the darkness signifying the radical unknowability of the divine essence seems to act as a stimulus to an unchecked passage towards union, in which created being seeks to pass beyond itself, opening itself infinitely to deifying participation without ever being satiated.

Here the object of vision is the divine light contemplated "in the pure atmosphere of the heart"—the kingdom of heaven within us. But in Gregory of Nyssa, contrary to Evagrius, it is not the vision of God in the νοῦς which procures beatitude by showing the "connaturality" of the human spirit with God. It is precisely consciousness of the radical lack of correspondence between the creature and God which makes union preferable to knowledge. "Beatitude consists not in knowing something about God but in having Him within us," says Gregory (*On the Beatitudes* Hom. 6). It is union with God that conditions knowledge of God, and not vice versa. The infinite and never completed character of this union with the transcendent God is signified by darkness, which seems to be, for St. Gregory of Nyssa, a metaphor whose purpose is to remind us of a dogmatic fact.

This is even clearer in Pseudo-Dionysius, as H.-Ch. Puech has well shown.[5] It is enough to read the first *Letter* of Dionysius, an appendix to his treatise on *Mystical Theology,*

---

[4] "La ténèbre mystique chez le Ps. Denys l'Aréopagite et dans la tradition patristique," *Études Carmélitaines* 23.2 (1938) pp. 33-53.
[5] *Ibid.*

in order to have to recognize that here we are concerned less with mystical experience of ecstacy than with dogmatic speculation about the conditions in which the knowledge of God is possible—speculation presented in the form of a dialectic of light and darkness, knowledge and ignorance, affirmation and negation.

"Darkness," says Dionysius, "becomes invisible in light and above all in abundant light. Knowledge purges ignorance, and above all abundant knowledge. If thou shalt think of this not in the sense of something being taken away, but in the sense of something being lifted up, thou shalt be able to affirm this, which is more true than very truth: ignorance concerning God remains hidden from those who have positive light and knowledge of things which are. Indeed, the transcendent darkness of God allows itself to be concealed by all that is light, but it also throws into the shadow all that is knowledge. . . If it happened that, in seeing God, one were to understand what he saw, that would mean that he was not seeing God in Himself, but only something that is knowable that belongs to Him. For in Himself, He surpasses all understanding and all essence; He exists in a manner above essence and is known beyond all understanding only inasmuch as He is totally unknown and does not exist at all. And it is this perfect lack of knowledge, taken in the best sense of the word, which is the knowledge of Him who surpasses all that can be known."

This dialectical movement in which contrasted light and darkness are mutually exclusive can be expressed in an inverse manner, as it is, for example, in one passage from *Divine Names* (4, 5), where light and knowledge are placed above darkness. Here God appears as the light which frees us from all darkness and ignorance—these understood in this passage in a subjective and privative sense. In that He manifests Himself and can be contemplated, God is light; and if divine darkness enters into Dionysius' line of thought concerning the conditions in which knowledge of God is possible, this is not in order to indicate a new mode of ecstatic experience which would necessitate the suppression of all mysticism of light, but rather to supply this mysticism of light with a necessary dogmatic corrective.

The fifth *Letter* begins by saying: "The divine darkness is the inaccessible light (ἀπρόσιτον τὸ φῶς) where God dwells." If God is light, this light has neither kinship nor connaturality with the νοῦς, with the human spirit. God by His very nature remains transcendent, even in the immanence of His manifestation. Hence the necessity that created being should continually pass beyond itself—the necessity of "union beyond the νοῦς," which is not depersonalization but an opening of the human person to communion with uncreated reality. Basically this is the same idea of infinite progress that one finds in the thought of Gregory of Nyssa, except that the author of the Areopagitic writings puts it in different terms. If infinite passage through the night does not appear here, that is because Dionysius made no use of the imagery of the Song of Songs and the theme of mystical marriage remained foreign to him. He confined himself to the allegorization of Moses' ascent of Sinai, which could best be adapted to his purpose: that of transforming the apophasis of the Platonists into an expression of the absolute transcendence of the divine essence— something that Clement did not know how to do. God is not light, says Dionysius at the end of *Mystical Theology,* but neither is He darkness. He transcends both affirmation and negation. Christian transcendence is beyond all opposition. And in the last analysis, it goes beyond the opposition between transcendence and immanence.

Here, however, we are in the presence not of the impersonal One of Plotinus, but of the superessence of the Trinity, which is "union and distinction in Union and ineffable Substance" (*De div. nom.* 2, 5). God is transcendent in His essence—in the darkness which is "His covering around Him" (or, if you will, in His "inaccessible light")— but God proceeds outside His essence. He continually bursts forth from this hiding-place, and this bursting forth, these "processions" or δυνάμεις, are a mode of existing in which the Divinity can communicate itself to created beings: they are an immanent aspect of God, His manifesting descent, "the superessential ray of the divine darkness" (*De myst. theol.* 1, 3). This image gives simultaneous expression to the two distinct but inseparable aspects of God: immanence, in that the Divinity proceeds in the δυνάμεις like light ("ray") and transcendence ("darkness"), in that it remains inaccessible in its essence.

Here we recognize the distinction between the unknowable οὐσία and the manifesting energies, according to which the divine names are formed—a distinction suggested in the works of St. Basil and St. Gregory of Nyssa. With Pseudo-Dionysius it is the pivotal point of all his theological thought. If this doctrine, developed above all in the second chapter of *Divine Names,* is neglected (and this too often happens), the central nerve of Dionysius' thought will not be perceived and, inevitably, he will be interpreted in the sense of the Neo-Platonism to which he is clearly opposed. The δυνάμεις (or energies) of Dionysius are not diminished emanations of the divine nature, which become weaker as they descend from their starting point in the unity of this nature until they reach the lowest degrees of created being. Dionysius insists on the integrity of the divine processions on each level of participation. That is why he often speaks of the processions in the singular, calling them "the ray." The Divinity is fully manifested and entirely present in the δυνάμεις, but created beings participate therein according to the proportion or analogy proper to each; whence arises the hierarchical arrangement of the universe, which unfolds according to the decreasing degrees of participation in, and analogy to the Divinity among created beings.[6] The hierarchy of Dionysius does not in any way limit the fulness of union. At each step of the ladder, union with God is fully realized, but this fulness is not uniform: it is personal. In the analogy of each created nature, there is an encounter and a synergy

---

[6]See our article "La notion des 'Analogies' chez Denys le pseudo-Aréopagite," *Archives d'histoire doctrinale et littéraire du Moyen-Age* 5 (1930) pp. 279-309. See also the more recent work of R. Roques, "La notion de hiérarchie selon le Pseudo-Denys," *Archives d'histoire doctrinale et littéraire du Moyen-Age* 17 (1949) pp. 183-222, and especially his *L'univers dionysien* (Paris, 1954).

of two wills: the liberty of the creature and predetermination (προορισμός)—the idea (παράδειγμα) or divine will addressed to each being. A double movement pervades this hierarchically arranged universe: God reveals Himself by His δυνάμεις in all beings ("multiplying Himself without abandoning His unity"), and creatures rise towards deification, by transcending the manifestations of God in creation. Here there is an impetus towards the "superessential ray," towards a communication which transcends the created order, being connatural with God and, in this sense, "a ray of darkness." If we want to translate this image into the terms of a more precise theology, we should call it "deifying grace."

In the age to come, the vision of the face of God will not exclude this impetus towards the Unknowable, which Dionysius this time describes in terms of light: "Then, when we shall become incorruptible and immortal, having reached the state of blessedness and having become like Christ (χριστοειδεῖς), we shall be forever with the Lord, as Scripture says, enjoying His visible theophany in most pure contemplations, illumined by His bright rays just as the disciples were at the time of His divine Transfiguration; then, with intelligence which is without passion and without matter, we shall share in His intelligible participation, and also in a union beyond all intelligence, in the unknowable yet blessed shining of rays which are more than bright, in a state which is like that of the heavenly spirits. For as the word of the Truth says, we shall be like the angels and sons of God, being sons of the resurrection" (*De div. nom.* 1, 4).

This text contains a synthesis of all that we have seen up to now in other authors. There is no trace of the intellectualism of Origen; it is the whole man, not only the spirit or the intelligence (the νοῦς), that enters into communion with God. As in St. John Chrysostom and the Antiochenes, the vision is of the incarnate Son. But in Dionysius the doctrine of the spiritual senses (which was absent from the writings of the Antiochene theologians) finds all its value in the "visible theophany"—the vision of the light of the transfigured Christ. At the same time, the intelligence (νοῦς) receives intelligible illumination, and man knows God in this same light; here Dionysius agrees with St. Gregory of Nazianzus and St. Cyril of Alexandria. But in union with God, which is a movement towards the unknowable nature of God, the human person goes beyond all knowledge and transcends the νοῦς; and here we find again St. Gregory of Nyssa's idea of "infinite progress." Thus simultaneously Christ is seen face to face, God is fully manifested, He is known in His revealing διακρίσεις; and yet, in the union, He surpasses all vision and all knowledge, for His superessential nature always remains inaccessible.

With Dionysius we enter the world of Byzantine theology in the proper sense of the term. For the Dionysian doctrine of the dynamic manifestation of God, implying a distinction between the unknowable essence of God and His natural processions or energies (as they will be termed, since the term "energy" used by the Cappadocians will receive preference to the term δυνάμεις used by Pseudo-Dionysius), will serve as a dogmatic basis for teaching concerning the vision of God in later theology, above all in the fourteenth century.

In that period, as dogmatic teaching about grace is clearly defined by the councils of the Orthodox Church, the image of the divine darkness, as we have met it in St. Gregory of Nyssa and Dionysius, no longer will have the same importance. The theology of darkness—which was but a metaphor of a dogmatic truth—will give way to a theology of the uncreated light, a real element in mystical experience. The darkness of Mount Sinai will be changed into the light of Mount Tabor, in which Moses at last was able to see the glorious face of God incarnate.

3

The Theology of Light in the Thought of St. Gregory Palamas

The mystical theology of St. Gregory Palamas, Archbishop of Thessalonica, evoked stormy polemics in the West, which have not ceased after six centuries. I have no intention of reviving old confessional disputes in raising one of the doctrinal points which separate Christian East and West. It seems to me, however, that for us to know one another better it would be preferable to put down in all frankness what is particularly precious to us in our spiritual traditions instead of being silent about the characteristic features of our spiritualities, which, often remaining badly understood by both sides, have engendered so many quarrels in the past.

I realize very well how strange and unusual the name of Gregory Palamas is for the majority of Western theologians. The doctrine which he professed raised violent criticism in the West. It is sufficient to recall the pages which Denis

Pétau[1] devoted to him. Even in purely historical studies (such as the works of Jugie and Guichardan)[2] the authors seem to see in the man whose thought they are studying only an adversary. Whence arise the numerous misconceptions which are a great obstacle to an understanding of the true value of what in the West is called "Palamism" and, I dare say, to an understanding of the very essence of the tradition of the Christian East. In fact, for us St. Gregory of Thessalonica, far from being the author of a new doctrine, is only a witness of this Tradition, as are, for example, Sts. Athanasius the Great, Basil the Great, Gregory of Nazianzus, or Maximus the Confessor. The personal character of his teaching is chiefly due to the special emphasis he places on certain doctrinal positions—which one finds, however, in the writings of other Fathers of the Church—and also perhaps to his bold and concise way of posing of problems which surpass human understanding. Thus it will be somewhat difficult for me to disengage the thought of Palamas from the common treasure of the Orthodox Church. But it is precisely because of this that his theology ought to interest us, in its capacity as one of the authentic expressions of the doctrinal foundation of Orthodox spirituality—Byzantine, Russian, or any other.

There are men whose lives and activities are linked so intimately with the great events of their epoch that it is impossible to isolate their biography from the general history

---

[1]Petavius, *Opus de theologicis dogmaticis* I.1, caps. 12, 13; III, cap. 5 (Thomas edition, 1864, pp. 145-160, 273-276).

[2]M. Jugie, the articles "Palamas" and "Palamite" (controversy), *Dictionnaire de théologie catholique* II, cols. 1735-1776 and 1777-1818. By the same author: "De theologia Palamitica," in his *Theologia dogmatica christianorum orientalium* II (1933) pp. 47-183 (a work of purely doctrinal character). See also various articles by Jugie in *Échos d'Orient*. Jugie gives the following appreciation of the theology of St. Gregory of Thessalonica: "...a doctrine which one might view as a punishment permitted by God, that has managed to be imposed as official dogma." (Article "Palamas," col. 1817). S. Guichardan, *Le problème de la simplicité divine en Orient et en Occident aux XIV⁰ et XV⁰ siècles: Grégoire Palamas, Duns Scot, Georges Scholarios* (Lyons, 1933). This work, rather simplistic in the manner in which it interprets a doctrine profoundly alien to the mentality of the critic, has earned a number of justifiable reproaches in the review by V. Grumel, *Échos d'Orient* 38 (1935) pp. 84-96.

of their age. Thus, for example, one cannot speak of the life of St. Athanasius and disregard the history of the Arian disputes, the councils and conciliabula, and all the religious and political troubles of the fourth century. The same can be said about St. Gregory Palamas. This is why, putting aside his entire biography—which would lead us too far from our theme—I shall limit myself here to a few observations, chiefly of a chronological nature. St. Gregory Palamas was born towards the end of the thirteenth century (probably in 1296) in Constantinople or Asia Minor. Born into a family of imperial court dignitaries, he was able to pursue serious philosophical and theological studies. At about the age of twenty, Palamas became a monk on Mount Athos, from which he was drawn in 1340 by the necessity of taking an active part in the dogmatic struggle. In 1347 he became Archbishop of Thessalonica. The rest of his life (Palamas died in 1359) was spent between Constantinople, where several councils and synods took place during the space of fifteen years, and Thessalonica, his archiepiscopal see.[3]

Certainly it is impossible to exaggerate the intimate link between St. Gregory Palamas and the spiritual milieu of Mount Athos. But it would be a grave mistake to see in him only a defender of the ascetic and monastic practice of the

---

[3]The principal biographical sources are the two *Lives* of St. Gregory Palamas written by two Patriarchs of Constantinople, St. Philotheus (d. 1376) and Nilus (d. 1387), both disciples of Palamas (P.G. 151, cols. 551-656, 655-678). Among the studies of the life and work of Palamas, see especially that of G. Papamichaïl, Ὁ ἅγιος Γρηγόριος Παλαμᾶς (Alexandria, 1911). A biographical notice is found in the article already cited of Fr. Jugie, as well as in that of Ph. Meyer, "Palamas," *Realencyklopaedie für protestantische Theologie* vol. 14, 599-601. In addition A. Vasiliev, *History of the Byzantine Empire* (2 vols. University of Wisconsin, 1958, newly revised) can be consulted. Vol. 2, ch. 9 gives a general tableau of the political, cultural, and religious life of Byzantium in the fourteenth and fifteenth centuries. Pages 640-670 are devoted to St. Gregory Palamas and to the so-called "Palamite" councils. [The fundamental work on St. Gregory Palamas is now that of Fr. John Meyendorff, *Introduction à l'étude de Grégoire Palamas* (Paris, 1959); English translation: *A Study of Gregory Palamas* (Tuckahoe: St. Vladimir's Press, 1964)—*trans.*].

"hesychast" monks.[4] It is true that the polemics which snatched Palamas from the silence of the cloister began with his apology for the hesychast method of prayer, which was violently criticized by the Calabrian monk Barlaam. The latter, interesting himself exclusively in certain external practices of the practitioners of contemplative prayer (for example, the immobile and inclined position of the body, mastery of breathing, and other technical procedures recommended to facilitate concentration of the spirit during mental prayer), tried to ridicule the Athonite monks; he wished to present them as ignorant rustics who imagined that spiritual faculties were concentrated in the navel and that by way of mechanical actions one could achieve the contemplation of God. Barlaam did not stop here: basing himself on the assertion of the hesychasts that certain of the contemplatives enjoyed the vision of the uncreated Light, he accused them of what he thought was Messalianism.[5] The debate centered on the nature of this light; and, carried

---

[4]Father Irénée Hausherr's article, "La méthode d'oraison hésychaste," *Orientalia christiana* 9 (1927) pp. 101-210, despite the incontestable erudition of the author, can in no way serve as a guide to the study of hesychasm: the polemical goal of the author lends the character of an impassioned pamphlet to a work which ought to have been an historical study. Unfortunately the same thing must be said of Fr. Jugie's article, "Les origines de la méthode d'oraison des hésychastes," *Échos d'Orient* 30 (1931). On the contrary, one can point with approval to G. Ostrogorsky's brief study, "The Hesychasts of Mount Athos and their Opponents" (in Russian), *Annales de l'Institut Scientifique Russe à Belgrade* 5 (1931) pp. 349-370.

[5]This reproach of Messalianism applied to St. Gregory of Thessalonica has in mind his doctrine of the possibility of seeing the divine light with corporeal eyes; but the Messalians maintained that one could attain by prayer a kind of material vision of the divine essence. St. John of Damascus, among the *capitula* in which he objects to the Messalians, notes (cap. 17) that they maintain that it is possible to see the hypostasis of the Holy Spirit with all its properties (*Liber de haeresibus*, P.G. 94, col. 7328). Likewise St. Timothy objects to the Messalians' claim to see with corporeal eyes the Holy Trinity in its essence (*De receptione haereticorum*, P.G. 86, cols. 48-49). St. Gregory Palamas remarks in *Theophanes* that the opinion according to which the saints could participate in the very essence of God is proper to the Messalians (P.G. 150, col. 933D-936A); he also ascribes to Messalianism the doctrine of the possibility of seeing the very essence of God (P.G. 151, col. 448C). The Bogomils, who basically professed the same errors, were often designated by the name "Messalians" by Byzantine authors. It is known that Palamas, a short time before the beginning of the Barlaamite disputes,

away with polemics, Barlaam affirmed that the light in which
Christ appeared to His disciples on Mount Tabor at the
moment of the Transfiguration was nothing but a created
phenomenon, on the order, so to speak, of the purely
atmospheric, thus lower in its nature than human thought.
This stirred up the entire Byzantine Empire.

At the council called in Constantinople in 1341, Palamas
posed the question on dogmatic grounds.[6] For him the question concerned the reality of mystical experience, the possibility of knowing God, the nature of this knowledge-vision,
and finally the nature and experience of grace. Such was
the theme of the teaching professed by St. Gregory Palamas,
the spokesman of the councils of this period.[7] Let us now
pass to an examination of several fundamental points of
this mystical theology.[8]

2

The Orthodox Church has never made a fine distinction

---

had to defend Orthodoxy against these heretics, who were attempting to
disseminate their doctrines on Mount Athos.

   Certain critics (J. Bois, "Les hésychastes avant le XIV° siècle," *Échos
d'Orient* 5 [1901] pp. 1-11) have continued in part Barlaam's thesis, wishing
to see a Messalian or Bogomil influence. This opinion—which makes Palamas
a tributary of Messalian doctrines—is as unjust as that which would affirm,
for example, an Averroist doctrinal influence on Thomas Aquinas. On
Messalianism see the articles "Euchites" (by G. Bareille) and "Messaliens"
(by E. Amann), *Dictionnaire de théologie catholique* 5, cols. 1434-65,
and 10, cols. 792-795; G. L. Marriot, "The Messalians and the Discovery
of their Ascetic," *Harvard Theological Review* 19 (1926) pp. 131-138,
should also be consulted.

   [6]Mansi, *Coll. concil.* 25, cols. 1147-1150.

   [7]See the conciliar acts of the fourteenth century in Mansi 25, col. 1147 ff.
and 26, *passim*. There is a good exposition of Palamas' doctrine in the
article by Fr. (now Abp.) Basil Krivoshein, "La doctrine ascétique et
théologique de saint Gregoire Palamas," *Seminarium Kondakovianum* 8
(Prague, 1936) pp. 99-154 (in Russian, with a French résumé; translated into
English in *The Eastern Churches Quarterly* 3 [1938]).

   [8]We use the term "mystical theology" in the same sense in which Gilson
uses it, when he entitles his study of St. Bernard *The Mystical Theology of
St. Bernard* (New York, 1940): "The subject is strictly limited by the very
title of this work. It does not discuss either the life of St. Bernard or his
theology in general, or even his mysticism taken all together, but only that
part of his theology on which his mysticism is based" (Preface).

between the realm of theology and that of mysticism.[9] All truly dogmatic work has a basis in mystical experience. On the other hand, all mystical work is connected to the realm of dogma, in that it expresses and exposes the content of the experience of divine things. If a purely "mystical" author like St. Symeon was named "the New Theologian," this indicates that mysticism is considered to be theology *par excellence*. However it belongs to a secret and mysterious profundity, so to speak, which ought not be divulged. The writings of St. Symeon the New Theologian, for example, were destined only for monks already experienced in the contemplative life.[10]

The *Hagioritic Tome,* compiled by the monks of Mount Athos under the inspiration and supervision of St. Gregory Palamas, allows us to be precise about Palamas' view of what belongs to the realm of mystical theology.[11] The authors of the *Tome* want to find in the Old Testament, alongside the dogmas of the ancient law, prophetic foreshadowings relating to what future dogmas should be, the dogmas of the age of the Gospel; these latter appeared to the men of the Old Testament as mysteries which could not be clearly expressed. So also for us who live in the age of the Gospel, things of the future age—the Kingdom of God—appear as mysteries. These mysteries cannot be fully known (or, rather, experienced) except by the saints—by those who live in perfect union with God, transformed by grace and belonging rather to the future life than to our earthly life.[12] One can

---

[9] I am not speaking here, of course, about theological textbooks and other such writings, in which only "juxtaposed" notions are found, to use Bergson's expression.

[10] P.G. 120, col. 289 (Leo Allatius' comment). Nicetas Stethatos, *Vie de Syméon le Nouveau Théologien,* ed. Fr. I. Hausherr, *Orientalia Christiana* 12 (Rome, 1928).

[11] The *Hagioritic Tome* ('Ο άγιορειτικὸς τόμος ὑπὲρ τῶν ἡσυχαζόντων) was compiled in 1339-1340 by Palamas' friend and disciple Philotheus Kokkinos (later Patriarch of Constantinople). It is a theological work devoted to the Light of the Transfiguration. The *Hagioritic Tome,* signed by numerous abbots and monks of Mount Athos, served as the basis for St. Gregory in the later controversy.

[12] P.G. 150, cols. 1225-1227. Jugie and Guichardan seek to find in this text acknowledgement of the "novelty" of this doctrine of the divine light by its defenders. But this extremely clear text, establishing the distinction

easily understand what St. Gregory Palamas felt when faced with the obligation of expressing in dogmatic form what belongs to the realm of mystery, what ought rather to be preserved in the silence of contemplation than to be made known to everyone in intelligible concepts.

Two kinds of theology exist. One, wanting to see in God an eminently simple object, narrows all possible knowledge about the attributes of God to this primordial simplicity, by reason of which the nature of God can be known only by means of analogies, which refer to an essence surpassing our understanding—our understanding naturally being dedicated to the knowledge of things complex and multiple. But there is another theological attitude for which the unknowable character of God has a more radical value. This unknowability cannot be founded on the eminent simplicity of the divine Being; in effect this would suppose an essence, if not knowable, then at least capable of being seen imperfectly with the aid of analogical concepts: a simple essence, identical to its attributes. On the contrary, using unknowability as a point of departure, one would sooner affirm that God cannot be termed a simple essence than allow His absolute unknowability to be weakened. Nonetheless, the same theology affirms with no less force the possibility of knowing God.

We are then in the presence of an antinomic theology which proceeds by oppositions of contrary but equally true propositions. St. Gregory Palamas himself recognizes this aspect of his theological method when he says: "It is an attribute of all theology which wishes to respect piety to affirm now one thing, now another, when both affirmations are true; to contradict oneself in one's own affirmations is appropriate only for people completely deprived of reason."[13] It is necessary, he says, to maintain an equilibrium between

between knowledge revealed to sons of the Church and mysteries which will be fully known only in the future life, does not provide any basis for an interpretation which would ascribe to Palamas and the Athonite monks a Joachimite philosophy of history.

[13]*Capitula physica, theologica, moralia, et practica* 121; P.G. 150, col. 1205.

the two members of the antinomy,[14] in order not to lose contact with revealed realities, replacing them by concepts of a human philosophy. Thus, for example, in speaking of God, it is appropriate to say that He is a not-one.[15] Sabellius, who did not know how to maintain this antinomy, seeing above all the unity of substance, lost the notion of the Trinity of Persons and replaced the living God of the Christians by the divine essence of the pagan philosophers. The goal of this antinomic theology is not to forge a system of concepts, but to serve as a support for the human spirit in the contemplation of divine mysteries. Every antinomic opposition of two true propositions gives way to a dogma, *i.e.* to a real distinction, although ineffable and unintelligible, which cannot be based on any concepts or deduced by a process of reasoning, since it is the expression of a reality of a religious order. If one is forced to establish these distinctions, it is precisely to safeguard the antinomy, to prevent the human spirit from being led astray, breaking the antinomy and falling then from the contemplation of divine mysteries into the platitude of rationalism, replacing living experience with concepts. The antinomy, on the contrary, raises the spirit from the realm of concepts to the concrete data of Revelation.

3

The point of departure in the theological work of St. Gregory Palamas is an antinomy concerning the knowable and the unknowable in God. It is the antinomy of two theological ways, the positive and the negative, established by Dionysius the Areopagite. One can know God positively, attributing to Him the perfections which one finds in the created world: goodness, wisdom, life, love, being. One can also know Him negatively, through ignorance, denying to His subject all that pertains to the realm of being, since God

---

[14]*Theophanes sive De divinitatis et rerum divinarum communicabilitate et incommunicabilitate,* P.G. 150, col. 917A.
[15]*Ibid.* col. 917B.

is above being, above everything which can be named. The opposition between these two ways, between these two theologies, cannot be resolved by any reconciliation whatsoever, according to Palamas, faithful in this to the thought of the Areopagite. It would be interesting to compare the attitude of Palamas on this point (and, in general, of the entire Dionysian tradition in the East) with the attitudes of other theologians, especially of Western theologians, who also have been more or less the inheritors of Areopagitic thought. For Thomas Aquinas, for example, the antinomy of the two theological ways does not exist; the positive and negative ways can and ought to be harmonized or, rather, reduced to a single way, that of positive theology; the negative way then would be nothing more than a complement, a corrective to the positive way, which would simple indicate that all affirmations touching the nature of God ought to be understood in a more sublime sense (*modo sublimiore*). For Nicholas of Cusa, that great mystical dialectician, more impregnated by the Dionysian tradition (as is, indeed, the entire German school of mysticism), the antinomy of the two theological ways keeps all its value; these two ways remain irreducible for the human spirit, but their opposition is resolved in God, who is "the accord of opposites" (*coincidentia oppositorum*), the nature in relation to which contrary propositions coincide, like two parallel lines which are rejoined in infinity. For St. Gregory Palamas—who does nothing more here than make the dominant idea of Dionysius more precise—the antinomy between the positive and negative theologies has a real foundation in God. Like all theological antinomies—like that of unity and trinity, which postulates a distinction between nature and persons[16]—the antinomy of the two ways discloses to our spirit a mysterious distinction in God's very being. This is the distinction between essence and divine operations or energies.

This distinction—affirmed as dogma of the Church by

---

[16]See, for example, the text cited above concerning the antinomy between unity and trinity and the one-sided doctrine of Sabellius, who did not want to accept the distinction postulated by the antinomy of Trinitarian dogma; P.G. 150, col. 917D.

the councils which are called "Palamite"—is the very source of the entire theological development of St. Gregory Palamas, whose goal was to give a dogmatic basis to mystical experience, to base the reality of this experience on a dogma touching the mode of God's existence. However Palamas was not the author of this distinction between the essence and the energies of God; he merely underscored one point of doctrine common to a number of the Fathers. The words of St. Basil are often cited: "If the energies descend to us, the essence remains absolutely inaccessible."[17] St. John Damascene is more explicit in the distinction which he makes between essence, or nature properly so-called (οὐσία, φύσις) —unknowable, absolutely inaccessible—and "that which is close to the nature" (τὰ περὶ τὴν φύσιν), the virtues or divine energies,[18] "that which can be known about God" (τὸ γνωστὸν τοῦ Θεοῦ), according to the words of St. Paul (Rom. 1:19).

In order to understand more clearly what operations or energies are in relation to essence in the teaching of St. Gregory Palamas or the other Greek Fathers, we must first of all eliminate any idea relating to causality,[19] even that of the operative presence of the cause in its effects.

The energies are not effects foreign to the divine essence; they are not acts exterior to God, depending on His will, like the creation of the world or acts of providence. They are the *natural* processions of God Himself, a mode of existence which is proper to Him and according to which God exists not only in His essence, but also outside His essence. All the images borrowed from the created world—

---

[17]*Ad Amphilochium*, P.G. 32, col. 869AB.

[18]*De fide orthodoxa*, P.G. 94, col. 800BC.

[19]If St. Gregory Palamas sometimes employs expressions relating to causality in speaking of essence and energies (Council of 1351, P.G. 151, col. 738AB), it should not be forgotten that we are in the presence of a theology of the Dionysian tradition, where causality means manifestation. See some remarks on this subject in our articles: "La notion des 'Analogies' chez Denys le pseudo-Aréopagite," *Archives d'histoire doctrinale et littéraire du moyen âge* 5 (1930) p. 285; "La théologie négative dans la doctrine de Denys l'Aréopagite," *Révue des sciences philosophiques et théologiques* 28 (1939) p. 217. Several very characteristic texts of St. Maximus can be found on this point; P.G. 4, cols. 137, 380, 404-405.

images by which Palamas attempts to grasp the character of this ineffable distinction between what God is in His essence and in His energies—are, as he says himself, insufficient. He compares essence to the solar disk and energies to the rays.[20] He also compares God to human intelligence, whose faculties of apprehension are varied, passing from one object to another, while by its essence, the intellect does not pass to other substances.[21] St. John Damascene designates energies by the words "movement" (κίνησις) or "impulse from God" (ἔξαλμα Θεοῦ).[22]

It would be incorrect to consider that the divine energies exist only as a function of God's relation to what is exterior to Him, *i.e.* exist in view of the creation of the world. The entire created world only represents a limited participation, preestablished by the will of the Creator.[23] If the world had not been created, God would have always existed not only in His inaccessible essence, but also outside His essence, in the energies which are the overflowing of the essence.[24] In speaking of energies, St. Gregory Palamas sometimes calls them "inferior divinity" in opposition to essence as "superior divinity."[25] But he makes it clear that this by no means indicates that God is diminished in His natural processions outside the essence. Here is a basic difference with the Platonists, despite the resemblance of terms ("energy," "procession"). Essence can be said to be superior to energies in the same sense that the Father, the source of all divinity, is said to be superior to the Son and to the Holy Spirit. Moreover, distinction is not separation: it does not divide God into knowable and unknowable. God reveals Himself, totally gives Himself in His energies, and remains totally unknowable and incommunicable in His essence. He remains identical in these two

[20]*Capita physica*... 92, 94; P.G. 150, cols. 1185D, 1188CD.
[21]*Theophanes,* P.G. 150, col. 949AB.
[22]*De fide orthodoxa* I, 14; P.G. 94, col. 860B.
[23]*Capita physica*... 91, 103; P.G. 150, cols. 1184A, 1192B.
[24]*Ibid.* col. 1172C: Μόνος οὖν ὁ Θεὸς ἐξ αἰῶνος ἐνεργής τε καὶ παντοδύναμος, ὡς καὶ προαιωνίους ἔχων δυνάμεις τε καὶ ἐνεργείας.
[25]In his second letter to Akindynos, unpublished, found in ms. Coislin 99 and described by Montfaucon. See Jugie's citation in the article "Palamas," *Dictionnaire de théologie catholique* 11, col. 1755.

modes of existence: the same, and at the same time, different (τὸ ταυτὸν καὶ τὸ ἕτερον), according to Dionysius the Areopagite.[26] Most often St. Gregory Palamas avoids the term "essence" (οὐσία), finding it improper, insufficient to designate what God is by His nature; he prefers the word "superessence" (ὑπερουσιότης) borrowed from Dionysius, to designate what cannot be named. If one must distinguish in God essence and that which is not essence, that is precisely because God is not limited by His essence. He is more than essence, if He is truly the living God, the God of Abraham, of Isaac, and of Jacob, the Holy Trinity—and not the God of the philosophers and the scholars.

4

The first consequence of this real distinction in God concerns the object itself of the mystical experience. This is not God in His essence, incommunicable and unknowable by definition; for if we could at a given moment participate to some degree in the essence, we would not in that moment be what we are, but gods by nature; but we are created beings, called to become by grace what God is by His nature.[27] If St. Peter (II Peter 1:4) calls us "partakers of the divine nature" (*divinae consortes naturae*), it is to the degree that this nature becomes participable in the energies, but not in itself. The same is true concerning the knowledge of God, whose fulness in no way is reduced by the fact that we are not able to know Him other than in His energies. St. Gregory (like Orthodox theology in general) is ignorant of the vision of the divine essence: it is the face of the living and personal God which will be contemplated by the saints in the life of the age to come. The doctrine which would make of essence the object of the beatific vision seems, in this way of thinking, too abstract, replacing a religious reality by an intel-

[26]*De divinis nominibus* 9, 1; P.G. 3, col. 909B.

[27]If one could participate in the essence itself, God would no longer be Trinity, but a multitude of persons. See *Theophanes,* P.G. 150, cols. 941A, 944AC.

lectualist concept. When Palamas speaks of God, he always means the Holy Trinity. Outside the Divinity in three Persons, he says, I give nothing the name of divinity—neither Essence nor Person.[28] Therefore, if he designates energies by the word "divinities" (in the plural), it is because they are proper to the Three consubstantial Persons as their life, power, wisdom, sanctity, common to the Father, Son, and Holy Spirit.[29] Each energy shows us the Trinity, which is the source and summit of all mystical experience. Everything proceeds from the Trinity and everything leads to It: to the Father, who is the Source of all divinity; to the Son and to the Holy Spirit, who proceed from Him in the unity of the inaccessible nature. The energies which flow eternally from this nature, being communicated to us by the Holy Spirit, deify us and make us participate in the life of the Holy Trinity, which the Gospels call the Kingdom of God.

Another consequence of the distinction between essence and energies is the concrete and, so to speak, dynamic character of what the theology of the textbooks calls "the attributes of God." The attributes-energies for St. Gregory Palamas by no means are abstract concepts applicable to the divine essence, but living and personal forces—not in the sense of individual beings, as Palamas' opponents wanted to define them, accusing him of polytheism, but precisely in the sense of manifestations of a personal God. These attributes have quite concrete designations, taken most often from Holy Scripture, whose anthropomorphic expressions do not trouble Palamas at all. For this mystical theology has as its goal turning the spirit from abstract notions to the experience of divine realities. It practically does not know expressions taken "in a figurative sense." This is why, when St. Gregory Palamas replaces the overly abstract and philosophical term of "energy," used especially for convenience of dogmatic discussion, by the more concrete term of "divine light," it is in a real sense that he uses this word.

---

[28]Council of 1351, P.G. 151, col. 725B, Mansi, 26, col. 138.
[29]*Ibid.* See also *Theophanes*, P.G. 150, col. 941CD.

5

Holy Scripture—as well as liturgical chants and all of
patristic literature—abounds in expressions relating to the
divine light, to the glory of God, to God Himself, named
"light." Should we see in this only metaphors, only figures
of speech? Or is this light a true aspect of God, a reality
of the mystical order?

"God is called light not according to His essence, but
according to His energy," says Palamas.[30] If the energies
which manifest the nature of God are called light, this is
not only by analogy with the material light (energy pro-
pagating itself from a luminous body, for example, from
the solar disk); the divine light, for St. Gregory Palamas,
is a datum of mystical experience. It is the visible character
of the divinity, of the energies in which God communicates
Himself and reveals Himself to those who have purified
their hearts. This light (φῶς) or illumination (ἔλλαμψις)
which surpasses intelligence and the senses[31] is not of the
intellectual order, as illumination of the intellect, taken in an
allegorical and abstract sense, often is; neither is it of the
sensible order; however this light simultaneously fills reason
and the senses, manifesting itself to the total man, and not
to just one of his faculties. The divine light is immaterial
(ἄϋλον) and contains nothing sensible in it, but neither is
it an intelligible light. The *Hagioritic Tome* distinguishes:
(1) sensible light, (2) the light of the intelligence, (3) the
uncreated light which surpasses both the others equally:
"The light of the intelligence is different from that which
is perceived by the senses; in effect, the sensible light reveals
to us objects proper to our senses, whereas the intellectual
light serves to manifest the truth which is in the thoughts.
Consequently, sight and intelligence do not perceive one and
the same light, but it is proper to each of these two faculties
to act according to their natures and within their limits.
However, when those who are worthy of it receive grace

---

[30]*Against Akyndnos,* P.G. 150, col. 823.
[31]Homily 22, ed. Sophocles (Athens, 1861) p. 171, cited by Krivoshein,
op cit. pp. 114-115.

and spiritual and supernatural strength, they perceive by their senses as well as by their intelligence that which is above all sense and all intellect... How? That is not known except by God and by those who have had experience of His grace."[32]

This uncreated, eternal, divine, and deifying light is grace,[33] for the name of grace (χάρις) also refers to divine energies insofar as they are given to us and accomplish the work of our deification. The doctrine of grace for St. Gregory Palamas (as for all of Orthodox theology) thus is founded on the distinction of nature and energies in God: "Illumination or divine and deifying grace is not essence, but the energy of God," he says.[34] Grace is not only a function; it is more than a relation of God to man; far from being an action or an effect produced by God in the soul, it is God Himself, communicating Himself and entering into ineffable union with man. "By grace, God totally embraces those who are worthy, and the saints embrace God in His fulness."[35] Being the light of the divinity, grace cannot remain hidden or unnoticed;[36] acting in man, changing his nature, entering into a more and more intimate union with him, the divine energies become increasingly perceptible, revealing to man the face of the living God, "the Kingdom of God come with power" (Mark 9:1). This divine experience, says Palamas, is given to each according to his measure and can be more or less profound, depending on the worthiness of those who experience it.[37] The full vision of the divinity

[32]P.G. 150, col. 1833D.

[33]Caps. 69, 93; P.G. 150, cols. 1169, 1188.

[34]Cap. 69, *ibid*. See the same formulas in St. Mark of Ephesus, *Capitula syllogistica*, in W. Gass, *Die Mystik des Nicolaus Cabasilas* (Greiswald, 1849) appendix II.

[35]*Hagioritic Tome*, P.G. 150, col. 1229D.

[36]It is interesting to note that the "mystical night" is foreign to the spirituality of the Orthodox Church. The states similar to those which are given this name in the West are given the name "acedia" by masters of Eastern spirituality; such states are seen as a sin or a temptation against which one ought to struggle, always keeping watch over the light which shines in the darkness. "Acedia" is *ennui*, a sadness which ends in despair, the greatest sin, the beginning of eternal death.

[37]*Homily on the Transfiguration*, P.G. 151, col. 448B.

having become perceptible in the uncreated light, in its deifying grace, is "the mystery of the eighth day"; it belongs to the future age. However those who are worthy of it attain the sight of "the Kingdom of God come with power" in this life, as the three apostles saw it on Mount Tabor.

The Transfiguration of the Lord occupies a central place in the thought of St. Gregory Palamas. Almost the entire debate with Barlaam and Akindynos revolves around the question of whether the light of the Transfiguration was created or uncreated—a question which can appear to be a scholastic subtlety, a "Byzantinism," to persons alien to the religious life.[38] However this question contains many others, such as: the nature of grace, the possibility of mystical experience and the reality of this experience, the possibility of seeing God and the nature of this vision, and finally, the possibility of deification in the real and not the metaphorical sense of this word.

The majority of the Fathers who have spoken of the Transfiguration affirm the uncreated and divine nature of the mystical experience.[39] The light which the apostles saw on Mount Tabor belongs to God by nature: eternal, infinite,

---

[38]Ch. Diehl, *Byzance, Grandeur et Décadence* (Flammarion, 1920) p. 195.

[39]St. Gregory of Nazianzus, *Or.* 40 (*In sanctum baptisma*), 4; P.G. 36, col. 365A. St. Cyril of Alexandria, *Commentary on St. Luke;* P.G. 72, cols. 752D-756A. St. Maximus the Confessor, *Capita theologica et oeconomica* 2, 13; P.G. 90, cols. 1129D-1132A. St. Andrew of Crete, *Sermon on the Transfiguration,* P.G. 97, cols. 932-957 *passim.* St. John of Damascus, *Homily on the Transfiguration,* P.G. 96, cols. 545-576 *passim; Acrostic on the Transfiguration, ibid.* col. 848C. Euthymius Zigabenus, *Commentary on Matthew* 17; P.G. 129, col. 477B. Numerous other passages of the Greek Fathers on the divine nature of the light of the Transfiguration can be cited. Some traces of the same tradition can be found in the West. Thus, St. Leo the Great (Sermon 51; P.L. 54, col. 310B) speaks of the glory of the Kingdom of God which Christ made visible to the Apostles in His transfigured body. He distinguishes, it is true, this vision of the divine glory communicated to humanity by Christ from the "ineffable and inaccessible vision of divinity itself" in eternal life. Pseudo-Augustine (*De mirabilibus Sanctae Scripturae* 3, 10; P.L. 35, col. 2197f.), an unknown author who was writing, without doubt, in Ireland toward the end of the seventh century, does not make this distinction: "non tamen ipsa caro splenduit, sed divinitas latens in corpore luminis qui portiunculam conspiciendam foris videntibus, quantum poterant, concessit. Nisi forte ut per carnem divinitas foris illuxit, sic et caro illuminata de divinitate, per vestimenta radiavit."

existing outside of time and space, it is revealed in the theophanies of the Old Testament as the glory of God. At the moment of the Incarnation the divine light was concentrated, so to speak, in Christ, the God-Man, in whom "the fulness of deity dwells bodily" (Col. 2:9). This means that the humanity of Christ was deified by the hypostatic union with the divine nature; that Christ, during his terrestrial life, was always resplendent with the divine light, which remained invisible for most men. The Transfiguration was not a phenomenon circumscribed in time and space; no change took place in Christ at that moment, even in His human nature, but a change was produced in the consciousness of the apostles, who received for a moment the ability to see their Master as He was, resplendent in the eternal light of His divinity.[40] St. Gregory Palamas says in his *Homily on the Transfiguration:* "The light of the Lord's Transfiguration had no beginning and no end, it remained uncircumscribed [in space] and imperceptible to the senses, although it was contemplated by corporeal eyes... But by a transmutation of their senses the disciples of the Lord passed from the flesh to the Spirit."[41] In order to see the divine light with corporeal eyes, as the disciples did on Mount Tabor, one must participate in this light, one must be transformed by it to a greater or lesser degree. In another homily, St. Gregory of Thessalonica says, speaking of the mystical experience, "He who participates in the divine energy... becomes himself, in a sense, Light; he is united to the Light and with the Light he sees in full consciousness all that remains hidden for those who have not this grace; he thus surpasses not only the corporeal senses, but also all that can be known [by the mind]... for the pure of heart see God... who, being the Light, abides in them and reveals Himself to those who love Him, to His beloved ones...."[42]

---

[40]*Hagioritic Tome,* P.G. 150, col. 1232C.

[41]P.G. 151, col. 433B.

[42]Sermon for the Feast of the Presentation of the Blessed Virgin in the Temple, ed. Sophocles, pp. 176-177; cited by Krivoshein, *op. cit.* p. 138.

6

Palamas' opponents were scandalized by his teachings about the possibility of seeing God with corporeal eyes. For modern critics—*e.g.* for Fr. Jugie, who is prepared however to recognize certain theological merit in Palamas—this point of doctrine seems to be a puerility owing to a bias, to a desire to defend at all costs a mystical aberration. Nevertheless, however absurd it may seem to us, this point of the doctrine of St. Gregory Palamas is by no means inconsequential: it is perfectly in the apophatic line of his theology, of all the theology of the Greek Fathers.

We must be careful not to evaluate too easily as "absurd" everything which seems strange to our minds, which are by nature rationalistic. Otherwise we would also have to reject as absurd the greater part of the dogmas of Christianity— for example, that of the Ascension of Christ with His true human body into the uncreated realm, to the very source of the Trinity.

The possibility of seeing God with corporeal eyes seems absurd to us. But before rejecting it in Palamas, let us at least note that one finds the same "absurdity" in St. Symeon the New Theologian, in whose teaching, it is true, Combéfis would like to find "the source of the Palamite error";[43] in St. John Damascene;[44] in St. Andrew of Crete;[45] in St. Gregory of Nazianzus;[46] as well as in the writings of other Fathers. Before "saving the honor" of these Fathers of the Church, attributing to their affirmations the character of figures of speech, as Jugie does,[47] let us try to look a little

---

[43]F. Combéfis (in his preface to Manuel Calecas' *De essentia et operatione,* P.G. 152, col. 260B) confesses to having persuaded Henschenius and Papebroch not to include the life of St. Symeon in the Bollandists' *Acta Sanctorum* "tanquam is fuerit fons omnis Palamici erroris." I. Hausherr reproves him for this extreme zeal, but it must be recognized that Combéfis' attitude was perfectly logical: in rejecting the teaching of Palamas, it was impossible for him not to condemn St. Symeon's teaching.

[44]P.G. 96, cols. 560CD, 565C, 569A, *etc.*

[45]P.G. 97, col. 941C.

[46]P.G. 36, col. 365A: "The Divine Light which appeared to the Disciples on the mountain and was almost visible to the eyes..."

[47]Article "Palamas," col. 1760.

into ourselves, to understand what it is that renders unacceptable for us Palamas' doctrine on the visibility of God. A dualist philosophy which for three centuries and perhaps longer radically separated matter and spirit, body and soul, sense and intellect, is without any doubt at the origin of this attitude which makes us instinctively place God in the spiritual camp and thus to oppose Him to the physical world. This opposition, which places God and the immortal soul on one side and the flesh and the world in which we live on the other, often makes us forget that for Christian theology there is another separation which counts above all: that which opposes uncreated Being, which is God, and created being, which is the world called forth from nothingness with all the spiritual or corporeal entities which make it up. Is God only the God of spirits or is He also the God of all flesh? For Descartes' God-the-mathematician[48] the answer is clear: he is a God of spirits, a God of intelligences. But for God-the-Trinity, living in inaccessible Light and penetrating by His energies the created world—the world of pure spirits as well as that of physical beings—that is not so: He is at the same time equally far from and equally close to the intelligences as the senses.

There is also another obstacle in our consciousness: a certain aftertaste of Manicheism, almost imperceptible, which still remains in our piety and which at times makes us despise the flesh a little too much, not because of sin but by virtue of its material nature. Consequently we forget that this opposition between the body and the soul, this struggle of the flesh against the spirit and of the spirit against the flesh of which St. Paul speaks, is a result of sin; that the body and the spirit are in reality only two aspects of the human being; that our last end is not only an intellectual contemplation of God but the resurrection of the total man, soul and body, the beatitude of human beings who are going to see God face to face in the fulness of their created nature.

Unfortunately, we cannot pause here on the anthropology

---

[48]"Descartes did nothing more than disguise the God of the Middle Ages as a mathematician": from Gilson's course at the Collège de France, 1940-1941.

of St. Gregory Palamas, nor on the ascetic doctrine which flows from it. "We do not give the name 'man' separately to the soul or to the body," he says, "but to both together, for the entire man was created in the image of God."[49] Men, according to St. Gregory Palamas, have a fulness of being greater than that of the angels, precisely because of their corporeality; the human spirit is a vivifying force which penetrates the body, like the divine energies by which God penetrates everything. Therefore men are a more perfect image of God.[50] The human body, if it is in accord with the soul, ought to be apt for "spiritual dispositions."[51] The goal of the ascetic life does not consist in a mortification which suppresses the passions of the body, but rather in the acquisition of a new and better energy which would permit the body as well as the spirit to participate in the life of grace.

"If the body," says Palamas, "is to participate together with the soul in the ineffable good things [of the future age], it is certain that it ought to participate now, to the extent possible . . . for the body also has the experience of divine things when the passionate forces of the soul are not put to death but transformed and sanctified."[52]

7

As we said at the beginning of this account, it is very difficult to disengage the personal doctrine of St. Gregory Palamas from the common patrimony of the Orthodox Church; and this is so for two reasons: (1) because Orthodox theology is, in a certain sense, a common work, proper to all the sons of the Church, anchored in the experience of all to the degree of each one's spiritual faculties; (2) because the very goal of Palamas' work consisted in a dogmatic

---

[49]*Prosopopoeiae*, P.G. 150, col. 1361C. Jugie casts doubt on the authenticity of this text (article "Palamas," col. 1749), apparently without sufficient foundation.

[50]*Capita physica*. . . 38, 39; P.G. 150, col. 1145-1148.

[51]*Hagioritic Tome*, P.G. 150, col. 1233BD.

[52]*Ibid*. col. 1233C.

expression of the foundation of the mystical life proper to Orthodoxy. This is why the conclusions which one can draw from his mystical theology express the fundamental character of Orthodox spirituality. I can only make a few very brief remarks here on this subject in order not to undertake too vast a task.

All of this spirituality is directed towards the fulness of the life of the future age, which ought to begin here below by a change in created nature. More and more perfect union with God ought to terminate—after death and resurrection—at a deified state in which "the righteous will shine like the sun," according to the words of the Gospel (Matt. 13:43), for they will be by grace everything that God is by His nature.[53]

Like the divine Person of the Word who assumed human nature, human persons in whom union with God is being accomplished ought to unite in themselves the created and the uncreated, to become, so to speak, persons of two natures, with this difference, that Christ is a divine Person while deified men are and always will remain created persons. There is one human person who has attained this fulness in this life, and that is why death could not hold her: that is the Mother of God, who is "the limit of the created and the uncreated" according to Palamas' expression.[54]

The adoration of Christ's humanity is almost alien to Orthodox piety. For if Christ has ascended into Heaven, it is in order that the Holy Spirit might descend upon the Church. One can say, with a modern theologian, that if the visible has become invisible (by the Ascension), this has happened in order that the invisible—the fire of uncreated grace—might become visible in us. It is the risen Christ, Christ sitting at the right hand of the Father, who is adored, always with the Father and the Holy Spirit, never separated from the Trinity. Even on the cross, even in the tomb, He is glorified as "one of the Holy Trinity," come into the world in order to conquer death.

---

[53]See the classical text on deification in St. Maximus, *Ambigua* 222; P.G. 91, col. 1038.
[54]*Homily on the Assumption*, P.G. 91, col. 472B.

The work of our deification is accomplished by the Holy Spirit, Giver of grace. He is rarely named for He remains invisible, even while permitting grace to appear—divinity become manifest in the saints. One could cite numerous examples of these visible manifestations of grace, taken from Orthodox works of spirituality or hagiography, such as the lives of the Fathers of the desert or the writings of St. Macarius of Egypt[55] or of St. Symeon the New Theologian,[56] as well as of other masters of the spiritual life more or less well known in the West.[57] However we will limit ourselves to citing a more recent example, borrowed from the *Revelations of St. Seraphim of Sarov,*[58] to make understandable all the significance of the "theology of the Light" in the mystical life of the Orthodox Church.

In the course of a conversation which took place at the edge of a forest on a winter morning, a disciple of St. Seraphim, the author of the text which we are citing, says to his master: " 'Nevertheless, I do not understand how I can be firmly assured that I am in the Spirit of God. How can I myself recognize His true manifestation?'

"Father Seraphim replied: 'I have already told you, my son, that it is very simple, and have in detail narrated to you

---

[55]The debates on the authenticity of these writings and even their attribution to circles from which Messalianism later sprang do not reduce the high value of these homilies attributed to St. Macarius; their role in the tradition of Christian spirituality remains an incontestable fact. See Dom L. Villecourt, "La date et l'origine des Homélies spirituelles attribuées à Macaire," *Comptes rendus des séances de l'Académie des Inscriptions et Belles Lettres* 5 (1920). See also the remark of Fr. J. Stiglmayr, "Pseudomakarius und die Altermystik der Messalianer," *Zeitschrift für katholische Theologie* 49 (1925) pp. 244-260, and especially the remarkable refutation of Dom Villecourt's hypothesis by W. Jaeger, *Two Rediscovered Works of Ancient Christian Literature: Gregory of Nyssa and Macarius* (Leiden, 1954).

[56]See an example of theophany of the light in the *Life of St. Symeon* by Nicetas Stethatos, ed. I. Hausherr, pp. 92-96.

[57]Western hagiography presents a typical example of luminous theophany in the narrative of St. Benedict's ecstasy by St. Gregory the Great, *Dialogues* II, 35; P.L. 66, cols. 198, 200.

[58][A few extracts from this monument of Russian spirituality of the beginning of the last century have been published in English: "A Conversation of St. Seraphim of Sarov with Nicholas Motovilov concerning the Aim of the Christian Life," translated by A. F. Dobbie-Bateman in *A Treasury of Russian Spirituality*, ed. G. P. Fedotov—*trans.*].

how men dwell in the Spirit of God, and how one must apprehend His appearance in us. . . . What then do you need?'

" 'My need,' said I, 'is to understand this well!'

" 'We are both together, son, in the Spirit of God. . . Why lookest thou not on me?'

" 'I cannot look, Father, because lightning flashes from your eyes; your face is brighter than the sun and my eyes ache in pain.'

" 'Fear not,' he says, 'you too have become as bright as I. You too are now in the fulness of God's Spirit; otherwise you would not be able to look on me as I am.'

"Then, bending his head towards me, he whispered softly in my ear: 'Give thanks to the Lord God for His ineffable mercy towards us. You have seen that I did not even make the sign of the cross; and only in my heart I prayed mentally to the Lord God and said within myself: Lord, vouchsafe to him to see clearly with bodily eyes that descent of Thy Spirit which Thou vouchsafest to Thy servants, when Thou art pleased to appear in the light of Thy marvellous glory. And see, my son, the Lord has fulfilled in a trice the humble prayer of poor Seraphim. . . Surely we must give thanks to Him for this ineffable gift to us both! Not always, my son, even to the Fathers of the desert, does the Lord God show His mercy. See, the grace of God has come to comfort your contrite heart, as a loving mother, at the intercession of the Mother of God herself. . . Come, son, why do you not look me in the eyes? Just look and fear not: the Lord is with us.'

"Encouraged by these words, I looked in his face and there came over me an even greater reverential awe. Imagine in the center of the sun, in the dazzling brilliance of his midday rays, the face of the man who talks with you. You see the movement of his lips and the changing expression of his eyes, you hear his voice, you feel someone grasp your shoulders; yet you do not see the hands, you do not even see yourself or his figure, but only a blinding light spreading several yards around and throwing a sparkling radiance across the snow blanket on the glade and into the snowflakes which did not stop falling. . .'"

It would seem unlikely to suppose that St. Seraphim of Sarov had a profound knowledge of the theological doctrines of St. Gregory Palamas on the nature of the uncreated light, which we have just briefly retraced in this article. However we find once again in him, five centuries after the "Palamite Councils," in a cultural ambiance very different from that of Byzantium, in a corner of a Russian province in the first quarter of the nineteenth century, the same "theology of Light," tested by experience, distinctly affirmed as the foundation and criterion of the mystical life, of a knowledge of grace which is God Himself revealing Himself to us.

8

The theology of Light is not a metaphor, a literary fiction lending an affected disguise to some abstract truth. Nor is it a doctrine, properly speaking, in the sense where "doctrine" means an intellectual system tending to replace the realities of experience with abstract concepts. Its negative, "apophatic" character is expressed by antinomic oppositions, which we have tried to describe, and continues the theological method of the Fathers, who affirmed the fundamental dogmas of Christianity by always confronting us with antinomies: unity-trinity for Trinitarian dogma, duality-unity for Christological dogma. In fact, just as the dogmas of Nicaea and Chalcedon—which impose on us an ineffable distinction between Nature and Person in order to safeguard the mysterious reality of the Trinity and of Christ, true God and true Man—likewise the dogma of the real distinction between essence and energies—imposed on our minds by the antinomy of God unknowable and knowable, incommunicable and communicable, transcendent and immanent—has no other goal than to defend the reality of divine grace, to leave open the door to mystical experience, outside of which there is no spiritual life in the true sense of that word. For the spiritual life requires that the Christian dogmas not merely be confessed, but lived by the faithful. In this way of thinking one no longer experiences difficulties in accepting the severe word of St. Symeon the New Theologian, who refuses the name of Christian to those who have not had in this life the experience of the divine Light.

The theology of Light is inherent in Orthodox spirituality: the one is impossible without the other. One can be completely ignorant of Gregory Palamas, of his role in the doctrinal history of the Church of the East; but one can never understand Eastern spirituality if one makes an abstraction of its theological basis, which finds its definitive expression in the great archbishop of Thessalonica, "preacher of grace."[59] All the liturgical texts are impregnated with it. Are these only metaphors, Byzantine rhetoric? Or rather, ought what one habitually wishes to take as affected forms of a fixed religiosity, devoid of genuine speculative content, be taken as something living and concrete, as religious experience? It seems evident to us that outside of this theology of Light, whose outlines we have just traced, all the spiritual richness of the Christian East would appear to the eyes of a foreign observer as deprived of life, of that inner warmth which rightly represents an intimate quality of Orthodox piety.

The West long disregarded the religious art of Byzantium and the artistic value of Russian icons; it took a long time to appreciate the Western "primitives" which sprang from the same tradition. Will this also be the fate of the doctrinal and spiritual tradition of Eastern Christianity? Certainly it is unnecessary to demonstrate the need for more profound studies of the theological tradition of the East: it is evident to everyone. But if one wishes to have these studies serve the cause of rapprochement and mutual understanding, we must agree to see and judge this tradition otherwise than through the rigid concepts of an academic theology which is foreign to it. Then the doctrinal traits which appeared as points of disagreement in the past will perhaps become fruitful sources of spiritual renewal in the future.[60]

---

[59]Hymn from the second Sunday of Lent, which is dedicated to the memory of St. Gregory Palamas.

[60]"We can await from a renewed contact with the great catholic tradition of the East a rebirth of youth and fecundity in the study of sacred theology." M.-J. Congar, "La déification dans la tradition spirituelle de l'Orient," *La vie spirituelle*, no. 188 (May 1, 1935) p. 107.

4

The Procession
of the Holy Spirit
in Orthodox Trinitarian
Doctrine

Whether we like it or not, the question of the procession
of the Holy Spirit has been the sole dogmatic grounds for
the separation of East and West. All the other divergences
which, historically, accompanied or followed the first dogmatic controversy about the *Filioque*, in the measure in
which they too had some dogmatic importance, are more or
less dependent upon that original issue. This is only too easy
to understand, when we take into account the importance
of the mystery of the Trinity and its place in the whole body
of Christian teaching. Thus the polemical battle between
the Greeks and the Latins was fought principally about the
question of the Holy Spirit. If other questions have arisen and
taken the first place in more recent inter-confessional debates,
that is chiefly because the dogmatic plane on which the
thought of theologians operates is no longer the same as it

was in the medieval period. Ecclesiological problems increasingly determine the preoccupations of modern Christian thought. This is as it should be. However the tendency to underestimate and even to despise the pneumatological debates of the past which may be noticed among certain modern Orthodox theologians (and especially among Russians, who are too often ungrateful to Byzantium) suggests that these theologians, so ready to renounce their fathers, lack both dogmatic sense and reverence for the living tradition.

True, it is always necessary to revalue the truths which the Church affirmed in the past in order to meet the needs of the present. But this revaluation is never a devaluation. It is the restatement of the value of that which was said in a different epoch under different historical circumstances. It is the duty of the historian to inform us about the circumstances in which a dogma was first required and to state the historical implications of dogma. But it is not his duty, as a historian, to judge dogmatic values as such. If this is not remembered, there is a danger that historical theology will become a "Grey Eminence," or rather a "Lay Eminence," in the Church, seeking to establish by the methods of secular science a new canon of tradition. This is a sort of Caesaropapism of the scholars, which might succeed in imposing its authority over the Church, if tradition were not, for Her, a living reality of revelation in the Holy Spirit.

Thus, for example, the learned Russian theologian, V. Bolotov, an eminent historian of theology, on the occasion of the Bonn conversations with the Old Catholics, considered himself able to declare, on the basis of an analysis of Patristic texts, that the Filioque hardly constitutes an *impedimentum dirimens* in the path of dogmatic reconciliation.[1] According to Bolotov, the question concerned two "theologoumena," expressing in two different formulas—*a Filio* and διὰ Υἱοῦ— the doctrine of the procession of the Holy Spirit. Bolotov was too good a historian of theology to conclude that the

---

[1]"Thesen über das Filioque (von einen russischen Theologen)," *Révue internationale de théologie* (published at Berne by the Old Catholics) 6 (1898), pp. 681-712.

doctrine on both sides was identical. But he lacked the dogmatic sense to perceive the true place of these two formulas in two different triadologies. Even historically, he made a mistake in treating *a Filio* as the opposite of διὰ Υἱοῦ, as if these were the two formulas which express the doctrine of the hypostatic procession of the Holy Spirit. It was *a Patre Filioque* and ἐκ μόνου τοῦ Πατρὸς which, as formulas about the procession, came into conflict and thus exposed a divergence in the theology of the Trinity.[2] The formula διὰ Υἱοῦ, interpreted in the sense of a mediation of the Son in the hypostatic procession of the Holy Spirit, was a formula of concord adopted by partisans of union in the thirteenth century precisely because their triadology was not the same as that of the adversaries of the *Filioque*. By adopting the interpretation of διὰ Υἱοῦ proper to the Latinizing Greeks, Bolotov minimized the doctrinal divergence between the two triadologies; hence he could write about two tolerable "theological opinions."

Our task here will not be that of a historian. We shall leave aside questions concerning the origins of the two different formulas. We shall even admit the possibility of an Orthodox interpretation of *Filioque*, as it first appeared at Toledo for example.[3] We are not dealing with verbal formulas here, but with two established theological doctrines. We shall try to show the outlines of the Trinitarian theology which Orthodox theologians regard themselves as obliged to defend when they are confronted with the doctrine of the eternal personal procession of the Holy Spirit from the Father and the Son as from a single principle. We shall confine ourselves to setting forth certain theological prin-

---

[2]Bolotov must have recognized, implicitly, the radical character of the divergences, since, after all, he categorically denied the *causal character* of the mediation of the Son in the procession of the Holy Spirit: "Aber wenn auch in den innersten geheimnisvollsten Beziehungen des trinitarischen Lebens begründet, ist das 'durch den Sohn' frei von dem leisesten Anstrich einer *Kausalitäts*-Bedeutung" (*op. cit.* p. 700; italics Bolotov's).

[3]A study of the Filioquism of the Spanish councils of the fifth, sixth, and seventh centuries would be of capital importance, so that a dogmatic appreciation of these formulas might be made. Here the disinterested work of historical theology could be really useful to the Church.

ciples, of a general character, about the formulas ἐκ μόνου τοῦ Πατρὸς and διὰ Υἰοῦ. We shall not enter into the controversies of the past in detail. Our sole aim will be to make Orthodox triadology better understood.

2

Roman Catholic and Orthodox theologians agree in recognizing that a certain anonymity characterizes the Third Person of the Holy Trinity. While the names "Father" and "Son" denote very clear personal distinctions, are in no sense interchangeable, and cannot in any case refer to the common nature of the two hypostases, the name "Holy Spirit" has not that advantage. Indeed, we say that God is Spirit, meaning by that the common nature as much as any one of the persons. We say that He is Holy: The triple *Sanctus* of the canon of the Mass alludes to Three Holy Persons, having the common holiness of the same Godhead. Taken in itself, the term "Holy Spirit" thus might be applied, not to a personal distinction, but to the common nature of the Three. In that sense, Thomas Aquinas is right in saying that the Third Person of the Trinity has no name of His own and that the name "Holy Spirit" has been given to Him on the basis of Scriptural usage (*accomodatum ex usu Scripturae;* I, q. 36, a. 1).

We meet the same difficulty when we wish to define the mode of origin of the Holy Spirit, contrasting his "procession" with the "generation" of the Son. Even more than the name "Holy Spirit," the term "procession" cannot be considered to be, in itself, an expression which exclusively envisages the Third Person. It is a general term, which could be applied, *in abstracto*, to the Son; Latin theology even speaks of *duae processiones.* We leave aside, for the moment, the question of the extent to which such an abstract way of dealing with the mystery of the Trinity is legitimate. The one point which we stress here is that the term "procession" has not the precision of the term "generation." The latter term, while preserving the mysterious character of the divine

Fatherhood and Sonship, states a definite relationship between two persons. That is not the case with the term "procession"—an indefinite expression which confronts us with the mystery of an anonymous person, whose hypostatic origin is presented to us negatively: it is not generation, it is other than that of the Son.[4] If we seek to treat these expressions positively, we find an image of the economy of the Third Person rather than an image of his hypostatic character: we find the procession of a divine force or Spirit which accomplishes sanctification. We reach a paradoxical conclusion: all that we know of the Holy Spirit refers to his economy; all that we do not know makes us venerate his Person, as we venerate the ineffable diversity of the consubstantial Three.

In the fourth century the question of the Trinity was examined in a Christological context and was raised in connection with the *nature* of the Logos. The term ὁμοούσιος, while assuming the diversity of the Three Persons, was meant to express the identity in the Trinity, by stressing the unity of the common nature against all subordinationism. In the ninth century the Pneumatological controversy between the Latins and the Greeks raised the question of the Trinity in connection with the *hypostasis* of the Holy Spirit. Both contending parties, while assuming the natural identity of the Three, intended to express hypostatic diversity in the Trinity. The former party strove to establish personal diversity on the basis of the term ὁμοούσιος, starting from natural identity. The latter party, more conscious of the Trinitarian antinomy of οὐσία and ὑπόστασις, while taking into account consubstantiality, stressed the monarchy of the Father, as a safeguard against all danger of a new Sabellianism.[5] Two doctrines of the hypostatic procession of the Holy Spirit, *a Patre Filioque tanquam ab uno principio* and ἐκ μόνου τοῦ Πατρός, represent two different solutions of the question of

---

[4] St. Gregory of Nazianzus, *Or.* 20, 11; P.G. 35, col. 1077C. *Or.* 31, 8; P.G. 36, col. 141B.

[5] The expression is that of St. Photius, *Mystagogia* 9; P.G. 102, col. 289B: καὶ ἀναβλαστήσει πάλιν ἡμῖν ὁ Σαβέλλιος, μᾶλλον δέ τι τέρας ἕτερον ἡμισαβέλλειον.

personal diversity in the Trinity, two different triadologies. It is important that we should describe the general outlines of these triadologies.

3

Starting from the fact that the hypostatic character of the Holy Spirit remains undefined and "anonymous," Latin theology seeks to draw a positive conclusion as to his mode of origin. Since the term "Holy Spirit" is, in some sense, common to the Father and the Son (both are Holy and both are Spirit), it should denote a person related to the Father and the Son in respect of what they have in common.[6] Even when the matter at hand is the procession, taken as the mode of origin of the Third Person, the term "procession"—which in itself does not signify any mode of origin distinguishable from generation—should denote a relation to the Father and the Son together, to serve as the basis for a Third Person, distinct from the other two. Since a "relation of opposition"[7] can only be established between two terms, the Holy Spirit should proceed from the Father and the Son, inasmuch as they represent a unity. This is the meaning of the formula according to which the Holy Spirit is said to proceed from the Father and the Son as from one principle of spiration.[8] One cannot deny the logical clarity of this process of reasoning, which seeks to base hypostatic diversity on the principle of relations of opposition. This triadological principle, formulated by Thomas Aquinas, becomes unavoidable the moment that the doctrine of the procession of the Holy

---

[6]Thomas Aquinas, *Summa Theologica* I, qu. 36, a. 1, with a reference to St. Augustine, *De Trinitate* I, 11.

[7]Thomas uses the expressions *relativa oppositio, oppositio relationis* (this above all with reference to the essence), *relatio* (or *respectus*) *ad suum oppositum*, and *relationes oppositae* to signify what we here have called "relation of opposition." In using this expression, we do not in any way misrepresent Thomas' thought, for the idea of opposition is implied in his very definition of relation: "De ratione autem relationis est respectus unius ad alterum, secundum quem aliquid alteri opponitur relative" (I, qu. 28, a. 3).

[8]I, qu. 36, a. 2 and 4.

Spirit *ab utroque* is admitted. It presupposes the following conditions: (1) That relations are the basis of the hypostases,[9] which define themselves by their mutual opposition, the first to the second, and these two together to the third. (2) That two persons represent a non-personal unity, in that they give rise to a further relation of opposition. (3) That in general the origin of the persons of the Trinity therefore is impersonal, having its real basis in the one essence, which is differentiated by its internal relations. The general character of this triadology may be described as a pre-eminence of natural unity over personal trinity, as an ontological primacy of the essence over the hypostases.

The attitude of Orthodox thought, when confronted with the mysterious name of the Holy Spirit, denoting a divine economy rather than a hypostatic mark of distinction, is far from being simply a refusal to define his personal diversity. On the contrary, because that diversity, or (to speak more generally) the diversity of the Three Persons, is presented as something absolute, we refuse to admit a relation of origin which opposes the Holy Spirit to the Father and the Son, taken as a single principle. If this were admitted, personal diversity in the Trinity in effect would be relativized: Inasmuch as the Holy Spirit is one hypostasis, the Holy Spirit only represents the unity of the two in their identical nature. Here the logical impossibility of any opposition between *three* terms intervenes, and the clarity of this triadological system shows itself to be extremely superficial. Indeed, on these lines, we cannot reach a mode of distinguishing the three hypostases from each another without confounding them in one way or another with the essence. In fact, the absolute diversity of the Three cannot be based on their relations of opposition without admitting, implicitly or explicitly, the primacy of the essence over the hypostases, by assuming a relative (and therefore secondary) basis for personal diversity,

---

[9]Thomas Aquinas goes further: for him the persons of the Trinity *are* relations (*persona est relatio*, I, qu. 40, a. 2).

in contrast to natural identity.[10] But that is exactly what Orthodox theology cannot admit.

Against the doctrine of procession *ab utroque* the Orthodox have affirmed that the Holy Spirit proceeds from the Father alone—ἐκ μόνου τοῦ Πατρός. This formula, while verbally it may seem novel, represents in its doctrinal tenor nothing more than a very plain affirmation of the traditional teaching about the "monarchy of the Father," unique source of the divine hypostases. It may be objected that this formula for the procession of the Holy Spirit from the Father alone provides no place for any relation of opposition between the Second Person of the Trinity and the Third Person. But those who say this overlook the fact that the very principle of relations of opposition is unacceptable to Orthodox triadology—that the expression "relations of origin" has a different sense in Orthodox theology than it has among defenders of the *Filioque*.

When we state that the eternal procession of the Holy Spirit from the Father alone is distinguished in an ineffable manner from the eternal generation of the Son, who is begotten of the Father alone, no attempt is being made to establish a relation of opposition between the Son and the Holy Spirit. This is not merely because the procession is ineffable (the generation of the Son is no less ineffable)[11] but also because relations of origin in the Trinity—filiation, procession—cannot be considered as the basis for the hypostases, as that which determines their absolute diversity.[12]

---

[10]Fr. Th. de Régnon, inquiring why Filioquist considerations were never developed in the rich works of the Greek Fathers, asks: "Is this not proof that [such considerations] never occurred to them in their conception of the Trinity?" And he replies with a significant avowal: "In fact all these [Filioquist considerations] presuppose that, in the order of concepts, nature is anterior to person and that the latter represents a kind of efflorescence of the former" (*Études de théologie positive sur la Sainte Trinité* I (Paris, 1892), p. 309). He also writes: "Latin philosophy envisages first the nature in itself and then procedes to the expression; Greek philosophy envisages first the expression and then penetrates it to find the nature. The Latin considers personality as a mode of nature, the Greek considers nature as the content of the person" (*ibid.* p. 433).

[11]St. John of Damascus, *De fide orthodoxa* I, 8; P.G. 94, cols. 820-824A.

[12]Cf. St. Gregory of Nazianzus, *loc. cit.* n. 4 *supra*.

When we say that the procession of the Holy Spirit is a relation which differs absolutely from the generation of the Son, we indicate the difference between them as to mode of origin (τρόπος ὑπάρξεως)[13] from that common source in order to affirm that community of origin in no way affects the absolute diversity between the Son and the Spirit.

Here it may be stated that the relations only serve to *express* the hypostatic diversity of the Three; they are not the basis of it. It is the absolute diversity of the three hypostases which determines their differing relations to one another, not *vice versa*. Here thought stands still, confronted by the impossibility of defining a personal existence in its absolute difference from any other, and must adopt a negative approach to proclaim that the Father—He who is without beginning (ἄναρχος)—is not the Son or the Holy Spirit, that the begotten Son is neither the Holy Spirit nor the Father, that the Holy Spirit, "who proceeds from the Father," is neither the Father nor the Son.[14] Here we cannot speak of relations of opposition but only of relations of diversity.[15] To follow here the positive approach, and to envisage the relations of origin otherwise than as signs of the inexpressible diversity of the persons, is to suppress the absolute quality of this personal diversity, *i.e.* to relativize the Trinity and in some sense to depersonalize it.

---

[13]More exactly, "mode of subsistence." This expression is found, first of all, in St. Basil, *De spiritu sancto* 18; P.G. 32, col. 152B; and later *e.g.* in St. John of Damascus, *De fide orthodoxa* I, 8 and I, 10; P.G. 94, cols. 828D, 837C. It is heavily used by George of Cyprus, *Apologia,* P.G. 142, col. 254A *et passim.*

[14]"To be unbegotten, to be begotten, to proceed—these are the features which characterize the Father, the Son, and Him whom we call the Holy Spirit, in such a way as to safeguard the distinction of the three hypostases in the one nature and majesty of the Divinity; for the Son is not the Father, because there is only one Father, but He is what the Father is; the Holy Spirit, although He proceeds from God, is not the Son, because there is only one Only Begotten Son, but He is what the Son is. The Three are One in divinity and the One is Three in persons. Thus we avoid the unity of Sabellius and the triplicity of the odious present-day heresy." St. Gregory of Nazianzus, *Or.* 30, 9; P.G. 36, col. 141D-144A.

[15]In his polemic against the Latins, St. Mark of Ephesus, in affirming the principle of the *diversity* of the persons, criticizes the Thomist principle of *opposition* of the persons. *Capita syllogistica contra Latinos* 24; P.G. 161, cols. 189-193.

The positive approach employed by Filioquist triadology brings about a certain rationalization of the dogma of the Trinity, insofar as it suppresses the fundamental antinomy between the essence and the hypostases. One has the impression that the heights of theology have been deserted in order to descend to the level of religious philosophy. On the other hand, the negative approach, which places us face to face with the primordial antinomy of absolute identity and no less absolute diversity in God, does not seek to conceal this antinomy but to express it fittingly, so that the mystery of the Trinity might make us transcend the philosophical mode of thinking and that the Truth might make us free from our human limitations, by altering our means of understanding. If in the former approach faith seeks understanding, in order to transpose revelation onto the plane of philosophy, in the latter approach understanding seeks the realities of faith, in order to be transformed, by becoming more and more open to the mysteries of revelation. Since the dogma of the Trinity is the keystone of the arch of all theological thought and belongs to the region which the Greek Fathers called Θεολογία *par excellence*, it is understandable that a divergence in this culminating point, insignificant as it may seem at first sight, should have a decisive importance. The difference between the two conceptions of the Trinity determines, on both sides, the whole character of theological thought. This is so to such an extent that it becomes difficult to apply, without equivocation, the same name of theology to these two different ways of dealing with divine realities.

4

If personal diversity in God presents itself as a primordial fact, not to be deduced from any other principle or based on any other idea, that does not mean that the essential identity of the Three is ontologically posterior to their hypostatic diversity. Orthodox triadology is not a counter-blast to Filioquism; it does not run to the other extreme. As we already have said, relations of origin signify the personal diversity of the Three, but they indicate no less their essential identity. In that the Son and the Holy Spirit are distinguished from the Father, we venerate three Persons; in that they are one with Him, we confess their consubstantiality.[16] Thus the monarchy of the Father maintains the perfect equilibrium between the nature and the persons, without coming down too heavily on either side.[17] There is neither an impersonal substance nor non-consubstantial persons. The one nature and the three hypostases are presented simultaneously to our understanding, with neither prior to the other. The origin of the hypostases is not impersonal, since it is referred to the person of the Father; but it is unthinkable apart from their common possession of the same essence, the "divinity in division undivided."[18] Otherwise we should have Three Divine Individuals, Three Gods bound together by an abstract idea of Godhead. On the other hand, since consubstantiality is the non-hypostatic identity of the Three, in that they have (or rather *are*) a common essence, the unity of the three hypostases is inconceivable apart from the monarchy of the Father, who is the *principle* of the common possession of the same one essence. Otherwise we should be concerned with a simple essence, differentiated by relationships.[19]

It may be asked whether, in seeking to avoid the semi-Sabellianism of the Latins, their Greek adversaries did not fall into subordinationism because of their emphasis on the monarchy of the Father. This might perhaps seem all the more likely to happen, because in Greek patristic literature

---

[16]"For us there is one God, for the Godhead is one, and the Three in whom we believe proceed from and are referred to the One... Thus when we look at the Godhead, the First Cause, and the Monarchy, the One appears to us; but when we look at the Persons in whom the Godhead is, who timelessly and with equal glory come forth from the First Cause, we adore the Three." St. Gregory of Nazianzus, *Or.* 31, 14; P.G. 36, cols. 148D-149A.

[17]St. Photius compares the Trinity to a pair of scales, in which the needle represents the Father, and the two platforms represent the Son and the Holy Spirit. *Amphilochia* qu. 181; P.G. 101, col. 896.

[18]St. Gregory of Nazianzus, *Or.* 31, 14; P.G. 36, col. 148D.

[19]"The one nature in the Three is God; but the union (ἕνωσις) is the Father, from whom the others proceed and to whom they refer, not so as to be confounded but rather to have all in common with Him, without distinction of time, will, or power." St. Gregory of Nazianzus, *Or.* 42; P.G. 36, col. 476B.

one often finds the idea of causality applied to the person of the Father. The Father is called the cause (αἰτία) of the hypostases of the Son and the Holy Spirit, or even the "Godhead-source" (πηγαία Θεότης). Sometimes He is designated simply as "God," with the definite article ὁ Θεός, or even as αὐτοθεός.

It is worthwhile to recall here what we have said before about the negative approach characteristic of Orthodox thought—an approach which radically changes the value of philosophical terms applied to God. Not only the image of "cause," but also such terms as "production," "procession," and "origin" ought to be seen as inadequate expressions of a reality which is foreign to all becoming, to all process, to all beginning. Just as relations of origin mean something different from relations of opposition, so causality is nothing but a somewhat defective image, which tries to express the personal unity which determines the origins of the Son and the Holy Spirit. This unique cause is not prior to his effects, for in the Trinity there is no priority and posteriority. He is not superior to his effects, for the perfect cause cannot produce inferior effects. He is thus the cause of their equality with himself.[20] The causality ascribed to the person of the Father, who eternally begets the Son and eternally causes the Holy Spirit to proceed, expresses the same idea as the monarchy of the Father: that the Father is the personal principle of unity of the Three, the source of their common possession of the same content, of the same essence.

The expressions "Godhead-source" and "source of the Godhead" do not mean that the divine essence is subject to the person of the Father, but only that the person of the Father is the basis of common possession of the same essence, because the person of the Father, not being the sole person of the Godhead, is not to be identified with the essence. In a certain sense it can be said the Father *is* this possession of

---

[20]"For He would be the origin (ἀρχή) of petty and unworthy things, or rather the term 'origin' would be used in a petty and unworthy sense, if He were not the origin of the Godhead (τῆς Θεότητος ἀρχή) and of the goodness contemplated in the Son and in the Spirit: in the former as Son and Word, in the latter as Spirit which proceeds without separation." St. Gregory of Nazianzus, *Or.* 2, 38; P.G. 35, col. 445.

the divine essence in common with the Son and the Holy Spirit, and that he would not be a divine Person if he were only a monad: he would then be identified with the divine Essence. Here it may be useful to recall that St. Cyril of Alexandria regarded the name "Father" as superior to the name "God," because the name "God" is given to God in respect of his relations with beings of a different nature.[21]

If the Father is sometimes called simply God—ὁ Θεὸς or even αὐτοθεὸς—nevertheless we cannot find in orthodox writers expressions which treat consubstantiality as participation by the Son and the Holy Spirit in the essence of the Father.[22] Each Person is God by nature, not by participation in the nature of another.

The Father is the cause of the other hypostases in that He is not His essence, *i.e.* in that He does not have His essence for Himself alone. What the image of causality wishes to express is the idea that the Father, being not merely an essence but a person, is by that very fact the cause of the other consubstantial Persons, who have the same essence as He has.

5

With reference to the Father, causality expresses the idea that He is God-Person, in that He is the cause of other divine persons—the idea that He could not be fully and absolutely Person unless the Son and the Holy Spirit are equal to Him in possession of the same nature and *are* that same nature. This might lead to the idea that each person of the Trinity could be regarded as the cause of the other two, in that each person is not the common essence; this would amount to a new relativization of the hypostases, transforming them into conventional and interchangeable signs of three diversities. Roman Catholic theology avoids this *personal relativism* by

---

[21]*Thesaurus,* assert. 5; P.G. 75, cols. 65, 68.
[22]Such a concept may be found in the works of Origen, e.g. *Commentary on St. John* 2, 2; P.G. 14, col. 109. On this subject the excellent work of Th. Lieske, *Theologie der Logosmystik bei Origen* (Münster, 1938), may be usefully consulted.

professing belief in the procession of the Holy Spirit *ab utroque, i.e.* by falling into an *impersonal relativism*, that of relations of opposition, which are regarded as the basis of the three persons in the unity of a simple essence. Orthodox theology, while taking as its starting-point the initial antinomy of essence and hypostasis, avoids personal relativism by attributing causality to the Father alone. The monarchy of the Father thus sets up irreversible relationships, which enable us to distinguish the two other hypostases from the Father, and yet to relate them to the Father, as a concrete principle of unity in the Trinity. There is not only unity of the same one nature in the Three, but also unity of the Three Persons of the same one nature. St. Gregory of Nazianzus expresses this neatly: "Each considered in himself is wholly God, as the Father so the Son, as the Son so the Holy Spirit, but each preserves his own properties; considered together the Three are God; each (considered in himself is) God because of the consubstantiality, the Three (considered together are) God because of the monarchy."[23]

According to St. Maximus, God is "identically, a monad and a triad."[24] He is not merely one and three; he is $1 = 3$ and $3 = 1$. That is to say, here we are not concerned with number as signifying quantity: absolute diversities cannot be made the subjects of sums of addition; they have not even opposition in common. If, as we have said, a personal God cannot be a monad—if he must be more than a single person—neither can he be a dyad. The dyad is always an opposition of two terms, and, in that sense, it cannot signify an absolute diversity. When we say that God is Trinity we are emerging from the series of countable or calculable numbers.[25] The procession of the Holy Spirit is an infinite

---

[23]St. Gregory of Nazianzus, *Or.* 40 (*In Sanctum baptisma*), 41; P.G. 36, col. 417B.

[24]*Capita theologica et oeconomica* 2, 13; P.G. 90, col. 1125A.

[25]St. Basil appears to express this idea well: "For we do not count by way of addition, gradually making increase from unity to plurality, saying 'one, two, three' or 'first, second, third.' 'I am the first and I am the last,' says God (Isaiah 44:6). And we have never, even unto our own days, heard of a second God. For in worshipping 'God of God' we both confess the distinction of persons and abide by the Monarchy." *De spiritu sancto* 18; P.G. 32, col. 149B.

passage beyond the dyad, which consecrates the absolute (as opposed to relative) diversity of the persons. This passage beyond the dyad is not an infinite series of persons but the infinity of the procession of the Third Person: the Triad suffices to denote the Living God of revelation.[26] If God is a monad equal to a triad, there is no place in him for a dyad. Thus the seemingly necessary opposition between the Father and the Son, which gives rise to a dyad, is purely artificial, the result of an illicit abstraction. Where the Trinity is concerned, we are in the presence of the One or of the Three, but never of two.

The procession of the Holy Spirit *ab utroque* does not signify passage beyond the dyad but rather re-absorption of the dyad in the monad, the return of the monad upon itself. It is a dialectic of the monad opening out into the dyad and closing again into its simplicity.[27] On the other hand, procession of the Holy Spirit from the Father alone, by emphasizing the monarchy of the Father as the concrete principle of the unity of the Three, passes beyond the dyad without a return to primordial unity, without the necessity of God retiring into the simplicity of the essence. For this reason the procession of the Holy Spirit from the Father alone confronts us with the mystery of the "Tri-Unity." We have here not a simple, self-enclosed essence, upon which relations of opposition have been superimposed in order to masquerade a god of philosophy as the God of Christian revelation. We say "the simple Trinity," and this antinomic expression, characteristic of Orthodox hymnography,[28] points out a simplicity which the absolute diversity of the three persons can in no way relativize.

6

When we speak of the Personal God, who cannot be a monad, and when, bearing in mind the celebrated Plotinian

---

[26]St. Gregory of Nazianzus, *Or.* 23 (*De pace* 3), 10; P.G. 35, col. 1161. *Or.* 45 (*In sanctum pascha*); P.G. 36, col. 628C.
[27]The idea of the Holy Spirit as the mutual love of the Father and the Son is characteristic, in this sense, of Filioquist triadology.
[28]Cf. St. Andrew of Crete's Great Canon of repentance, odes 3, 6, 7.

passage in the works of St. Gregory of Nazianzus, we say
that the Trinity is a passage beyond the dyad and beyond
its pair of opposed terms,[29] this in no sense implies the Neo-
Platonist idea of *bonum diffusivum sui* or any kind of moral
basis for the doctrine of the Trinity, *e.g.* the idea of love
seeking to share its own plenitude with others. If the Father
shares His one essence with the Son and the Holy Spirit and
in that sharing remains undivided, this i ' neither an act of
will nor an act of internal necessity. In more general terms,
it is not an act at all, but the eternal mode of Trinitarian
existence in itself. It is a primordial reality which cannot be
based on any notion other than itself, for the Trinity is prior
to all the qualities—goodness, intelligence, love, power,
infinity—in which God manifests Himself and in which He
can be known.

When Roman Catholic theology presents the relations
of origin as notional acts and speaks of two processions *per
modum intellectus* and *per modum voluntatis,* it commits—
from the point of view of Orthodox triadology—an inadmis-
sible error of confusion concerning the Trinity. In effect,
the external qualities of God—intellect, will, or love—are
introduced into the interior of the Trinity to designate the
relations between the three hypostases. This line of thought
gives us a divine individuality rather than a Trinity of
persons—an individuality which in thought is conscious of its
own essential content (generation of the Word *per modum
intellectus*) and which, in knowing himself, loves himself
(the procession of the Holy Spirit *ab utroque, per modum
voluntatis* or *per modum amoris*). We are here confronted
with a philosophical anthropomorphism having nothing in
common with Biblical anthropomorphism; for the Biblical
theophanies, while showing us in human guise the acts and
manifestations of a personal God in the history of the world,
also place us face to face with the mystery of His unknowable

---

[29]"The monad is set in motion on account of its richness; the dyad is
surpassed, because Divinity is beyond matter and form; perfection is reached
in the triad, the first to surpass the composite quality of the dyad, so that
the Divinity neither remains constrained nor expands to infinity." St. Gregory
of Nazianzus, *Or.* 23 (*De pace* 3), 8; P.G. 35, col. 1160C. See also *Or.* 29
(*Theologica* 3), 2; P.G. 36, col. 76B.

Being, which Christians nevertheless dare to venerate and to invoke as the unique Being in Three Persons, Father, Son, and Holy Spirit, who live and reign in the inaccessible light of their essence.

For us the Trinity remains the *Deus absconditus,* the Holy of Holies of the divine existence, where no "strange fire" may be introduced. Theology will be faithful to tradition in so far as its technical terms—οὐσία, ὑπόστασις, consubstantiality, relations of origin, causality, monarchy—serve to present more and more clearly the initial mystery of God the Trinity, without obscuring it with "Trinitarian deductions" derived from another starting-point. By defending the hypostatic procession of the Holy Spirit from the Father alone, Orthodoxy professes its faith in the "simple Trinity," wherein relations of origin denote the absolute diversity of the Three while at the same time indicating their unity, as represented by the Father, who is not simply a monad but—in that he is the Father—the principle of the Tri-Unity. This means, if God is truly the Living God of revelation and not the simple essence of the philosophers, He can only be God the Trinity. This is a primordial truth, incapable of being based on any process of reasoning whatever, because all reasoning, all truth, and all thought prove to be posterior to the Trinity, the basis of all being and all knowledge.

As we have seen, all triadology depends on the question of the procession of the Holy Spirit:

(1) If the Holy Spirit proceeds from the Father alone, this ineffable procession confronts us with the absolute diversity of the three hypostases, excluding all relations of opposition. If He proceeds from the Father and the Son, the relations of origin, instead of being signs of absolute diversity, become determinants of the persons, which emanate from an impersonal principle.

(2) If the Holy Spirit proceeds from the Father alone, this procession presents us with a Trinity which escapes the laws of quantitative number, since it goes beyond the dyad of opposed terms, not by means of a synthesis or a new series of numbers, but by an absolutely new diversity which we call the Third Person. If the Holy Spirit proceeds *ab*

utroque, we get a relativized Trinity, submitted to the laws of number and of relations of opposition—laws which cannot serve as a basis for the diversity of the Three Persons without confusing them either with each other or with their common nature.

(3) If the Holy Spirit proceeds from the Father alone, as the hypostatic cause of the consubstantial hypostases, we find the "simple Trinity," where the monarchy of the Father conditions the personal diversity of the Three while at the same time expressing their essential unity. The balance between the hypostases and the οὐσία is safeguarded. If the Holy Spirit proceeds from the Father and the Son as from one single principle, essential unity takes precedence over personal diversity, and the Persons become relations of the essence, differentiating themselves from one another by mutual opposition. This is no longer the "simple Trinity" but an absolute simplicity of essence, which is treated as an ontological basis at a point where there can be no basis except the primordial Tri-Unity itself.

7

By the dogma of the *Filioque*, the God of the philosophers and savants is introduced into the heart of the Living God, taking the place of the *Deus absconditus, qui posuit tenebras latibulum suum*. The unknowable essence of the Father, Son, and Holy Spirit receives positive qualifications. It becomes the object of natural theology: we get "God in general," who could be the god of Descartes, or the god of Leibnitz, or even perhaps, to some extent, the god of Voltaire and of the dechristianized Deists of the eighteenth century. Manuals of theology begin with a demonstration of His existence, thence to deduce, from the simplicity of His essence, the mode in which the perfections found among creatures are to be attributed to this eminently simple essence. From His attributes they go on to a discussion of what He can or cannot do, if He is not to contradict Himself and is to remain true to His essential perfection. Finally a chapter about the relations of the essence—which do not at all abolish its simplicity—serves as a fragile bridge between the god of the philosophers and the God of revelation.

By the dogma of the procession of the Holy Spirit from the Father alone, the god of the philosophers is forever banished from "the Holy of Holies, which is hid from the gaze of the Seraphim and glorified through the Three Holinesses Who are united into a single Sovereignty and Divinity."[30] The ineffable essence of the Trinity escapes all positive qualification, including that of simplicity. If we speak of the "simple Trinity," this self-contradictory expression means that distinctions between the three hypostases and between them and the essence do not introduce into the Tri-Unity any division into "constituent elements." Where the idea of the monarchy of the Father remains unshakable, no distinction postulated by faith can introduce composition into the Godhead. Precisely because God is unknowable in that which He is, Orthodox theology distinguishes between the essence of God and His energies, between the inaccessible nature of the Holy Trinity and its "natural processions."[31]

When we speak of the Trinity in itself, we are confessing, in our poor and always defective human language, the mode of existence of the Father, Son, and Holy Spirit, one sole God who cannot but be Trinity, because He is the Living God of Revelation, Who, though unknowable, has made Himself known, through the incarnation of the Son, to all who have received the Holy Spirit, Who proceeds from the Father and is sent into the world in the name of the incarnate Son.

Every name except those of Father, Son, and Holy Spirit—even the names of "Word" and "Paraclete"—is inappropriate for designating the special characteristics of the hypostases in the inaccessible existence of the Trinity, and refers rather

---

[30]St. Gregory of Nazianzus, *Or.* 38 (*In theophaniam*), 8; P.G. 36, col. 320BC.

[31]See the acts of the councils of Constantinople in 1341, 1347, and 1350; Mansi, vol. 25, cols. 1147-1150, vol. 26, cols. 105-110, 127-212. St. Gregory Palamas, *Theophanes*, P.G. 150, cols. 909-960.

to the external aspect of God, to His manifestation,[32] or even to His economy. The dogma of the Trinity marks the summit of theology, where our thought stands still before the primordial mystery of the existence of the Personal God. Apart from the names denoting the three hypostases and the common name of the Trinity, the innumerable names which we apply to God—the "divine names" which textbook theology calls his attributes—denote God not in his inaccessible Being but in "that which surrounds the essence" (τὰ περὶ τῆς οὐσίας).[33] This is the eternal radiance of the common content of the Three Persons, who reveal their incommunicable nature in "energies." This technical term of Byzantine theology, denoting a mode of divine existence besides essence, introduces no new philosophical notion alien to revelation. The Bible, in its concrete language, speaks of nothing other than "energies" when it tells us of the "glory of God"—a glory with innumerable names which surrounds the inaccessible Being of God, making Him known outside Himself, while concealing what He is in Himself. This is the eternal glory which belongs to the Three Persons, which the Son "had before the world was." And when we speak of the divine energies in relation to the human beings to whom they are communicated and given and by whom they are appropriated, this divine and uncreated reality within us is called Grace.

8

The manifesting energies of God—which signify a mode of divine existence other than that of the Trinity in itself, in its incommunicable nature—do not make a breach in its unity; they do not abolish the "simple Trinity." The same monarchy of the Father, who is the cause of the consub-

---

[32]It is thus that the Logos of the Prologue to St. John's Gospel signifies the Son, in that he *manifests* the nature of the Father—the common nature of the Trinity. In this sense, the Logos also includes the manifesting role of the Holy Spirit: "In him was life, and the life was the light of men."

[33]St. Gregory of Nazianzus, *Or.* 38 (*In theophaniam*), 7; P.G. 36, col. 317B.

stantial hypostases of the Son and the Holy Spirit, also presides over the external manifestation of the unity of the Trinity. Here the term "causality," applied to the Person of the Father in that He is the principle of the absolute diversities of the Three consubstantial Persons (a term implying the hypostatic procession of the Holy Spirit from the Father alone), must be clearly distinguished from the revelation or manifestation of the Father by the Son in the Holy Spirit. Causality, with all its defects as a term, expresses what it stands for quite well: the hypostatic distinction of the Three which arises from the Person of the Father—a distinction between absolute diversities, brought about by the fact that the Father is not uniquely the essence. It is not possible to replace the conventional term "causality" by that of "manifestation" of the Father—as Fr. Bulgakov has tried to do[34]—without confounding the two planes of thought: that of the existence of the Trinity in itself, and that of existence *ad extra,* in the radiance of the essential glory of God.

If the Father is the personal cause of the hypostases, He is also, for that very reason, the principle of their common possession of one and the same nature; and in that sense, He is the "source" of the common divinity of the Three. The revelation of this nature, the externalization of the unknowable essence of the Three, is not a reality foreign to the Three hypostases. Every energy, every manifestation, comes from the Father, is expressed in the Son, and goes forth in the Holy Spirit.[35] This procession—natural, "energetic," manifesting—must be clearly distinguished from hypostatic procession, which is personal, internal, from the Father alone. The same monarchy of the Father conditions both the hypostatic procession of the Holy Spirit—His personal existence ἐκ μόνου τοῦ Πατρὸς—and the manifesting,

---

[34]S. Bulgakov, *Le Paraclet* (Paris: Aubier, 1946) pp. 69-75.

[35]Thus all the divine names, denoting as they do the common nature, can be applied to each of the Persons, but only in the *energetic* order—the order of the manifestation of the Divinity. See, for example, St. Gregory of Nyssa, *Adversus Macedonianos* 13; P.G. 45, col. 1317: "The source of power is the Father; the power is the Son; the spirit of power is the Holy Spirit." St. Gregory of Nazianzus, *Or.* 23, 11; P.G. 35, col. 1164A: "The True, the Truth, the Spirit of Truth."

natural procession of the common Godhead *ad extra* in the Holy Spirit, through the Son—διὰ Υἱοῦ.

If, as we have already said, the name "Holy Spirit" expresses more a divine economy than a personal quality, this is because the Third Hypostasis is *par excellence* the hypostasis of manifestation, the Person in whom we know God the Trinity. His Person is hidden from us by the very profusion of the Divinity which He manifests. It is this "personal kenosis" of the Holy Spirit on the plane of manifestation and economy which makes it hard to grasp His hypostatic existence.

The same plane of natural manifestation gives to the name "Logos," as applied to the Son, all its significance. The Logos is "a concise declaration of the nature of the Father," as St. Gregory of Nazianzus says.[36] When St. Basil speaks to us of the Son who "shows in Himself the whole of the Father, shining with all His glory in resplendence,"[37] he also is concerned with the manifesting and energetic aspect of the Trinity. Likewise all the patristic passages in which the Son is called "the image of the Father" and the Holy Spirit is called "the image of the Son"[38] refer to the energetic manifestation of the content common to the Three; for the Son is not the Father, but He is what the Father is; the Holy Spirit is not the Son, but He is what the Son is.[39] In the order of divine manifestation, the hypostases are not the respective images of the personal diversities but of the common nature: the Father reveals His nature through the Son, and the divinity of the Son is manifested in the Holy Spirit. This is why, in the realm of divine manifestation, it is possible to establish an order of Persons (τάξις) which, strictly speaking, should not be attributed to Trinitarian existence in itself, despite the "monarchy" and "causality" of the Father: these confer upon Him no hypostatic primacy over the other two

---

[36]*Or.* 30 (*Theologica* 4), 20; P.G. 36, col. 129A.

[37]*Adversus Eunomium* II, 17; P.G. 24, col. 605B.

[38]St. Cyril of Alexandria, *Thesaurus* assert. 33; P.G. 75, col. 572. St. John of Damascus, *De imaginibus* III, 18; P.G. 94, cols. 1337D-1340B; *De fide orthodoxa* I, 13; P.G. 94, col. 856B.

[39]St. Gregory of Nazianzus, *Or.* 31 (*Theologica* 5), 9; P.G. 36, col. 144A.

hypostases, since He is a person only because the Son and the Holy Spirit are also.

9

Confusion between Trinitarian existence and energetic radiance, between personal causality and natural manifestation, can arise in two different and, in a certain sense, opposite ways: (1) The Trinity may be conceived as an internal revelation of the divine nature in notional acts: the Father expresses His nature in the Word and the two cause the Holy Spirit to proceed as a mutual "bond of love." This is the triadology of Latin Filioquism. (2) The Trinity may be conceived as an internal revelation of the hypostases or of the "Tri-hypostatic subject" in the common nature. This is the triadology of Russian Sophiology, particularly of Fr. Bulgakov. In both cases, the equilibrium between essence and hypostases is broken. The Trinitarian antinomy is suppressed, with the former in favour of the essence, with the latter in favour of the hypostases.

The distinction between the unknowable essence of the Trinity and its energetic processions, clearly defined by the great councils of the fourteenth century, allows Orthodox theology to maintain firmly the difference between tri-hypostatic existence in itself and tri-hypostatic existence in the common manifestation outside the essence. In His hypostatic existence, the Holy Spirit proceeds from the Father alone; and this ineffable procession enables us to confess the absolute diversity of the Three Persons, *i.e.* our faith in the Tri-Unity. In the order of natural manifestation, the Holy Spirit proceeds from the Father through the Son (διὰ Υἱοῦ), after the Word; and this procession reveals to us the common glory of the Three, the eternal splendor of the divine nature.

It is curious to notice that the distinction between the hypostatic existence of the Holy Spirit, proceeding from the Father alone, and His eternal radiance—εἰς ἀΐδιον ἔκφανσιν—through the Son, was formulated in the course of discussions which took place in Constantinople towards the end of the thirteenth century, after the Council of Lyons.[40] The doctrinal continuity can be recognized here: defense of the doctrine of the procession of the Holy Spirit from the Father alone necessitates a decision as to the import of the phrase διὰ Υἱοῦ; this in turn opens the way for the distinction between essence and energies. This is not a "dogmatic development." Rather, one and the same tradition is defended, at different points, by the Orthodox from St. Photius to George of Cyprus and St. Gregory Palamas.

It would not be exact to say, as some Orthodox polemicists have, that the procession διὰ Υἱοῦ signifies solely the temporal mission of the Holy Spirit. In the case of the temporal mission of the persons of the Son and the Holy Spirit, a new factor is involved: that of will. This will, as we know, can only be the common will of the Trinity. The temporal mission is a specific case of divine manifestation _in the economy_, _i.e._ in relation to created being. Generally speaking, the divine economy in time expresses the eternal manifestation; but the eternal manifestation is not necessarily the basis of created beings, which could have not existed. Independently of the existence of creatures, the Trinity is manifested in the radiance of its glory. From all eternity, the Father is "the Father of glory" (Eph. 1:17); the Word is "the brightness of His glory" (Heb. 1:3); and the Holy Spirit is "the Spirit of glory" (I Peter 4:14).

Poverty of vocabulary sometimes makes it hard to recognize whether it is the hypostatic procession of the Holy Spirit or the procession of manifestation to which a writer is alluding: both are eternal, though having a different point of reference. Very often the Fathers simultaneously employ expressions referring to the hypostatic existence of the Holy Spirit and to the eternal manifestation of the divine nature in the Holy Spirit, even when defining His personal qualities or distinguishing His person from the other two. Nevertheless, they well distinguished between the two dif-

---

[40]See the expression εἰς ἀΐδιον ἔκφανσιν in the works of George of Cyprus: _Expositio fidei_, P.G. 142, col. 241A; _Confessio_, col. 250; _Apologia_, cols. 266-267; _De processione Spiritus Sancti_, cols. 290C, 300B.

ferent modes of hypostatic subsistence and of manifestation. In evidence, we can cite this passage from St. Basil: "From the Father proceeds the Son, through whom are all things, and with whom the Holy Spirit is ever inseparably known, for none can think of the Son without being enlightened by the Spirit. Thus on one hand the Holy Spirit, the source, of all good things distributed to created beings, is linked to the Son, with whom He is inseparably conceived; on the other hand His being is dependent on the Father, from whom He proceeds. Therefore the characteristic mark of His personal quality is *to be manifested* after the Son and with Him, and *to subsist* in proceeding from the Father."[41] Many other patristic texts could be cited, in which the writer is concerned simultaneously with the eternal manifestation of the Divinity in the Holy Spirit and with His personal existence.[42] It was on the basis of these texts that Latinizing Greeks sought to defend the hypostatic procession of the Holy Spirit "through the Son" in order to reconcile two such different triadologies.

10

It is easy to conceive the difficulties which the distinction between hypostatic existence of the Holy Spirit and eternal manifestation of the divine nature in His person presented to the theologically rude and uneducated minds of Western Christians of the Carolingian period. It may well be supposed that it was the truth of the eternal manifestation which the first Filioquist formulas, in Spain and elsewhere before the ninth century, were intended to express. It is possible that the Filioquism of St. Augustine can also be interpreted in the same sense, although here the problem is more difficult and a theological analysis of the treatise

---

[41]*Ep.* 38, 4; P.G. 32, col. 329C-332A. See also two passages in St. Gregory of Nyssa, *Adversus Eunomium* I; P.G. 45, cols. 369A and 416C.

[42]For example, the pneumatological formula of the *Synodicon* of St. Tarasius, read at the Seventh Ecumenical Council, in which the distinction between the plane of subsistence and that of eternal manifestation is not noticed; Mansi, vol. 12, col. 1122.

De Trinitate is needed—something which has not yet been done by the Orthodox. Filioquism as a doctrine of the hypostatic procession of the Holy Spirit from the Father and the Son as from a single principle reached its clear and definitively explicit form in the great centuries of scholasticism. After the councils of Lyons and Florence, it was no longer possible to interpret the Latin formula for the procession of the Holy Spirit in the sense of eternal manifestation of the Divinity. At the same time it also became impossible for Roman Catholic theologians to admit the energetic manifestation of the Trinity as something not contradicting the truth of the divine simplicity. No longer was there any place for the concept of the energies of the Trinity: nothing was admitted to exist outside the divine essence except created effects, acts of will analogous to the act of creation. Western theologians had to profess the created character of glory and of sanctifying grace, to renounce the concept of deification; and in doing this they are quite consistent with the premises of their triadology.

Reconciliation will be possible and *Filioque* will no longer be an *impedimentum dirmens* at that moment when the West, which has been frozen for so long in dogmatic isolation, ceases to consider Byzantine theology as an absurd innovation and recognizes that it only expressed the truths of tradition, which can be found in a less explicit form in the Fathers of the first centuries of the Church. Then it will be recognized that what may seem absurd for a theology in which faith seeks understanding is not so absurd for an understanding open to the full reception of Revelation—open to the acquisition of "the sense of the Scriptures," whose sacred words long ago were "foolishness" to the Greek philosophers. The Greeks have ceased to be Greeks in becoming sons of the Church. That is why they have been able to give to the Christian faith its imperishable theological armory. May the Latins in their turn cease to be solely Latins in their theology! Then together we shall confess our catholic faith in the Holy Trinity, who lives and reigns in the eternal light of His glory.

5

Redemption and Deification

"God made Himself man, that man might become God." These powerful words, which we find for the first time in St. Irenaeus,[1] are again found in the writings of St. Athanasius,[2] St. Gregory of Nazianzus,[3] and St. Gregory of Nyssa.[4] The Fathers and Orthodox theologians have repeated them in every century with the same emphasis, wishing to sum up in this striking sentence the very essence of Christianity: an ineffable descent of God to the ultimate limit of our fallen human condition, even unto death—a descent of God which opens to men a path of ascent, the unlimited vistas of the union of created beings with the Divinity.

The descent (κατάβασις) of the divine person of Christ makes human persons capable of an ascent (ἀνάβασις) in the Holy Spirit. It was necessary that the voluntary humilia-

---

[1] *Adversus haereses* V, preface; P.G. 7, col. 1120.
[2] *De incarnatione verbi* 54; P.G. 25, col. 192B.
[3] *Poema dogmatica* 10, 5-9; P.G. 37, col. 465.
[4] *Oratio catechetica magna* 25; P.G. 45, col. 65D.

tion, the redemptive κένωσις, of the Son of God should take place, so that fallen men might accomplish their vocation of θέωσις, the deification of created beings by uncreated grace. Thus the redeeming work of Christ—or rather, more generally speaking, the Incarnation of the Word—is seen to be directly related to the ultimate goal of creatures: to know union with God. If this union has been accomplished in the divine person of the Son, who is God become man, it is necessary that each human person, in turn, should become god by grace, or "a partaker of the divine nature," according to St. Peter's expression (II Peter 1:4).

Since, in the thought of the Fathers, the Incarnation of the Word is so closely linked to our ultimate deification, it could be asked whether the Incarnation would have taken place if Adam had not sinned. This question has often been raised, but it seems to us an unreal question. In fact, we have no knowledge of any condition of the human race except the condition resulting from original sin, in which our deification—the carrying out of the divine purpose for us— has become impossible without the Incarnation of the Son, a fact necessarily having the character of a redemption. The Son of God came down from heaven to accomplish the work of our salvation, to liberate us from the captivity of the devil, to destroy the dominion of sin in our nature, and to undo death, which is the wages of sin. The Passion, Death, and Resurrection of Christ, by which his redemptive work was accomplished, thus occupy a central place in the divine dispensation for the fallen world. From this point of view it is easy to understand why the doctrine of the redemption has such a great importance in the theological thought of the Church.

Nevertheless, when the dogma of the redemption is treated in isolation from the general body of Christian teaching, there is always a risk of limiting the tradition by interpreting it exclusively in terms of the work of the Redeemer. Then theological thought develops along three lines: original sin, its reparation on the cross, and the appropriation of the saving results of the work of Christ to Christians. In these constricting perspectives of a theology dominated by the idea of redemption, the patristic sentence, "God made Himself man that man might become God," seems to be strange and abnormal. The thought of union with God is forgotten because of our preoccupation solely with our own salvation; or, rather, union with God is seen only negatively, in contrast with our present wretchedness.

2

It was Anselm of Canterbury, with his treatise *Cur Deus Homo*, who undoubtedly made the first attempt to develop the dogma of redemption apart from the rest of Christian teaching. In his work Christian horizons are limited by the drama played between God, who is infinitely offended by sin, and man, who is unable to satisfy the impossible demands of vindictive justice. The drama finds its resolution in the death of Christ, the Son of God who has become man in order to substitute Himself for us and to pay our debt to divine justice. What becomes of the dispensation of the Holy Spirit here? His part is reduced to that of an auxiliary, an assistant in redemption, causing us to receive Christ's expiating merit. The final goal of our union with God is, if not excluded altogether, at least shut out from our sight by the stern vault of a theological conception built on the ideas of original guilt and its reparation. The price of our redemption having been paid in the death of Christ, the resurrection and the ascension are only a glorious happy end of His work, a kind of apotheosis without direct relationship to our human destiny. This redemptionist theology, placing all the emphasis on the passion, seems to take no interest in the triumph of Christ over death. The very work of the Christ-Redeemer, to which this theology is confined, seems to be truncated, impoverished, reduced to a change of the divine attitude toward fallen men, unrelated to the nature of humanity.

We find an entirely different conception of the redeeming work of Christ in the thought of St. Athanasius.[5] "Christ,"

---

[5] *De incarnatione verbi* 20; P.G. 25, col. 129D-132A.

he says, "having delivered the temple of His body to death, offered one sacrifice for all men to make them innocent and free from original guilt, and also to show Himself victorious over death and to create the first fruits of the General Resurrection with His own incorruptible body." Here the juridical image of the Redemption is completed by another image, the physical—or rather biological—image of the triumph of life over death, of incorruptibility triumphing in the nature which had been corrupted by sin.

In the Fathers generally, as well as in the Scriptures, we find many images expressing the mystery of our salvation accomplished by Christ. Thus, in the Gospel, the Good Shepherd is a "bucolic" image of the work of Christ.[6] The strong man, overcome by the "stronger than he, who taketh away his arms and destroys his power," is a "military" image,[7] which is often found again in the Fathers and in the Liturgy: Christ victorious over Satan, trampling upon the gates of hell, making the Cross his standard of triumph.[8] There is also a "medical" image, that of a sickly nature cured by salvation as the antidote to a poison.[9] There is an image which could be termed "diplomatic," the divine stratagem which deceives the devil in his cunning.[10] And so it goes. At last we come to the image used most often, taken by St. Paul from the Old Testament, where it was borrowed from the sphere of juridical relations.[11] Taken in this sense, redemption is a juridical image of the work of Christ, found

---

[6]Matt. 18:12-14, Luke 15:4-7, John 10:1-16.

[7]Matt. 12:29, Mark 3:27, Luke 11:21-22.

[8]St. Athanasius, *De incarnatione verbi* 30; P.G. 25, col. 148.

[9]St. John of Damascus, *De imaginibus* III, 9; P.G. 94, col. 1332D. The image of Christ as the physician of human nature, wounded by sin, is often found in connection with the parable of the Good Samaritan, which was interpreted in this way for the first time by Origen, Homily 34 on St. Luke, P.G. 13, cols. 1886-1888; *Commentary on St. John* 20, 28; P.G. 14, col. 656A.

[10]St. Gregory of Nyssa, *Oratio catechetica magna* 22-24; P.G. 45, cols. 60-65.

[11]Rom. 3:24, 8:23; I Cor. 1:30; Eph. 1:7, 14:30; Col. 1:14; Hebr. 9:15, 11:35, with the sense of deliverance. I Tim. 2:6; I Cor. 6:20, 7:22; Gal. 3:13, with the sense of a ransom paid.

side by side with many other images.[12] When we use the word "redemption," as we do nowadays, as a generic term designating the saving work of Christ in all its fulness, we should not forget that this juridical expression has the character of an image or simile: Christ is the Redeemer in the same sense that He is the Warrior victorious over death, the perfect Sacrificer, *etc.*

Anselm's mistake was not just that he developed a juridical view of the redemption, but rather that he wanted to see an adequate expression of the mystery of our redemption accomplished by Christ in the juridical relations implied by the word "redemption." Rejecting other expressions of this mystery as inadequate images, *quasi quaedam picturae,* he believed that he had found in the juridical image—that of the redemption—the very body of the truth, its "rational solidity," *veritatis rationabilis soliditas,* the reason why it was necessary for God to die for our salvation.[13]

The impossibility of proving rationally that the work of redemption was necessary, by making use of the juridical meaning of the term "redemption," was demonstrated by St. Gregory of Nazianzus in a magisterial *reductio ad absurdum.* He says: "We must now consider a problem and a doctrine often passed over silently, which, in my view, nevertheless needs deep study. The blood shed for us, the most precious and glorious blood of God, the blood of the Sacrificer and the Sacrifice—why was it shed and to whom was it offered? We were under the reign of the devil, sold to sin, after we had gained corruption on account of our sinful desire. If the price of our ransom is paid to him who has us in his power, I ask myself: Why is such a price to be paid? If it is given to the devil, it is outrageous! The brigand receives the price of redemption. Not only does he receive it from God, he receives God Himself. For his violence

---

[12]For St. Paul, the sacrificial or sacerdotal image of the work of Christ is basically identical to the juridical image—that of purchase or redemption properly so-called—but it also completes and deepens it. In effect, the idea of propitiation in blood (Rom. 3:26) ties together the two images—the juridical and the sacrificial—in the notion of the expiatory death of the just man, a notion characteristic of the messianic prophecies (Isaiah 53).

[13]*Cur Deus homo* I, 4; P.L. 158, col. 365.

he demands such a disproportionate ransom that it would
be more just for him to set us free without ransom. But if
the price is paid to the Father, why should that be done?
It is not the Father who has held us as His captives. Moreover, why should the blood of His only Son be acceptable
to the Father, who did not wish to accept Isaac, when Abraham offered Him his son as a burnt-offering, but replaced
the human sacrifice with the sacrifice of a ram? Is it not
evident that the Father accepts the sacrifice not because He
demanded it or had any need for it but by His dispensation?
It was necessary that man should be sanctified by the humanity of God; it was necessary that He Himself should free
us, triumphing over the tyrant by His own strength, and
that He should recall us to Himself by His Son who is the
Mediator, who does all for the honor of the Father, to whom
He is obedient in all things. . . . Let the rest of the mystery
be venerated silently."[14] What emerges from the passage we
have just quoted is that, for St. Gregory of Nazianzus, the
idea of redemption, far from implying the idea of a necessity
imposed by vindictive justice, is rather an expression of the
dispensation, whose mystery cannot be adequately clarified
in a series of rational concepts. He says, in later passage,
that "it was necessary for us that God should be incarnate
and die that we might live again" (c. 28). "Nothing can
be compared with the miracle of my salvation: a few drops
of blood re-make the whole universe" (c. 29).

After the constricted horizons of an exclusively juridical
theology, we find in the Fathers an extremely rich idea of
redemption which includes victory over death, the first
fruits of the general resurrection, the liberation of human
nature from captivity under the devil, and not only the
justification, but also the restoration of creation in Christ.
Here the Passion cannot be separated from the Resurrection
nor the glorious body of Christ, seated at the right hand of
the Father, from the life of Christians here below. Even if
redemption appears as the central aspect of the incarnation,
i.e., of the dispensation of the Son toward the fallen world,

---

[14]*Or.* 45, 22; P.G. 36, col. 653.

it is but one aspect of the vaster dispensation of the Holy Trinity toward being created *ex nihilo* and called to reach deification freely—to reach union with God, so that "God may be all in all." The thought of the Fathers never shuts out this ultimate vision. Redemption has our salvation from sin as an immediate aim, but that salvation will be, in its ultimate realization in the age to come, our union with God, the deification of the created beings whom Christ ransomed. But this final realization involves the dispensation of another divine Person, sent into the world after the Son.

The work of the Holy Spirit is inseparable from that of the Son. To be able to say with the Fathers, "God became man that man might become God," it is not enough to supplement the insufficiencies of Anselm's theory by returning to the wider and richer idea of redemption found in the Fathers. We must, above all, recover the true place of the dispensation of the Holy Spirit, distinct but not separable from that of the Incarnate Word.[15] If the thought of Anselm could stop at the redeeming work of Christ, isolating it from the rest of Christian teaching, constricting the horizons of tradition, it was precisely because in his time the West had already lost the true idea of the Person of the Holy Spirit, relegating Him to a secondary position by making Him into a kind of lieutenant or deputy of the Son. We shall leave this question aside, for we have already attempted to analyze the dogma of the *processio ab utroque* and its consequences for all Western theology. We confine ourselves here to the positive task of showing why the idea of our ultimate deification cannot be expressed on a Christological basis alone, but demands a Pneumatological development as well.

---

[15]We find in St. Athanasius some hints of a pneumatological explication of the sentence: "God became man, that man might become god." This is above all manifest in the celebrated opposition of Christ, "God bearing flesh," and Christians, "men bearing the Spirit." The Word assumed flesh so that we might receive the Holy Spirit. *De incarnatione et contra Arianos* 8; P.G. 26, col. 996C.

3

In the West, the theological thought of our day is making a great effort to return to the patristic sources of the first centuries—particularly to the Greek Fathers—in order to incorporate them into a catholic synthesis. Not only Post-Tridentine theology, but also medieval scholasticism, with all its philosophical richness, nowadays appears theologically inadequate. A powerful effort is being made to put back into use the notion of the Church as the body of Christ, as a new creature recapitulated by Christ, a nature or a body having the Risen Christ as her Head.

Since the first Adam missed his vocation of free attainment of union with God, the Second Adam, the divine Word, accomplished this union of the two natures in His Person, when He was incarnate. Entering the actuality of the fallen world, He broke the power of sin in our nature, and by His death, which reveals the supreme degree of His entrance into our fallen state, He triumphed over death and corruption. In baptism we die with Christ, symbolically, to rise again, really, in Him, in the new life of His victorious body, to become members of this unique body, historically and concretely existing on earth, but with its Head in heaven, in eternity, in the mystery of the Holy Trinity. Christ, who is both the Sacrificer and the Sacrifice, offers on the heavenly altar the unique sacrifice which is done here below on numberless earthly altars in the eucharistic mystery. Thus there is no schism between the invisible and the visible, between heaven and earth, between the Head seated on the Father's right hand, and the Church, His body, in which flows unceasingly His most precious blood.

"That which was visible in our Redeemer now has passed into the sacraments."[16] This conception of the unity of the Christians who form the unique body of Christ is now being revived everywhere in the West. It is above all a liturgical and sacramental conception, which underscores the organic character of the Church, as our unity in the whole Christ.

---

[16] St. Leo the Great, Sermon 74, 2; P.L. 54, col. 398.

It is unnecessary to emphasize the importance of this theology of the body of Christ, which recovers in a new way the riches of patristic tradition. What is important at present is to notice that this way of regarding the doctrine of redemption reopens the way to a wider Christology and a wider ecclesiology, in which the question of our deification, of our union with God, can again be raised. We can now say again what the Fathers said: "God became man, so that man might become God." But when one tries to interpret these words solely on a Christological and sacramental basis, in which the part of the Holy Spirit is that of a liaison between the heavenly Head of the Church and His earthly members, we get into grave difficulties and reach insoluble problems.[17]

In this conception of the Church as the body of the whole Christ, who contains in Himself the human beings who are members of the Church (a conception which we fully accept, in any case), there is a kind of Christian totalitarianism. Is it possible, one may ask, to safeguard the idea that all human persons are distinct from each other and, above all, from the unique Person of Christ, who here seems to be identified with the person of the Church? Is there not also a danger of losing the idea of personal liberty and of replacing the determinism of the sinful state from which we are saved by some sort of sacramental determinism, in which the organic process of salvation, accomplished in the collective totality of the Church, tends to suppress personal encounter with God? In what sense are we all one single body in Christ, and in what sense is it true that we are not and cannot be one without ceasing to exist as human persons or hypostases, each of whom is called to realize in his person union with God? For it would appear that there are as many unions with God as there are human persons, each person having an absolutely unique relation with the Divinity, and

---

[17]To have an idea of the difficulties in which Roman Catholic theology of our times flounders—hardly able to reconcile personal deification with the notion of the Church as the body of Christ—it is useful to consult Fr. L. Bouyer, *Mystère pascal* (Paris, 1945) pp. 180-194.

that as many possible sainthoods exist in heaven as there are personal destinies on earth.

4

When we wish to speak about human persons in relation to the body of Christ of which we are members, we should resolutely renounce the sense of the word "person" which belongs to sociology and to most philosophers. We should go to seek our norm or "canon" of thinking in a higher region, in the idea of person or hypostasis as it is found in trinitarian theology. The dogma of the Trinity, which places our spirit before the antinomy of absolute identity and of no less absolute diversity, is expressed in the distinction between nature and persons or hypostases. Here each person exists not by excluding others, not by opposition to the "Not-I," but by a refusal to possess the nature for himself (to use psychological language, which is very much out of place when we speak of the Trinity). Personal existence supposes a relation to the other; one person exists "to" or "towards" the other: Ὁ λόγος ἦν πρὸς τὸν Θεόν, as the preface to St. John's Gospel says. To put it briefly, let us say that a person can be fully personal only in so far as he has nothing that he seeks to possess for himself, to the exclusion of others, *i.e.,* when he has a common nature with others. It is then alone that the distinction between persons and nature exists in all its purity; otherwise we are in the presence of individuals, dividing nature among themselves. There is no partition or division of nature among the three Persons of the Holy Trinity. The Hypostases are not three parts of a whole, of the one nature, but each includes in Himself the whole divine nature. Each is the whole, because He has nothing for Himself: even will is common to the Three.

If we now turn to human beings, created in the image of God, we can find, by taking the dogma of the Trinity as our starting-point, a common nature existing in many created hypostases. However, in the actuality of the fallen world, human beings tend to exist by excluding each other. Each affirms himself by contrasting himself with others, *i.e.,* in dividing—in parceling out—the unity of nature, each owning a portion of human nature for himself, so that "my" will contrasts "myself" with all that is "not I." From this point of view, what we habitually call a human person is not truly a person but an individual, a part of the common nature, more or less like the other parts or human individuals of which humanity is composed. But in the measure in which he is a person in the true theological sense of the word, a human being is not limited by his individual nature. He is not only a part of the whole, but potentially includes the whole, having in himself the whole of the earthly cosmos, of which he is the hypostasis.[18] Thus each person is an absolutely original and unique aspect of the nature common to all. The mystery of a human person, which makes it absolutely unique and irreplaceable, cannot be grasped in a rational concept and defined in words. All our definitions inevitably have reference to an individual, more less like other individuals; and the most perfect word for indicating personality in its absolute diversity will always be the wrong word. Persons, as such, are not parts of nature. Although linked with individual parts of the common nature in created actuality, they potentially contain in themselves, each in his fashion, the whole of nature. In our habitual experience we know neither true personal diversity nor true unity of nature. We see on the one hand human individuals, and on the other hand human collective totalities, in perpetual conflict.

We find in the Church the unity of our nature perpetually being realized, for the Church is more united than a collective totality: St. Paul calls it "the body." It is human nature, whose unity is no longer represented by the old Adam, the head of the human race in its extension into individuals. This human nature, ransomed and renewed, is reassembled and recapitulated in the Hypostasis or divine Person of the Son

---

[18]In speaking of the "earthly cosmos"—the nature of which man is the hypostasis (or the hypostases)—we are leaving aside the question of the "celestial cosmos," the angelic world. This is a completely different subject, not directly relating to the problem with which we are concerned here.

of God who has become man. If in this new reality our individualized natures are freed from their limitations (there is neither Greek nor Scythian, freeman nor slave), and if the individual, existing by opposition to his "Not-I," is called to disappear by becoming a member of a single body, this does not mean that human persons or hypostases are thereby suppressed. On the contrary. Only in the Church can they realize themselves in their true diversity. Not being parts of a common nature, as is the case with individuals, persons are not confused with each other on account of the unity of nature which is in the process of realization in the Church.[19] They do not become portions of the Person of Christ. They are not included in the Person of Christ as in a super-person. That would be contrary to the very idea of a person. We are *one* in Christ by virtue of our nature, in that He is the Head of our nature, forming in Himself one sole Body.

One conclusion must be drawn: if our individual natures are incorporated into the glorious humanity of Christ and enter the unity of His Body by baptism, conforming themselves to the death and resurrection of Christ, our persons need to be confirmed in their personal dignity by the Holy Spirit, so that each may freely realize his own union with the Divinity. Baptism—the sacrament of unity in Christ—needs to be completed by chrismation—the sacrament of diversity in the Holy Spirit.

5

The mystery of our redemption leads up to what the Fathers call the recapitulation of our nature by Christ and in Christ. This is the Christological foundation of the Church, which expresses itself above all in the sacramental life, with its quality of absolute objectivity. But if we wish to safeguard

---

[19]"In whatever way we are divided into well defined personalities, according to which someone is Peter or John, Thomas or Matthew, we are, as it were, established in one sole body in Christ, by being nourished by one sole flesh." St. Cyril of Alexandria, *Commentary on St. John* 11, 11; P.G. 74, col. 560.

another aspect of the Church, which has a quality of subjectivity no less absolute, it must be based on the dispensation of another divine Person, independent, in His origin, of the Person of the Incarnate Son.[20] Without this, we risk depersonalizing the Church, by submitting the freedom of her human hypostases to a kind of sacramental determinism. On the other hand, if the subjective aspect alone is stressed, we will lose—along with the idea of the Body of Christ—the "logical," objective basis of the Truth and will fall into the vagaries of "individual" faith.

The point is that the Incarnation and the redeeming work of Christ, considered apart from the dispensation of the Holy Spirit, cannot justify the Church's personal multiplicity—something which is as necessary as her natural unity in Christ. The mystery of Pentecost is as important as the mystery of the Redemption. The redeeming work of Christ is an indispensable pre-condition of the deifying work of the Holy Spirit. The Lord Himself affirmed that when He said, "I came to cast fire on the earth, and would that it were already kindled!" (Luke 12: 49). But, on the other hand, one may say that the work of the Spirit serves that of the Son, for it is by receiving the Spirit that human persons can bear witness in full consciousness to the divinity of Christ. The Son has become like us by the incarnation; we become like Him by deification, by partaking of the divinity in the Holy Spirit, who communicates the divinity to *each* human person in a particular way. The redeeming work of the Son is related to our nature. The deifying work of the Holy Spirit concerns our persons. But the two are inseparable. One is unthinkable without the other, for each is the condition of the other, each is present in the other; and ultimately they are but one dispensation of the Holy Trinity, accomplished by two Divine Persons sent by the Father into the world. This double dispensation of the Word

---

[20]"The Holy Spirit is found present in each of those who receive Him as though He had been communicated to him alone, and nevertheless He pours out complete grace on all." St. Basil, *De spiritu sancto* 9, 2; P.G. 32, cols. 108-109.

and of the Paraclete has as its goal the union of created beings with God.

Considered from the point of view of our fallen state, the aim of the divine dispensation can be termed salvation or redemption. This is the negative aspect of our ultimate goal, which is considered from the perspective of our sin. Considered from the point of view of the ultimate vocation of created beings, the aim of the divine dispensation can be termed deification. This is the positive definition of the same mystery, which must be accomplished in each human person in the Church and which will be fully revealed in the age to come, when, after having reunited all things in Christ, God will become all in all.

6

The Theological Notion of the Human Person

I do not intend to discourse on the notion of the human person either in the doctrines of the Church Fathers or in the works of other Christian theologians. Even if I had wanted to do so, I would have had to ask myself originally, to what degree this wish to find a doctrine of the human person among the Fathers of the first centuries is legitimate. Would this not be trying to attribute to them certain ideas which may have remained unknown to them and which we would nevertheless attribute to them, without realizing how much, in our way of conceiving of the human person, we depend upon a complex philosophical tradition—upon a line of thought which has followed paths very different from the one which could claim to be part of a properly theological tradition? To avoid such unconscious confusion, as well as conscious anachronisms—inserting Bergson into the work of St. Gregory of Nyssa or Hegel into the work of St. Maximus the Confessor—we will refrain for the moment from all attempts at finding in these texts the outlines of a developed

111

doctrine (or doctrines) of the human person such as might have arisen in the course of the history of Christian theology. For my part, I must admit that until now I have not found what one might call an elaborated doctrine of the human person in patristic theology, alongside its very precise teaching on divine persons or hypostases. However there is a Christian anthropology among the Fathers of the first eight centuries, as well as later on in Byzantium and in the West; and it is unnecessary to say that these doctrines of man are clearly personalist. It could not have been otherwise for a theological doctrine based upon the revelation of a living and personal God who created man "according to his own image and likeness."

Thus I shall not put forward an historian's examination of Christian doctrines, but simply some theological reflections on the questions which must be answered by the notion of the human person in the context of Christian dogma. We shall have to say a few words about the divine Persons before posing the question: What is the human person according to theological thought? This brief triadological study will not divert us from our main subject.

In order better to express personal reality in God or, rather, the reality of a personal God—a reality which is not only an economic mode of expressing an impersonal monad in itself but the absolute and primordial condition of a Trinitarian God in His transcendence—the Greek Fathers preferred the term ὑπόστασις to πρόσωπον for designating the divine persons. The line of thought which distinguishes οὐσία and ὑπόστασις in God uses metaphysical vocabulary; it expresses itself in terms of an ontology—in terms which here have the value of conventional signs rather than of concepts—in order to point out both absolute identity and absolute difference. It was a great terminological discovery to introduce a distinction between two synonyms, in order to express the irreducibility of the ὑπόστασις to the οὐσία and of the person to the essence, without, however, opposing them as two different realities. This will enable St. Gregory of Nazianzus to say, "The Son is not the Father, because there is only one Father, but He is what the Father is; the

Holy Spirit, although he proceeds from God, is not the Son, because there is only one Only Begotten Son, but He is what the Son is" (*Or.* 31, 9). The ὑπόστασις is the same as the οὐσία; it receives all the same attributes—or all the negations—which can be formulated on the subject of the "superessence"; but it nonetheless remains irreducible to the οὐσία. This irreducibility cannot be understood or expressed except in the relation of the Three Hypostases who, strictly speaking, are not "three" but "Tri-Unity." In speaking of three hypostases, we are already making an improper abstraction: if we wanted to generalize and make a *concept* of the "divine hypostasis," we would have to say that the only common definition possible would be the impossibility of any common definition of the three hypostases. They are alike in the fact that they are dissimilar; or, rather, to go beyond the relative idea of resemblance, which is out of place here, one must say that the absolute character of their difference implies an absolute identity. Beyond this one cannot speak of hypostases of the Tri-Unity. Just as the Three here is not an arithmetic number but indicates in the Triad of pure difference—a Triad which remains equal to the Monad—an infinite passage beyond the dyad of opposition, so the hypostasis as such, inasmuch as it is irreducible to the οὐσία, is no longer a conceptual expression but a sign which is introduced into the domain of the non-generalizable, pointing out the radically personal character of the God of Christian revelation.

However, οὐσία and ὑπόστασις remain synonyms, and each time one wants to establish a distinction between the two terms, by attributing to them a different content, one inevitably falls back into the domain of conceptual knowledge: one opposes the general to the particular, the "second οὐσία" to the individual substance, the genus or species to the individual. This is what we find, for example, in a passage of Theodoret:[1] "According to secular philosophy, there is no difference between οὐσία and ὑπόστασις. For οὐσία signifies that which is (τὸ ὄν), and ὑπόστασις

---

[1] *Eranistes* I; P.G. 83, col. 33.

signifies that which subsists (τὸ ὑφεστός). But, according
to the doctrine of the Fathers, there is between οὐσία and
ὑπόστασις the same difference as between the common and
the particular, that is to say, the same difference as between
the genus or the species and the individual." The same
surprise awaits us in the writings of St. John of Damascus.
In the "Dialectic," which is a type of philosophical prelude
to his account of Christian dogma, he says:[2] "The word
ὑπόστασις has two meanings. Sometimes it simply means
existence (ὕπαρξις). Following this meaning, οὐσία and
ὑπόστασις are the same thing. This is why certain Fathers
have said 'natures (φύσεις) or hypostases'. Other times it
designates what exists by itself and according to the subsistence constituted by itself (τὴν καθ' αὐτὸ καὶ ἰδια-
σύστον ὕπαρξιν). Following this meaning, it designates
the individual (τὸ ἄτομον) numerically different from all
others, *e.g.:* Peter, Paul, a particular horse."

It is clear that such a definition of the hypostasis could
only serve as a preamble to Trinitarian theology—as a
conceptual starting-point leading towards a deconceptualized
notion which is no longer that of an individual of a species.
If certain critics have wanted to see in St. Basil's Trinitarian
doctrine a distinction between ὑπόστασις and οὐσία which
should correspond to the Aristotelian distinction between
πρώτη and δευτέρα οὐσία, this is because they have not
been able to distinguish either the point of arrival from the
point of departure or the theological construct, which is
beyond concepts, from its conceptual scaffolding.

In Trinitarian theology (which is theology *par excellence,
Theologia* in the true sense of the word for the Fathers of
the first centuries) the notion of hypostasis is neither that
of an individual of the species "Divinity" nor that of an
individual substance of divine nature. Thus the distinction
between two synonyms which Theodoret attributes to the
Church Fathers is, in its conceptual form, nothing but an
approximation of that which cannot be conceptualized. On
the whole, Theodoret was wrong when he opposed the

---

[2]Cap. 42; P.G. 94, col. 612.

conceptual distinction introduced by the Fathers to the identity of the two terms in "secular philosophy." More in keeping with the historian which he was than with the theologian, he was able to see in the original identical meaning of the two terms chosen to designate the "common" and the "particular" in God, only an historical curiosity. But why choose this identical meaning except to maintain in what is common the sense of the concrete οὐσία and to eliminate from the particular all limitations proper to the individual, so that the ὑπόστασις might apply itself to the whole of the common nature instead of dividing it? If this is so, the theological truth of the distinction between οὐσία and ὑπόστασις established by the Fathers is not to be sought in the letter of its conceptual expression but rather between that expression and the identity of the two concepts which would have been proper to "secular philosophy." That is to say, one must situate this theological truth beyond concepts: concepts here divest themselves of regular meaning to become signs of the personal reality of a God who is not the God of philosophers nor (very often) the God of theologians.

Let us now look in Christian anthropology for the same non-conceptual meaning of the distinction between ὑπόστασις and οὐσία or φύσις. (These two notions coincide without being completely identical.) We will ask ourselves whether this irreducibility of hypostasis to essence or nature —an irreducibility which forced us to give up equating the hypostasis with the individual in the Trinity by revealing the non-conceptual character of the notion of hypostasis—must take place in the realm of created being as well, especially when one is dealing with human hypostases or persons. By asking this question, we will be asking at the same time whether Trinitarian theology has had any repercussion on Christian anthropology—whether it has opened up a new dimension of the "personal" by discovering a notion of the human hypostasis not reducible to the level of natures or individual substances, which fall under the hold of concepts and which can be classed so comfortably in the logical tree of Porphyry.

We will answer this question, *more scholastico,* first by negation, cautiously saying: it seems not, *videtur quod non.* It seems that the human person is nothing other than an individual numerically different from all other men. In fact, even if thus far it has been necessary to give up the notion of individuals—a notion which has no place in the Trinity— to rise to the unencumbered idea of the divine hypostasis, it is quite another matter in created reality, where there are individual human beings whom we call persons. We can also call them "hypostases," but then this term will apply to each individual of a given species, as was the case in the example given by St. John of Damascus: "Peter, Paul, a particular horse." Others (St. Gregory of Nazianzus, for example) reserve the term "hypostasis" for individuals of a reasonable nature, exactly as Boethius does in his definition of person: *substantia individua rationalis naturae* (and let us note that *substantia* here is a literal translation of ὑπόστα- σις). Thomas Aquinas received intact this concept formulated by Boethius for designating created being. Like the Greek Fathers, he sought to transform it in order to apply it to the persons of the Trinity; but in the context of a Trinitarian doctrine different from that of the East, the philosopher's *persona* becomes the theologian's *relatio.*[3] It is curious to note that Richard of Saint-Victor, who refused to accept Boethius' definition of person, ended by conceiving of the divine hypostasis as *divinae naturae incommunicabilis existentia,* which, according to Fr. Bergeron, would bring him close to the concept of the Greek theologians. However (and this is the one point which should interest us at this moment) it seems that neither the Church Fathers nor Thomas Aquinas nor even Richard of Saint-Victor, who criticized Boethius, abandoned the notion of human person = individual substance in his anthropology, after having transformed it for use in Trinitarian theology.

Thus in theological language, in the East as in the West,

---

[3] The path of this transformation, from Boethius to William of Auxerre and Thomas Aquinas, has been traced in the excellent study of Fr. Bergeron, *La structure du concept latin de personne,* (= *Études d'histoire littéraire et doctrinale du XIII* siècle, 2nd series, Paris, Ottawa, 1932).

the term "human person" coincides with that of "human individual." But we cannot stop at this declaration. Since it seems that Christian anthropology has not given a new sense to the *term* "human hypostasis" or "person," let us try to disclose the presence of a different notion, which is no longer identical to that of "individual" and yet remains unfixed by any term, as a basis implied but most often not expressed in all theological or ascetic teaching which deals with man.

Before all else, let us see (and this will be our task here) whether the notion of the human person reduced to that of a φύσις or individual nature can be maintained in the context of Christian dogma. The dogma of Chalcedon, whose fifteenth centenary the Christian world celebrated in 1951, shows us Christ "consubstantial with the Father in divinity, consubstantial with us in humanity." We can conceive of the reality of God's incarnation without admitting any transmutation of the Divinity into humanity, without confusion or mixture of the uncreated and the created, precisely because we distinguish the person or hypostasis of the Son from His nature or essence: a person who is not formed *from* two natures, ἐκ δύο φύσεων, but who is *in* two natures, ἐν δύο φύσεσιν. The expression "hypostatic union" (despite its convenience and general use) is improper because it makes us think of a human nature or substance existing before the incarnation which would enter into the hypostasis of the Word, while in fact the human nature or substance assumed by the Word in the Virgin Mary only began to exist as this particular nature or substance at the moment of the incarnation, *i.e.* in the unity of the Person or Hypostasis of the Son of God become Man. Thus the humanity of Christ, by which He is "consubstantial with us," never had any other hypostasis than that of the Son of God; however no one would deny that His human nature has the character of an "individual substance," and the Chalcedonian dogma insists on the fact that Christ is "perfect in his humanity," "truly man," ἐκ ψυχῆς λογικῆς καὶ σώματος—"with a reasonable soul and a body." In these conditions, the human subject of Christ has the same character as other particular substances or natures of humanity that one calls "hypostases" or "persons." Nevertheless, if one were to apply this understanding of "hypostasis" to Him, one would fall into the Nestorian error of dissecting the hypostatic unity of Christ into two distinct "personal" beings. Since, according to Chalcedon, a divine Person made himself consubstantial with created beings, this is because He has become an Hypostasis of human nature without transforming Himself into the hypostasis of a human person. Thus, if Christ is a divine Person, all the while being totally man by his "enhypostasized" nature, one has to admit (at least in Christ's case) that here the hypostasis of the assumed humanity cannot be reduced to the human substance, to that human individual who was registered with the other subjects of the Roman Empire under Augustus. But at the same time, one can say that it is God who was registered according to His humanity precisely because that individual human, that "atom" of human nature counted with the others, was not a human "person."

It seems that, in order to be logical, it should be necessary to give up designating the individual substance of reasonable nature by the term "person" or "hypostasis." Otherwise the Nestorian controversy risks seeming like a dispute over words: One or two hypostases in Christ? Two, if in the first case (that of the divine hypostasis) "hypostasis" means irreducibility to nature, while in the second case "hypostasis" only signifies the individual human substance. But if in both cases one finds the same irreducibility of person to nature, one will say one hypostasis or person of Christ. And this refusal to admit two distinct personal beings in Christ means at the same time that one must also distinguish in human beings the person or hypostasis from the nature or individual substance. Thus, in the light of Christological dogma, Boethius' definition, *substantia individua rationalis naturae,* appears insufficient for establishing the concept of human person. It can only be applied to the "enhypostasized nature" (to use the expression created by Leontius of Byzantium) and not to the human hypostasis or person itself. We understand why Richard of Saint-Victor rejected Boethius' definition, remarking with finesse that substance

answers the question *quid,* person answers the question *quis.*
Now, to the question *quis* one answers with a proper noun
which alone can designate the person.[4] Hence the new
definition (for the divine persons): *persona est divinae
naturae incommunicabilis existentia.*

However, let us leave Richard to ask ourselves how one
ought to distinguish between the human person or hypostasis
and man taken as an individual or particular nature. What
should "person" mean in relation to the individual human?
Is it a superior quality of the individual—a quality which
would be his perfection, inasmuch as he is a being created
in the image of God, and, at the same time, a principle of
his individuality? This might appear likely, especially if one
considers that attempts to show in the human being the
distinctive marks of what is "in the image of God" almost
always aim at the superior ("spiritual") faculties of man.
(Let us recall, however, that St. Irenaeus extended the
"image" to the corporeal nature of man.) The superior
faculties of man which usually serve to bring out the
distinctive marks of the image receive, in a tripartite anthropology, the name of νοῦς—a term which is difficult to
translate and which we are forced to render as "human
mind." In this case, man, as a person, would be an incarnate
νοῦς—an incarnate mind, linked to an animal nature which
it "enhypostasizes" or, rather, to which it remains juxtaposed
while dominating it. In fact one can find, especially among
the Fathers of the fourth century and in particular in St.
Gregory of Nyssa, development of such ideas concerning the
νοῦς—the seat of liberty (αὐτεξουσία), the faculty of
self-determination which lends to man his character of being
created in the image of God or what we could call his
dignity of personhood.

But let us try to submit this new schema, which seems
based on the authority of the Fathers, to the judgment of
Christological dogma. We see immediately that we must
abandon it. In fact, if the νοῦς in a human being did
represent the "hypostatic" element which makes him a per-

---

[4]*De Trinitate* IV, 7; P.L. 196, cols. 934-935.

son, it would be necessary, in order to safeguard the unity of the hypostasis of the God-Man, to take away the human mind from the nature of Christ and to replace the created νοῦς by the divine Logos, *i.e.* we ought to accept the Christological formula of Apollinarius of Laodicea. It is important to notice that it was precisely Gregory of Nyssa who criticized most pertinently Apollinarius' error. This leads us to think that, despite the intellectualist accent of Gregory's doctrine of the image of God, the human νοῦς in his thinking cannot be interpreted in the sense of the hypostatic element which confers on man his personal being.

If this is so, there will be no place for the idea of the hypostasis or person of man as one element in the composite of his individual nature. Now this corresponds exactly to that irreducibility of the human hypostasis to the human individual which we had to admit in speaking of Chalcedon. But on the other hand, in distinguishing the human hypostasis from that which constitutes its complex nature—body, soul, spirit (if one wants to accept this trichotomy)—we will not find any definable property or any attributes which would be foreign to the φύσις and would belong exclusively to the person taken in itself. Under these conditions, it will be impossible for us to form a concept of the human person, and we will have to content ourselves with saying: "person" signifies the irreducibility of man to his nature—"irreducibility" and not "something irreducible" or "something which makes man irreducible to his nature" precisely because it cannot be a question here of "something" distinct from "another nature" but of *someone* who is distinct from his own nature, of someone who goes beyond his nature while still containing it, who makes it exist as human nature by this overstepping and yet does not exist in himself beyond the nature which he "enhypostasizes" and which he constantly exceeds. I would have said "which he ecstacizes," if I did not fear being reproached for introducing an expression too reminiscent of "the ecstatic character" of the *Dasein* of Heidegger, after having criticized others who allowed themselves to make such comparisons.

Fr. Urs von Balthasar in his book on St. Maximus the

Confessor, in speaking of Post-Chalcedonian theology, makes a remark which seems to be both correct and erroneous at the same time. He says:[5] "Besides the tree of Porphyry, which tries to place all existing being into categories of essence (οὐσία), class, type, specific difference, and finally individual (ἄτομον εἶδος), there appear new ontological categories. These new categories, irreducible to the categories of essence, refer at the same time to the domain of existence and to the domain of person. These two domains are still linked in the new expressions (ὕπαρξις, ὑπόστασις) . . . to contours still vague which are looking for a precise quality. It will take a long time before the Middle Ages is able to formulate the distinction between essence and existence and to make of it the framework for the mode of being of the creature . . . . However, we are most assuredly going in that direction when we see this new order of existence and person arise next to the old Aristotelian order of essences."

Fr. von Balthasar touches here on a group of extremely important questions; but, having made this comparison, instead of pursuing his investigation further, he digresses and remains at the surface. He compared, as we have seen, the "new ontological categories" of hypostasis or person and the existential *esse* which Thomas Aquinas discovered beyond the Aristotelian order of substantiality—the presence of existence which, as Gilson says, "transcends the concept because it transcends essence."[6] We believe Gilson is right in saying that only a Christian metaphysician could go so far in the analysis of the concrete structure of created beings. But faced with Fr. von Balthasar's comparison one asks: Did the real distinction between essence and existence— though it finds at the root of each individual being the act of existing, which places him in his own existence—attain at the same time the root of personal being? Is the non-conceptualizable character of existence of the same order as that of the person, or does this new ontological order, discovered by Thomas Aquinas, still fail to reach the personal?

---

[5]H. Urs von Balthasar, *Liturgie cosmique* (Paris, 1947) p. 21.
[6]*L'Etre et l'essence* (Paris, 1948) p. 111.

It is certain that there is a close link between the two, at least in Thomas' thought. Answering the question *Utrum in Christo sit tantum unum esse (Sent.* III, d. 6, q. 2, a. 2; III, q. 17, a. 2), Thomas affirms the unity of the existence of the God-Man in speaking of the unicity of His hypostasis. But will he push this comparison between the existential and the personal any further, so as to affirm three existences in God? Richard of Saint-Victor did this by speaking of three divine hypostases; but he did not reform the notion of human person. Thomas Aquinas reconstructed the notion of individual substances, finding in them the multiple creative energy which actualizes all that exists; but this new ontological category applies to all created beings and not only to human or angelic persons. At the same time, the God of Thomas Aquinas is one sole existence, identical to its essence: pure Act or *Ipsum Esse subsistens.* This forces us to correct one of Fr. von Balthasar's remarks. In the notion of the created hypostasis, Maximus the Confessor may have reached the new domain of that which cannot be conceptualized because it cannot be reduced to its essence; but one will not find in the Thomistic distinction between essence and existence—a distinction which penetrates to the existential depths of *individual* beings—the ontological solution of the mystery of the human person.

Thomas Aquinas' natural theology does not reach this solution; and he cannot be reproached for this fact, because such was not his task. If I am permitted to speak in the language of the "Palamite" theology which is natural to me, I will say that Thomas Aquinas, as a metaphysician, attained God and created beings at the level of energy and not at the level of the "superessence" in Three Hypostases and of the polyhypostasity of the created cosmos. The creature, who is both "physical" and "hypostatic" at the same time, is called to realize his unity of nature as well as his true personal diversity by going in grace beyond the individual limits which divide nature and tend to reduce persons to the level of the closed being of particular substances.

Thus the level on which the problem of the human person is posed goes beyond that of ontology as we normally understand it; and if it is a question of metaontology, only God can know—that God whom the story of Genesis shows stopping His work to say in the Council of the Three Hypostases: "Let us create man in our image and likeness."

7

The Theology
of the Image

The theme of the *image*, in the knowledge of God and man, is of such importance for Christian thought that I think we are justified in speaking of a "theology of the image" in the New Testament or in the work of a particular Christian writer without fear of magnifying a doctrinal element of secondary value out of all due proportion. Thus (to mention only one work among many which have appeared recently), Fr. Henri Crouzel's study, *Théologie de l'image de Dieu chez Origène*,[1] touches on all the fundamental problems of Origen's thought; and this in spite of the fact that the writer apologizes in his introduction for having limited the "theology of the image" to a single aspect—that of the relationship of God to man by the intermediary of the Word. Even this concentration on the role of the second hypostasis cannot reduce the scope of the theme of the image of God in Origin's thought: if the

---

[1](Paris: Aubier, 1956).

Logos is the Image which makes known the paternal Archetype, all the problems connected with the manifestation of
God belong to the "theology of the Image"—whether
"cosmic," in nature created by the Word, or "historic," in
the revelation given to a people chosen to receive the Message of God. If man is λογικός, to use here an expression
of Origen's, if he is "in the image" of the Logos, everything
which touches the destiny of man—grace, sin, redemption
by the Word made man—must also be related to the theology
of the image. And we may say the same of the Church, the
sacraments, spiritual life, sanctification, and the end of all
things. There is no branch of theological teaching which
can be entirely isolated from the problem of the image without danger of severing it from the living stock of Christian
tradition. We may say that for a theologian of the catholic
tradition in the East and in the West, for one who is true
to the main lines of patristic thought, the theme of the
image (in its twofold acceptation—the image as the principle
of God's self-manifestation and the image as the foundation
of a particular relationship of man to God) must belong to
the "essence of Christianity." The little book by Romano
Guardini which bears this title gives a prominent place to
the idea of the image. But on the contrary, one looks in
vain for the theme of the image in Harnack's *Das Wesen des
Christentums*.

The reasons usually advanced by certain Protestant theologians who would like to exclude the "theology of the
image" from the essentials of Christianity can find support
in a sound knowledge of Biblical vocabulary. Thus Karl
Barth in his *Dogmatik*[2] declares that the teachings of the
Fathers of the Church about the "theology of the image"
were entirely invented, without any scriptural foundation.
Emil Brunner,[3] who is less categorical, nevertheless concludes
that "the doctrine of the *Imago Dei*, if one equates the

<hr>

[2]III. 1 (Zurich, 1945) p. 216 ff. [English trans. *Church Dogmatics* III. 1
(Edinburgh, 1958) p. 191 ff.].
[3]*Der Mensch im Widerspruch* (Berlin, 1937) p. 519. [English trans. *Man
in Revolt: A Christian Anthropology* (London, 1939) p. 499].

phrase with the truth for which it stands, does not play a very important part in the Bible." Anders Nygren in *Agape and Eros* eliminates the theme of the image, quoting E. Lehmann, who says: "The strongest argument against 'creation in God's image' is the complete silence of the rest of the Old Testament on this subject, which, if it had been a prevalent idea, might have been expected to be very frequently used, and used to the full, in the constantly recurring treatment of the relation between God and men. But no Prophet, no Psalm, not Job, not even the humane Deuteronomy, has any suggestion of such a likeness of nature between God and man." And the same writer adds: "It is no accident that this doctrine of the image of God was first developed at a time when the Greek language was making its way into the religious literature of the Jews."

"It is no accident": here is a phrase which merits attention. Lehmann and Nygren simply wanted to say that the theme of the image of God is foreign to Revelation: it is an Hellenic contribution which we owe to the Platonic and Stoic associations already latent in the terms εἰκών and ὁμοίωσις used in the translation of the book of Genesis by the Septuagint, about the third or second century before Christ.

These ideas are developed in the book of Wisdom, written in Greek about the middle of the first century before our era. In fact, we find there (2:23) a paraphrase of "Let us make man in our image" which gives to man's vocation the attributes of incorruptibility and conformity with God in what is proper to Him (ἰδιότητος), or, according to another version, conformity with His eternity (αἰδιότητος). In the same book (7:26) Wisdom, co-creator of the universe, makes God known in creation: she is the ἀπαύγασμα —the reflection (or radiance) of the eternal light, "a spotless mirror of the working of God," the "image (εἰκών) of his goodness." This is almost the second hypostasis of Middle Platonism or the Logos of Philo.

Certainly the fact that the sudden development of the

---

⁴*Eros et Agapé* I, p. 257. [English trans. (London, 1953) p. 230n.].

theme of the image coincided with the entry of the Greek language into the religious literature of Judaism was not fortuitous. But one may wonder if this recourse to a new vocabulary, rich in philosophical tradition, was not the answer to an internal need of Revelation itself, which thus received in the last stage of the Old Covenant an increase of light which was to lend new coloring to the sacred books of the Jews. "It is no accident" that the Jewish diaspora, in order to keep alive the word of Truth revealed to Israel, chose to give it an Hellenic expression, which allowed the authors of the deuterocanonical books to open up a theology of the image on the eve of the advent of Christianity.

The precise facts appealed to by theologians who are opposed to the patristic doctrine of the image must be admitted by all who, as they face the texts of the Old Testament, are unwilling to close their eyes to the history of the formation of the Biblical canon. Thus they will recognize that the Hebraic expressions *selem* and *demut,* governed by the prepositions *be* and *ke,* in Genesis 1:26 (which give: "in our image, after our likeness") have not the positive and direct force of κατ' εἰκώνα ἡμῶν, καθ' ὁμοίωσιν ἡμῶν of the translation of the Septuagint. In the context of the sacerdotal narrative of Genesis, the creation of man "in the image" of God confers on human beings a dominion over the animals analogous to that which God enjoys over the whole of his creation. If, as is sometimes supposed, this text is aimed against the Egyptian cult of theriomorphic gods, the expression "in the image" would have a mainly negative meaning: animals have nothing of the divine, for only man is made "in the image" of God. But it has also been noticed that the expression "after our likeness" ought to limit still further the positive force of "in our image," perhaps to avoid at the same time the Iranian myth of the "heavenly man": man is *only in the image*—he has only a certain distant analogy with the Lord through the place which he occupies among earthly creatures. Obviously all this is too thin for us to be able to speak of an Old Testament doctrine of the "image of God" except in negative terms: the God of Israel, Creator of heaven and earth, has nothing in common with the divinities of the other nations. He has no image in human or animal form which could be worshipped. This is in complete harmony with the formal prohibition of any plastic representation of God: "Therefore take good heed to yourselves. Since you saw no form on the day that the Lord spoke to you at Horeb out of the midst of the fire, beware lest you act corruptly by making a graven image for yourselves, in the form of any figure" (Deut. 4:15-16). "Then the Lord spoke to you out of the midst of the fire; you heard the sound of words, but saw no form; there was only a voice" (Deut. 4:12).

Let us concede this much to the opponents of the theology of the image: in the purely Hebraic text of the Bible, interpreted in the historic context in which the books of the Old Testament were composed, there is nothing (or almost nothing) which would permit us to base either a theognosis or a religious anthropology on the notion of the image of God. Nevertheless, this God who hides Himself—the God of Isaiah (45:15)—the "God of Israel, the Savior" who does not show his nature by means of any image, does not remain an unknown God: He speaks and He exacts a response; He reveals His Name and He calls His chosen by their name: Abraham, Isaac, Jacob. He is a personal Absolute who enters into relationships with human persons. For Judaism before Christ, as for a believing Jew today, this is so. To quote the witness of Martin Buber:[5] "The great achievement of Israel is not to have taught the one true God, who is the only God, the source and end of all that is; it is to have shown that it was possible *in reality* to speak to Him, to say 'Thou' to Him, to stand upright before His face." "It was Israel who first understood and—much more—lived life as a dialogue between man and God."

This God reveals Himself as transcendent to every image which could make known His nature, but He does not refuse personal relationship, living intercourse with men, with a people; He speaks to them and they reply, in a series of concrete situations which unfold as sacred history. Never-

---

[5]"Le message hassidique," *Dieu Vivant* 2, p. 16.

theless the depths of His nature remain forbidden to all enquiry. If there is a gnosis which is purely Hebraic, it is not a knowledge of the divine nature, but the revelation of the mysterious designs of God given to the prophets, a revelation of the divine economy being realized in a history directed towards one end, a history which finds its meaning in the promise of an eschatological event. Some Hebraizers will tell us that even the tetragrammaton of Exodus, the name of God, says nothing about the divine Being, about God considered in His nature. The Septuagint translated this declaration thus: ἐγώ εἰμι ὁ ˝Ων—"I am the one who is" (or, "who am"). According to some modern exegetes the translation ought to be "I am who I am," in the sense of a refusal to give the name. For others, the declaration means: "I am He who remains faithful." This personal Absolute is the God of history, a God who takes seriously the engagement He demands of men, for He commits Himself by entering into relationship with those whom He chooses. Intolerable folly to the Greeks: can one say "Thou" to the transcendent principle of becoming?

Indeed, in the religions and metaphysics which are foreign to the revelation given to Israel, the "I—thou" relationship can only be maintained on the level of polytheism, at a level which remains below that of a philosophical theology. As soon as one approaches the Absolute, dialogue with the divinity becomes impossible, absurd, for even to call him God would not be proper. He must be named otherwise, in order not to sully his impersonally objective purity: "That which truly is," "the Good transcending being," the One. Or—even better—deny him all names, embracing a way of negative knowledge which will end in a mysticism of absorption in the Unknowable. "Of Him there is no name, no definition (λόγος), nor knowledge nor feeling nor opinion." This conclusion to the first hypothesis of the *Parmenides* was to become a kind of "Scriptural authority" for the whole Platonic tradition of negative theognosis down to Pseudo-Dionysius, who introduced this text into Christian literature, though without mentioning the name of Plato.

Unlike the monotheism of the Jewish prophets, this

monotheism (or rather, "henotheism") of the Greek philosophers does not refuse to justify the image: rather, its legitimateness is taken for granted. One could not practise apophatic ascent towards the Deity, unknowable and nameless in itself, if what comes later, at the level of being and knowing, was not the Deity's expression on a less elevated plane. Thus the νοῦς—the Intelligence—of Plotinus is the εἰκών of the One (*Enneads* V, 1, 7), while the Soul of the world is called εἴδωλον of the Intelligence (V, 1, 6). This impersonal God, whom it would not enter one's head to address in prayer as "Thou," is certainly not the God of sacred history. Doubtless, we avoid applying the term "nature" to him; and yet, since he is the Archetype of what comes after him, the perceptible nature of the cosmos is also, in the last resort, a distant image of this God who transcends all that makes him known outside his absolute identity with himself (VI, 8, 18). The One of Plotinus thus appears, when all is said and done, as a God of holy nature. And this is even more true for the God of Middle Platonism (as, for example, the God of the Hermetic writings), not to mention the God of the Stoics. Now nature, sanctified because it is the image of the Unimaginable, is full of gods who, though never masters of history, yet receive sacrifices from mortals and reply to their supplications by oracles, revealing the inexorable laws of the universe.

This is scandal to the Jews: can one admit a world without history, subject to necessity, a beautiful and ordered world, no doubt, but where nothing new can happen? We do find this view in the Bible, the pessimistic view of Ecclesiastes: for the author of this strange book, written after the exile, the necessity which rules and orders the whole of created nature is "vanity." St. Paul takes up this expression again, to say that creation did not subject itself to "vanity" of its own will, but as a consequence of the sin of man (Romans 8:19-20); there are also men, the "sons of God," who must finally liberate nature from its bondage to corruption. And in the same Epistle to the Romans (1:19-23) the apostle of the Gentiles, while giving his due

to the God of the philosophers—knowable from created
nature, manifested in images which show the invisible and
eternal—condemns the "vanity" of the wise men who, after
having had the merit of knowing the God of cosmic nature,
did not glorify Him as the personal God of Revelation, the
God of history, the God of the promises—Him to whom
one says "Thou"; they persisted in making their prayers to
idols.

In considering this passage of St. Paul, the disciple of
Gamaliel, we have the right to wonder: did the tradition
of Israel really ignore the aspect of "nature" in this God
who remains always uniquely personal and refuses not only
images which might make Him manifest in the cosmos,
but also theology (in the Greek sense of the word), intellectual or mystical seeking which would dare to climb
towards His mystery, going beyond images? Several texts
in the Wisdom books, the multiplication of gnostic writings
in more recent Judaism, and above all the work of Philo
(who notwithstanding his Hellenism remained nevertheless
a believing Jew) ought to prove the contrary. But people
want at all costs to oppose the "God of Abraham, of Isaac
and of Jacob" to the "God of the philosophers and scholars,"
without, however, meeting as Pascal did the living God of
a living Bible. For there is also a dead God, the God of a
particular school of Biblical purists who are too wedded to
the Hebraic letter, which they study in the historical context
of its redaction, to be able to recognize the life (dynamic,
and in this sense never "pure") and the living tradition which
leads to the discovery in the most ancient texts of a meaning
ever new, adapted to each new stage of the divine economy
before Christ. It is in the name of a God reduced to the
categories of an abstract Judaism, the God of an inert book
duly studied, that Biblical science, setting itself up as a
theology, wants to proscribe the theology of the image by
declaring it foreign to Revelation.

It is true that the God of Greek thought who admits
images is not yet He of the Jewish Revelation who forbids
them: an act of folly is needed to reach Him by faith, by
crossing an abyss. But on the other hand it could not be

said that the God of the philosophers is "another God," a stranger to that hidden God of Israel who "dwells in thick darkness" (III Kings 8:12). If He excludes images and condemns the curiosity of those who would pry into His transcendent nature, it is because the initiative of revelation belongs to Him alone in the history of the people which He has chosen for the recapitulation, in one unique event, of the whole of history and of the whole nature of the universe. This personal God is no mere Existence, devoid of nature; but He hides the depths of His Being until the decisive moment, only making Himself known to His elect by His authority. "Theology" in the proper sense, as the Fathers of the Church were to understand it, remains a closed book to Israel until the Incarnation of the Word. What was allowed to the Greeks was forbidden to the Jews, but this prohibition was their privilege as well as a restriction. It was to be lifted at the moment when God chose to reveal Himself fully to all men, to Jews and to Greeks, by the perfect Image who is of the same nature with Him, and to allow Himself to be known in the Spirit who searches the depths of His nature. Through the Incarnation, which is the fundamental dogmatic fact of Christianity, "image" and "theology" are linked so closely together that the expression "theology of the image" might become almost a tautology— which it is, if one chooses to regard theology as a knowledge of God in His Logos, who is the consubstantial Image of the Father.

Yet there is a series of problems which the term "image," in Christian theology, must inevitably raise. Let us pause first on the image in Trinitarian theology. St. Paul calls the Son "the image of the invisible God" (εἰκὼν τοῦ Θεοῦ τοῦ ἀοράτου—Col. 1:15, II Cor. 4:4). In the context of an Hellenistic theognosis this expression would imply a correspondence of the image to its archetype: the Logos would be the image of the first hypostasis (unknowable in itself) in so far as it made the first hypostasis known. This would be a correspondence of likeness, based on a natural participation of the inferior in the superior. There would therefore be a non-identity of nature (or of level) but nevertheless a kinship, a συγγένεια. This means that it would be possible to go further and to raise the level of God-image to that of God-archetype, only if one could attain to the inexpressible nature of the God-archetype in itself. In the Christian context of a Trinitarian theology this relationship of the image to the archetype must be utterly transformed, as can be seen from the following text of Gregory of Nyssa:[6] "The Son is in the Father as the beauty of the image resides in the archetypal form... the Father is in the Son as the archetypal beauty remains in its image... and we must think both these things simultaneously."

Indeed, we are here dealing with a new doctrinal element which is foreign to Greek thought and foreign also to the thought of a Hellenizing Jew like Philo, for whom the personal God of the Bible, identified with the impersonal God of Hellenism, remains nonetheless a closed monad, a person-nature transcending by his essence the Logos who is his image, his mediator vis-à-vis the created world—the Hebraic Utterance personified rather than personal. The new element, peculiar to Christian theology, is the distinction between Nature or Essence and Person or Hypostasis in God, a distinction which cannot be avoided by those who recognize the divinity of Christ. Not identical in person, the Father, the Son and the Holy Spirit are identical in nature or essence. This is the exact meaning of the term ὁμοούσιος, which is approximately translated by the adjective "consubstantial." Since the Logos of Christians is the consubstantial image of the Father, the relationship of the image to the archetype (if one wishes to keep this last term, which was familiar to Origen but was already an archaism in Gregory of Nyssa) —this relationship of the image to that which it manifests— can no longer be thought of as a participation (μέθεξις) or a kinship (συγγένεια), for it is a matter of identity of nature. So it would seem that this relationship of the image to the model which it manifests ought to be interpreted as the personal relation of the Son to the Father. This is what Fr. Leys chose to do in the last chapter of his book *L'Image*

---

[6]*Adversus Eunomium* I; P.G. 44, col. 636.

de Dieu chez S. Grégoire de Nysse.[7] But if we introduce the theme of the Image-which-makes-manifest into intra-Trinitarian relationships, we cannot avoid a new difficulty: how could the personal relationship which indicates non-identity by itself give rise to the manifestation of one person by another? True, the notion of the Son as Image of the Father implies personal relationship; but what is manifested by the Image is not the person of the Father but His nature, identical in the Son. It is identity of essence which is shown in the difference of persons: the Son, in his function of εἰκών, bears witness to the divinity of the Father.

This is a commonplace of Greek patristic writings. Thus, for St. Gregory of Nazianzus, the name of Logos would be applied to the Son "because He remains united to the Father and reveals the Father . . . because He is, in relation to the Father, as the definition is to that which is defined. For *logos* also means definition, and 'He who knows the Son, knows the Father also.' The Son is therefore a concise declaration of the nature of the Father, for every being that has been begotten is a silent definition of his begetter."[8] This last example is rather illuminating: a human individual is "the picture of his father" by the family characteristics which he has in common with him, not by the personal qualities which distinguish his father. Therefore, when one wishes to apply the theology of the image to the Trinity, one ought, in order to prevent any ambiguity, to speak of the "natural image," as did St. John Damascene,[9] for whom the Son is an εἰκών φυσική, "complete, in everything like the Father, excepting the characteristics of unbegottenness and fatherhood." The same thing can be said of the Holy Spirit, who is "the image of the Son," for " 'no man can say, Jesus is Lord, except in the Holy Spirit'. So it is in the Holy Spirit that we know Christ as Son of God and God, and it is by the Son that we see the Father."

The Trinitarian theology of "images" can have its place

---

[7](Paris, 1951).
[8]*Or.* 30 (*Theologica* 4), 20; P.G. 36, col. 129A.
[9]*De imaginibus* III, 18; P.G. 94, col. 1340AB.

only in a vertical perspective, that of the self-manifesting action of the divine nature, to which the old patristic formula corresponds: "from the Father, by the Son, in the Holy Spirit." This manifestation is not the act of an impersonal divinity surviving from unconquered Hellenism, for it presupposes the "monarchy of the Father" who manifests the attributes of His nature by the Logos in the Spirit. So, for example, in this theology of the image, the attribute of wisdom will have the Father as the source of wisdom, the Logos as hypostatic wisdom, expressing fully the Archetype in his person, the Holy Spirit as the energetic radiance of wisdom, common to the three hypostases, revealed outwardly and communicable as a gift to created persons. The theme of the image in Trinitarian theology, when placed in its proper perspective, can help in understanding the true meaning of the "energetic" theory of the divine attributes in the Byzantine theology of the fourteenth century. At the same time it justifies the Trinitarian theology of the Ante-Nicene Fathers, by permitting us to remove from the wealth of their speculative thought the (usually unmerited) reproach of subordinationism.

I shall not have time to develop certain observations on the theme of the "image" in Christology. The idea of the "Image of God" is attached here to the hypostasis of the Son who, in becoming man, makes visible in the human nature which He assumes His divine Person, consubstantial with the Father. Yet one cannot recognize the divinity of Christ (and consequently His character of "perfect image of the invisible God") except in the grace of the Holy Spirit.

It is in the context of the Incarnation (say rather: it is by the fact, by the event of the Incarnation) that the creation of man in the image of God receives all its theological value, which remained unperceived (or somewhat impoverished) in the letter of the sacerdotal narrative of the creation as seen by critical exegesis. It is not that one wishes to deny the importance or depreciate the merits of the historical study of the Bible: it is most valuable and ought to be taken into consideration by theologians. But never must this exegesis usurp a place which does not belong to it: that of a judge in theological matters.

The positive sense of a particular relationship to God, which does not appear in the Hebrew expressions *selem* and *demut*, begins to be more precise in the Greek translation of the Septuagint, where εἰκών and ὁμοίωσις, governed by the preposition κατά, are already loaded with a promise of future theology, denoting a progress of tradition, a "preparation for the Gospel" in a brighter light of Revelation. Proclamation of the Image of God manifested in Christ, the God-Man, makes use of this translation, discovering new connections favourable to an anthropology revealed, though latent, in the letter of the Biblical writings (for example Psalm 8:6, quoted in Hebrews 2:6).

The idea of kinship—συγγένεια, οἰκείωσις—implied in the Hellenic notion of the image was insufficient, as has been said, for a Christian doctrine of the Logos, the consubstantial Image of the Father: indeed, here no difference at all of nature may be admitted. In Christian anthropology, on the other hand, the idea of kinship would have been excessive, for the διάστημα, the distance between uncreated and created natures is infinite. Thus, as in Trinitarian theology, the term "image"—or, rather, "in the image"—applied to man must be given a new meaning along the same line of thought which made us distinguish in God the personal or hypostatic from the essential or natural. Man is not merely an individual of a particular nature, included in the generic relationship of human nature to God the Creator of the whole cosmos, but he is also—he is chiefly—a person, not reducible to the common (or even individualized) attributes of the nature which he shares with other human individuals. Personhood belongs to every human being by virtue of a singular and unique relation to God who created him "in His image." This personal element in anthropology, discovered by Christian thought, does not indicate, in itself, a relationship of participation, much less a "kinship" with God, but rather an analogy: like the personal God, in whose image he is created, man is not only "nature." This bestows on him liberty in regard to himself, taken as an individual of a particular nature. Though not explicit in patristic anthropology, this new category of the human person or hypostasis is nonetheless always presupposed by it. What is important to notice, in speaking of the theology of the image applied to man, is how the human person manifests God.

In its Trinitarian use, the term "image" denoted one divine Person who shows in Himself the nature or the natural attributes while referring them to another Hypostasis: the Holy Spirit to the Son, the Son to the Father. This presupposed, as we said, identity of nature or consubstantiality, something which is obviously out of the question for a created person who must be thought of as an "image" of God.[10] "Image," or "in the image," the human person could not truly be either; it could not make God manifest, transcending the nature which it "enhypostasizes," if it did not have the faculty of becoming like God, of assimilation to Him. Here enters the theme of ὁμοίωσις, of resemblance, with all that it can imply of Platonic heritage, going back to the *Phaedrus* and the *Theaetetus*. Of course, in Christian anthropology resemblance or assimilation to God can never be thought of otherwise than as by grace coming from God, which excludes the natural συγγένεια of Greek philosophy, replacing it with the idea of filial adoption.

Nevertheless—and this is the last remark I should like to make—theologians who try to find the "image of God" (or "what is in the image") in the human being by distinguishing it, as "a certain something," from the rest of human nature which "is not in the image," will never succeed in freeing themselves entirely from the συγγένεια of Greek thought. This remains true of Origen, though Fr. Crouzel has succeeded in clearing him of several charges which had become almost traditional. It is true in a certain degree of St. Gregory of Nyssa: thus, whenever Gregory tries to locate the "image of God" only in the higher faculties of man, identifying it with the νοῦς, he seems to want to make the

---

[10]This expression, stronger than "in the image," is found in I Cor. 11:7: εἰκὼν καὶ δόξα Θεοῦ.

human spirit the seat of grace by reason of a certain proximity which it has with the divine nature; this is again a survival of the idea of συγγένεια inherited from Origen. On the other hand, other texts, which Fr. Leys is right to emphasize, show a dynamic concept of human nature, rich in possibilities, poised, like a μεθόριον, between likeness and possible unlikeness; this would presuppose, it seems to me, another conception of the image, closely linked with the condition of personhood—and which would extend to the whole human make-up, not excepting the "cloak of skin."

Quite apart from the interpretation of the doctrine of the image in the works of St. Gregory of Nyssa, I for my part believe that this is the only conception of the image (or of "in the image") which can fulfill the demands of a Christian anthropology. Man created "in the image" is the person capable of manifesting God in the extent to which his nature allows itself to be penetrated by deifying grace. Thus the image—which is inalienable—can become similar or dissimilar, to the extreme limits: that of union with God, when deified man shows in himself by grace what God is by nature, according to the expression of St. Maximus; or indeed that of the extremity of falling-away which Plotinus called "the place of dissimilarity" (τόπος τῆς ἀνομοιώτητος), placing it in the gloomy abyss of Hades. These are the two extremes between which the personal destiny of man may veer in the working-out of his salvation, which is already realized in hope for everyone in the incarnate Image of the God who willed to create man in His own image.

8

Tradition and Traditions

Tradition (παράδοσις, *traditio*) is one of those terms which, through being too rich in meanings, runs the risk of finally having none. This is not only due to a secularization which has depreciated so many words of the theological vocabulary—"spirituality," "mystic," "communion"—detaching them from their Christian context in order to make of them the current coin of profane language. If the word "tradition" has suffered the same fate, this has happened all the more easily because even in the language of theology itself this term sometimes remains somewhat vague. In fact, if one tries to avoid mutilation of the idea of tradition by eliminating some of the meanings which it can comprise and attempts to keep them all, one is reduced to definitions which embrace too many things at a time and which no longer capture what constitutes the real meaning of "Tradition."

As soon as precision is desired, the over-abundant content has to be broken up and a group of narrow concepts created, the sum of which is far from expressing that living reality called the Tradition of the Church. A reading of the erudite work of Fr. A. Deneffe, *Der Traditionsbegriff*,[1] raises the question of whether tradition is capable of being expressed in concepts, or indeed whether, as with all that is "life," it "overflows the intelligence" and would have to be described rather than defined. There are, in fact, in the works of some theologians of the romantic epoch, such as Möhler in Germany or Khomiakov in Russia, beautiful pages of description, in which tradition appears as a catholic plenitude and cannot be distinguished from the unity, the catholicity (Khomiakov's *sobornost'*), the apostolicity, or the consciousness of the Church, which possesses the immediate certitude of revealed truth.

Faced with these descriptions, faithful in their general outline to the image of Tradition in the patristic writings of the first centuries, one is anxious to recognize the quality of pleroma which belongs to the tradition of the Church, but all the same one cannot renounce the necessity of drawing distinctions, which is imposed on all dogmatic theology. To distinguish does not always mean to separate, nor even to oppose. In opposing Tradition to Holy Scripture as two sources of Revelation, the polemicists of the Counter Reformation put themselves from the start on the same ground as their Protestant adversaries, having tacitly recognized in Tradition a reality other than that of Scripture. Instead of being the very ὑπόθεσις[2] of the sacred books—their fundamental coherence due to the living breath passing through them, transforming their letter into "a unique body of truth"—Tradition would appear as something added, as an external principle in relation to Scripture. Henceforth, patristic texts which attributed a character of *pleroma* to the Holy Scripture[3] became incomprehensible, while the Protestant doctrine of the "sufficiency of Scripture" received a negative meaning, by the exclusion of all that is "tradition." The defenders of Tradition saw themselves obliged to prove the necessity of

---

[1] In the collection *Münsterische Beiträge zur Theologie* 18 (Münster, 1931).
[2] The expression is from St. Irenaeus, *Adversus haereses* I, 1, 15-20.
[3] See the article of Fr. L. Bouyer, "The Fathers of the Church on Tradition and Scripture," *Eastern Churches Quarterly* 7 (1947), special number on Scripture and Tradition.

uniting two juxtaposed realities, each of which remained insufficient alone. Hence a series of false problems, like that of the primacy of Scripture or of Tradition, of their respective authority, of the total or partial difference of their content, *etc*. How is the necessity of knowing Scripture in the Tradition to be proved? How is their unity, which was ignored in separating them, to be found again? If the two are "fulness," there can be no question of two *pleromas* opposed to one another, but of two modalities of one and the same fulness of Revelation communicated to the Church.

A distinction which separates or divides is never perfect nor sufficiently radical: it does not allow one to discern, in its purity, the difference of the unknown term which it opposes to another that is supposed to be known. Separation is at the same time more and less than a distinction: it juxtaposes two objects detached from one another, but in order to do this it must first of all lend to one the characteristics of the other. In the present case, in seeking to juxtapose Scripture and Tradition as two independent sources of Revelation, Tradition is inevitably endowed with qualities which belong to Scripture: it becomes the ensemble of "other writings" or of unwritten "other words," that is, all that the Church can add to the Scripture on the horizontal plane of her history. Thus we find on the one hand Scripture or the Scriptural canon and on the other hand the Tradition of the Church, which in its turn can be divided into several sources of Revelation or *loci theologici* of unequal value: acts of ecumenical or local councils, writings of the Fathers, canonical prescriptions, liturgy, iconography, devotional practices, *etc*. But can this still be called "Tradition"? Would it not be more exact to say, with the theologians of the Council of Trent, "the traditions"? This plural well expresses what is meant when, having separated Scripture and Tradition instead of distinguishing them, the latter is projected onto the written or oral testimonies which are added to the Holy Scripture, accompanying or following it. Just as "time projected in space" presents an obstacle to the intuition of Bergsonian "duration," so too this projection of the qualitative notion of Tradition into the quantitative domain of "traditions" disguises rather than reveals its real character, for Tradition is free of all determinations which, in situating it historically, limit it.

An advance is made towards a purer notion of Tradition if this term is reserved to designate solely the oral transmission of the truths of faith. The separation between Tradition and Scripture still subsists, but instead of isolating two sources of Revelation, one opposes two modes of transmitting it: oral preaching and writing. It is then necessary to put in one category the preaching of the apostles and of their successors, as well as all preaching of the faith performed by a living teaching authority, and in another category the Holy Scripture and all other written expressions of the revealed Truth (these latter differing in the degree of their authority recognized by the Church). This approach affirms the primacy of Tradition over Scripture, since the oral transmission of the apostles' preaching preceded its recording in written form in the canon of the New Testament. It even might be said: the Church could dispense with the Scriptures, but she could not exist without Tradition. This is right only up to a certain point: it is true that the Church always possesses the revealed Truth, which she makes manifest by preaching and which equally well could have remained oral and passed from mouth to mouth, without ever having been fixed by writing.[4] But however much the separability of Scripture and Tradition is affirmed, they have not yet been radically distinguished: we remain on the surface, opposing books written with ink to discourses uttered with the living voice. In both cases it is a question of the word that is preached: "the preaching of the faith" here serves as a common foundation which qualifies the opposition between the two. But is not that to attribute to Tradition something which still makes it akin to Scripture? Is it not possible to go further in search of the pure notion of Tradition?

Among the variety of meanings that can be noted in the Fathers of the first centuries, Tradition sometimes receives that of a teaching kept secret, not divulged, lest the mystery

---

[4]St. Irenaeus envisages this possibility: *Adversus haereses* III, 4, 1.

be profaned by the uninitiate.[5] This is clearly expressed by
St. Basil in the distinction which he makes between δόγμα
κήρυγμα.[6] "Dogma" here has a sense contrary to that given
to this term today: far from being a doctrinal definition loudly
proclaimed by the Church, it is a "teaching (διδασκαλία),
unpublished and secret, that our fathers kept in silence, free
from disquiet and curiosity, well knowing that in being
silent one safeguards the sacred character of the mysteries."[7]
On the other hand the κήρυγμα (which means "preaching"
in the language of the New Testament) is always an open
proclamation, whether it be a doctrinal definition,[8] the official
prescription of an observance,[9] a canonical act,[10] or public
prayers of the Church.[11] Although they call to mind the
doctrina arcana of the Gnostics, who also laid claim to a
hidden apostolic tradition,[12] the unwritten and secret traditions of which St. Basil speaks differ from it notably. First,
the examples that he gives in the passage that we have
mentioned show that St. Basil's expressions relating to the
"mysteries" do not concern an esoteric circle of a few perfect
men in the interior of the Christian community, but rather
the ensemble of the faithful participating in the sacramental
life of the Church, who are here opposed to the "uninitiate"—
those whom a progressive catechism must prepare for the
sacraments of initiation. Secondly, the secret tradition
(δόγμα) can be declared publicly and thus become "preaching" (κήρυγμα) when a necessity (for example the struggle against a heresy) obliges the Church to make its pro-

---

[5]Clement of Alexandria, *Stromata* VI, 61.
[6]St. Basil, *De spiritu sancto* 27; P.G. 32, cols. 188A-193A.
[7]*Ibid.* cols. 188C-189A.
[8]St. Basil (*Ep.* 51; P.G. 32, col. 392C) calls ὁμοούσιος "the great
declaration of piety (τὸ μέγα τῆς εὐσεβείας κήρυγμα) which has
made manifest the doctrine (δόγμα) of salvation." Cf. *Ep.* 125; P.G. 32,
col. 548B.
[9]*Homilia de ieiunio,* P.G. 31, col. 185C.
[10]*Ep.* 251; P.G. 32, col. 933B.
[11]*Ep.* 155; P.G. 32, col. 612C.
[12]Ptolemy, *Letter to Flora* 7:9.

nouncement.[13] So, if the traditions received from the apostles remain unwritten and subject to the discipline of secrecy, if the faithful did not always know their mysterious meaning,[14] this is due to the wise economy of the Church, which surrenders its mysteries only to the extent that their open declaration becomes indispensable. One is here faced with one of the antinomies of the Gospel: On the one hand one must not give what is holy to the dogs, nor cast pearls before swine (Matt. 7:6). On the other hand "nothing is covered that will not be revealed, or hidden that will not be known" (Matt. 10:26; Luke 12:2). The "traditions guarded in silence and in mystery," that St. Basil opposes to oral preaching in public, make one think of the words that were told "in the dark," "whispered," but which will be spoken "in the light," "upon the housetops" (Matt. 10:27; Luke 12:3).

This is no longer an opposition between the ἄγραφα and the ἔγγραφα, oral preaching and written preaching. The distinction between Tradition and Scripture here penetrates further into the heart of the matter, placing on one side that which is kept in secret and which, for this reason, must not be recorded in writing, and on the other all that is the subject of preaching and which, once having been publicly declared, can henceforth be ranged on the side of the "Scriptures" (Γραφαί). Did not Basil himself judge it opportune to reveal in writing the secret of several "traditions," thus transforming them into κηρύγματα?[15] This new distinction puts the accent on the secret character of Tradition, by thus opposing a hidden fund of oral teachings, received from the apostles, to that which the Church offers for the knowledge of all; hence it immerses "preaching" in a sea of apostolic traditions, which could not be set aside or underestimated without injury to the Gospel. Even more, if one did this "one would transform the teaching that is

---

[13]The example of ὁμοούσιος is typical in this sense. The economy of St. Basil on the subject of the Divinity of the Holy Spirit is explained not only by a pedagogue's care, but also by this conception of the secret tradition.

[14]St. Basil, *De spiritu sancto* 27; P.G. 32, cols. 189C-192A.

[15]*Ibid.* cols. 192A-193A.

preached (τὸ κήρυγμα) into a simple name," devoid of meaning.[16] The several examples of these traditions offered by St. Basil all relate to the sacramental and liturgical life of the Church (sign of the Cross, baptismal rites, blessing of oil, eucharistic epiclesis, the custom of turning towards the east during prayer and that of remaining standing on Sunday and during the period of Pentecost *etc.*). If these "unwritten customs" (τὰ ἄγραφα τῶν ἐθῶν), these "mysteries of the Church" (ἄγραφα τῆς Ἐκκλησίας μυστήρια), so numerous that one could not expound them in the course of a whole day,[17] are necessary for understanding the truth of the Scripture (and in general the true meaning of all "preaching"), it is clear that the secret traditions point to the "mysterial character" of Christian knowledge. In fact, the revealed truth is not a dead letter but a living Word: it can be attained only in the Church, through initiation by the "mysteries" or sacraments[18] into the "mystery hidden for ages and generations but now made manifest to his saints" (Col. 1:26).

The unwritten traditions or mysteries of the Church, mentioned by St. Basil, constitute then the boundary with Tradition properly so-called, and they give glimpses of some of its features. In effect, there is participation in the revealed mystery through the fact of sacramental initiation. It is a new knowledge, a "gnosis of God" (γνῶσις Θεοῦ) that one receives as grace; and this gift of gnosis is conferred in a "tradition" which is, for St. Basil, the confession of the Trinity at the time of baptism: a sacred formula which leads us into light.[19] Here the horizontal line of the "traditions" received from the mouth of the Lord and transmitted by the apostles and their successors crosses with the vertical, with *Tradition*—the communication of the Holy Spirit, which opens to members of the Church an infinite perspective of

[16]*Ibid.* col. 188AB.

[17]*Ibid.* cols. 188A, 192C-193A.

[18]On the identification of these two terms and on the "mysterial" meaning of the sacraments in the writers of the first centuries, see Dom Odo Casel, *Das christliche Kultusmysterium* (Regensburg, 1932) p. 105 ff.

[19]St. Basil, *De spiritu sancto* 10; P.G. 32, col. 113B.

mystery in each word of the revealed Truth. Thus, starting from traditions such as St. Basil presents to us, it is necessary to go further and admit Tradition, which is distinguished from them.

In fact, if one stops at the boundary of the unwritten and secret traditions, without making the last distinction, one will still remain on the horizontal plane of the παρα-δόσεις, where Tradition appears to us as "projected into the realm of the Scriptures." It is true that it would be impossible to separate these secret traditions from the Scriptures or, more generally, from "preaching," but one could always oppose them as words spoken in secret or guarded in silence and words declared publicly. The fact is that the final distinction has not yet been made so long as there remains a last element which links Tradition with Scripture, with the *word*—which serves as a basis for opposing hidden traditions to open preaching. In order to isolate the pure notion of Tradition, in order to strip it of all that is its projection on the horizontal line of the Church, it is necessary to go beyond the opposition of secret words and words preached aloud, placing "the traditions" and "preaching" together rather than in opposition. The two have this in common, that, secret or not, they are nonetheless expressed by word. They always imply a verbal expression, whether it is a question of words properly so-called, pronounced or written, or whether of the dumb language which is addressed to the understanding by visual manifestation (iconography, ritual gestures, *etc.*). Taken in this general sense, the word is not uniquely an external sign used to designate a concept, but above all a content which is defined intelligibly and declared in assuming a body, in being incorporated in articulate discourse or in any other form of external expression.

If such is the nature of the word, nothing of what is revealed and makes itself known can remain foreign to it. Whether it be the Scriptures, preaching, or the "apostles' traditions guarded in silence," the same word λόγος or λόγια can equally be applied to all that constitutes expression of the revealed Truth. In fact, this word ceaselessly recurs in patristic literature to designate equally the Holy

Scripture and the Symbols of faith. Thus, St. John Cassian says on the subject of the symbol of Antioch: "It is the abridged word (*breviatum verbum*) that the Lord has given ... contracting into a few words the faith of His two Testaments, in order for it to contain in a brief way the meaning of all the Scriptures."[20] If one next considers that the Scriptures are not a collection of words about God, but the Word of God (λόγος τοῦ Θεοῦ), one will understand why, above all since Origen, there has been a desire to identify the presence of the divine Logos in the writings of the two Testaments with the incarnation of the Word, by which the Scriptures were "accomplished." Well before Origen, St. Ignatius of Antioch refused to see in the Scriptures merely an historical document—"archives"—and to justify the Gospel by the texts of the Old Testament, declaring: "For me, my archives are Jesus Christ; my inviolable archives are His Cross and His Death and His Resurrection, and the Faith which comes from Him... He is the Door of the Father, by which enter in Abraham, Isaac and Jacob, and the prophets, and the apostles, and the Church."[21] If by the fact of the incarnation of the Word the Scriptures are not archives of the Truth but its living body, the Scriptures can be possessed only within the Church, which is the unique body of Christ. Once again one returns to the idea of the sufficiency of Scripture. But here there is nothing negative: it does not exclude, but assumes the Church, with its sacraments, institutions and teachings transmitted by the apostles. Nor does this sufficiency, this *pleroma* of the Scripture, exclude any other expressions of the same Truth which the Church could produce (just as the fulness of Christ, the Head of the Church, does not exclude the Church, the complement of His glorious humanity). One knows that the defenders of the holy images founded the possibility of Christian icono-

---

[20]"Hoc est ergo breviatum verbum quod fecit Dominus...fidem scilicet duplicis Testamenti sui in pauca colligens, et sensum omnium Scripturarum in brevia concludens." *De incarnatione* VI, 3; P.L. 50, col. 149A. The "breviatum verbum" is an allusion to Rom. 9:27, which in its turn quotes Is. 10:22. Cf. St. Augustine, *De symbolo* 1; P.L. 40, col. 628; and St. Cyril of Jerusalem, *Catechesis V*, 12; P.G. 33, col. 521AB.

[21]Philadelphians 8:2, 9:1.

graphy on the fact of the incarnation of the Word: icons, just as well as the Scriptures, are expressions of the inexpressible, and have become possible thanks to the revelation of God which was accomplished in the incarnation of the Son. The same holds good for the dogmatic definitions, the exegesis, the liturgy—for all in the Church of Christ that participates in the same fulness of the Word as is contained by the Scriptures, without thereby being limited or reduced. In this "totalitarian" quality of the incarnate Word, all that expresses the revealed Truth thus is related to Scripture and, if all were in fact to become "scripture," the world itself could not contain the books that should be written (John 21:25).

But since expression of the transcendent mystery has become possible by the fact of the incarnation of the Word, since all that expresses it becomes in some way "scripture" alongside the Holy Scripture, the question arises as to where finally is that Tradition which we have sought by detaching progressively its pure notion from all that can relate it to scriptural reality?

As we have said, it is not to be sought on the horizontal lines of the "traditions" which, just as much as the Scripture, are determined by the Word. If again we wished to oppose it to all that belongs to the reality of the Word, it would be necessary to say that the Tradition is Silence. "He who possesses in truth the word of Jesus can hear even its silence (τῆς ἡσυχίας αὐτοῦ ἀκούειν)," says St. Ignatius of Antioch.[22] As far as I know, this text has never been used in the numerous studies which quote patristic passages on Tradition in abundance, always the same passages, known by everyone, but with never a warning that texts in which the word "tradition" is not expressly mentioned can be more eloquent than many others.

The faculty of hearing the silence of Jesus, attributed by St. Ignatius to those who in truth possess His word, echoes the reiterated appeal of Christ to His hearers: "He who has ears to hear, let him hear." The words of Revelation have

---

[22]Ephesians 15:2.

then a margin of silence which cannot be picked up by the
ears of those who are outside. St. Basil moves in the same
direction when he says, in his passage on the traditions:
"There is also a form of silence, namely the obscurity used
by the Scripture, which is intended in order to make it difficult to gain understanding of the teachings, for the profit
of readers."[23] This silence of the Scriptures could not be
detached from them: it is transmitted by the Church with
the words of Revelation as the very condition of their reception. If it could be opposed to words (always on the
horizontal plane, where they express the revealed Truth),
this silence which accompanies words implies no kind of
insufficiency or lack of fulness of Revelation, nor the necessity of adding to it anything whatever. It signifies that the
revealed mystery, to be truly received as fulness, demands
a conversion towards the vertical plane, in order that one
may be able to "comprehend with all saints" not only what
is the "breadth and length" of Revelation, but also its "depth"
and its "height" (Eph. 3:18).

At the point which we have reached, we can no longer
oppose Scripture and Tradition, nor juxtapose them as two
distinct realities. We must, however, distinguish them, the
better to seize their indivisible unity, which lends to the
Revelation given to the Church its character of fulness. If
the Scriptures and all that the Church can produce in words
written or pronounced, in images or in symbols liturgical
or otherwise, represent the differing modes of expression of
the Truth, Tradition is the *unique mode* of receiving it. We
say specifically *unique mode* and not *uniform mode,* for to
Tradition in its pure notion there belongs nothing formal.
It does not impose on human consciousness formal guarantees
of the truths of faith, but gives access to the discovery of
their inner evidence. It is not the content of Revelation, but
the light that reveals it; it is not the word, but the living
breath which makes the words heard at the same time as the
silence from which it came;[24] it is not the Truth, but a com-

[23]*De spiritu sancto* 27; P.G. 32, col. 189BC.
[24]Cf. St. Ignatius of Antioch, Magnesians 8:2.

munication of the Spirit of Truth, outside which the Truth cannot be received. "No one can say 'Jesus is Lord' except by the Holy Spirit" (I Cor. 12:3). The pure notion of Tradition can then be defined by saying that it is the life of the Holy Spirit in the Church, communicating to each member of the Body of Christ the faculty of hearing, of receiving, of knowing the Truth in the Light which belongs to it, and not according to the natural light of human reason. This is true gnosis, owed to an action of the divine Light (Φωτισμὸς τῆς γνώσεως τῆς δόξης τοῦ Θεοῦ, II Cor. 4:6), the unique Tradition, independent of all "philosophy," independent of all that lives "according to human tradition, according to the elemental spirits of the universe, and not according to Christ" (Col. 2:8). This freedom from every condition of nature, every contingency of history, is the first characteristic of the vertical line of Tradition; it is inherent in Christian gnosis: "You will know the Truth, and the Truth will make you free" (John 8:32). One cannot know the Truth nor understand the words of Revelation without having received the Holy Spirit, "and where the Spirit of the Lord is, there is freedom" (II Cor. 3:17).[25] This freedom of the children of God, opposed to the slavery of the sons of this world, is expressed by the "freeness" (παρρησία) with which those can address God who know Him whom they worship, for they worship the Father "in Spirit and Truth" (John 4:23, 24).

Wishing to distinguish Tradition from Scripture, we have sought to strip the notion of all that could make it akin to scriptural reality. We have had to distinguish it from the "traditions," ranking these latter, together with the Scriptures and all expressions of the Truth, on the same horizontal line, where we have found no other name for designating Tradition than that of Silence. When therefore Tradition has been detached from all that could receive its projection on the horizontal plane, it is necessary to enter another dimension in order to reach the conclusion of our analysis. Contrary to

---

[25]See St. Basil's interpretation of this text, *De spiritu sancto* 20; P.G. 32, cols. 164C-165C.

analyses such as philosophy since Plato and Aristotle conceives
them, which end in dissolving the concrete by resolving it
into general ideas or conceptions, our analysis leads us finally
towards the Truth and the Spirit, the Word and the Holy
Spirit, two Persons distinct but indissolubly united, whose
twofold economy, while founding the Church, conditions at
the same time the indissoluble and distinct character of
Scripture and of Tradition.

2

The culmination of our analysis—Incarnate Word and
Holy Spirit in the Church, as the twofold condition of the
fulness of the Revelation—will serve us as a turntable from
which to set forth now on the way of synthesis and to
assign to Tradition the place which belongs to it in the
concrete realities of ecclesiastical life. It will first of all be
necessary to establish a double reciprocity in the economy of
the two divine Persons sent by the Father. On the one hand,
it is by the Holy Spirit that the Word is made incarnate of
the Virgin Mary. On the other hand, it is by the Word, following His incarnation and work of redemption, that the
Holy Spirit descends on the members of the Church at
Pentecost. In the first case, the Holy Spirit comes first, but
with a view to the incarnation, in order that the Virgin
may be able to conceive the Son of God, come to be made
Man. The role of the Holy Spirit here, then, is functional:
He is the power of the incarnation, the virtual condition of
the reception of the Word. In the second case, it is the
Son who comes first, for He sends the Holy Spirit who comes
from the Father; but it is the Holy Spirit who plays the
principal role: It is He who is the aim, for He is communicated to the members of the Body of Christ in order
to deify them by grace. So here the role of the Incarnate
Word is, in its turn, functional in relation to the Spirit: it is
the form, so to speak, the "canon" of sanctification, a formal
condition of the reception of the Holy Spirit.

The true and holy Tradition, according to Filaret of

Moscow, "does not consist uniquely in visible and verbal
transmission of teachings, rules, institutions and rites: it is at
the same time an invisible and actual communication of
grace and of sanctification."[26] If it is necessary to distinguish
what is transmitted (the oral and written traditions) and
the unique mode according to which this transmission is
received in the Holy Spirit (Tradition as the principle of
Christian knowledge), it will nonetheless be impossible to
separate these two points; hence the ambivalence of the term
"tradition," which designates simultaneously the horizontal
line and the vertical line of the Truth possessed by the
Church. Every transmission of a truth of faith implies then
a communication of the grace of the Holy Spirit. In fact,
outside of the Spirit "who spoke by the prophets," that
which is transmitted cannot be recognized by the Church
as word of truth—word akin to the sacred books inspired
by God and, together with the Holy Scriptures, "recapitulated" by the Incarnate Word. This wind of Pentecostal
fire, communication of the Spirit of Truth proceeding from
the Father and sent by the Son, actualizes the supreme faculty
of the Church: the consciousness of revealed Truth, the
possibility of judging and of discerning between true and
false in the Light of the Holy Spirit: "It has seemed good
to the Holy Spirit and to us" (Acts 15:28). If the Paraclete
is the unique Criterion of the Truth revealed by the Incarnate
Word, He is also the principle of the incarnation, for the
same Holy Spirit by whom the Virgin Mary received the
faculty of becoming Mother of God, acts as function of the
Word as a power for expressing the Truth in intelligible
definitions or sensible images and symbols—documents of
the faith which the Church will have to judge as to whether
or not they belong to its Tradition.

These considerations are necessary to enable us to find
again, in concrete cases, the relationship between Tradition
and the revealed Truth, received and expressed by the Church.
As we have seen, Tradition in its primary notion is not the

---

[26]Quoted by Fr. G. Florovsky, *The Ways of Russian Theology* (In Russian;
Paris, 1937) p. 178.

revealed content, but the unique mode of receiving Revelation, a faculty owed to the Holy Spirit, who renders the Church capable of knowing the Incarnate Word in His relationship with the Father (supreme gnosis which is, for the Fathers of the first centuries, Theology in the proper meaning of the word) as well as the mysteries of the divine economy, from the creation of heaven and earth of Genesis to the new heaven and new earth of the Apocalypse. Recapitulated by the incarnation of the Word, the history of the divine economy makes itself known by the Scriptures, in the recapitulation of the two Testaments by the same Word. But this unity of the Scriptures can be recognized only in the Tradition, in the Light of the Holy Spirit communicated to the members of the unique Body of Christ. The books of the Old Testament, composed over a period of several centuries, written by different authors who have often brought together and fused different religious traditions, have only an accidental, mechanical unity for the eyes of the historian of religions. Their unity with the writings of the New Testament will appear to him factitious and artificial. But a son of the Church will be able to recognize the unity of inspiration and the unique object of the faith in these heteroclitic writings, woven by the same Spirit who, after having spoken by the prophets, preceded the Word in rendering the Virgin Mary apt to serve as means for the incarnation of God.

It is only in the Church that one is able to recognize in full consciousness the unity of inspiration of the sacred books, because the Church alone possesses the Tradition—the knowledge in the Holy Spirit of the Incarnate Word. The fact that the canon of the writings of the New Testament was formed relatively late, with some hesitations, shows us that the Tradition is in no way automatic: it is the condition of the Church having an infallible consciousness, but it is not a mechanism which will infallibly make known the Truth outside and above the consciousness of individuals, outside all deliberation and all judgment. In fact, if Tradition is a faculty of judging in the Light of the Holy Spirit, it obliges those who wish to know the Truth in the Tradition to make incessant efforts: one does not remain in the Tradition by a certain historical inertia, by keeping as a "tradition received from the Fathers" all that which, by force of habit, flatters a certain devout sensibility. On the contrary, it is by substituting this sort of "traditions" for the Tradition of the Holy Spirit living in the Church that one runs the most risk of finding oneself finally outside the Body of Christ. It must not be thought that the conservative attitude alone is salutary, nor that heretics are always "innovators." If the Church, after having established the canon of Scripture, preserves it in the Tradition, this preservation is not static and inert, but dynamic and conscious—in the Holy Spirit, who purifies anew "the words of the Lord . . . words that are pure, silver refined in a furnace on the ground, purified seven times" (Ps. 12:6). If that were lacking, the Church would have conserved only a dead text, witness of an ended epoch, and not the living and vivifying Word, perfect expression of the Revelation which it possesses independently of the existence of old discordant manuscripts or of new "critical editions" of the Bible.

One can say that Tradition represents the critical spirit of the Church. But, contrary to the "critical spirit" of human science, the critical judgment of the Church is made acute by the Holy Spirit. It has then quite a different principle: that of the undiminished fulness of Revelation. Thus the Church, which will have to correct the inevitable alterations of the sacred texts (that certain "traditionalists" wish to preserve at any price, sometimes attributing a mystical meaning to stupid mistakes of copyists), will be able at the same time to recognize in some late interpolations (for example, in the *comma* of the "three that bear record in heaven" in the first epistle of St. John) an authentic expression of the revealed Truth. Naturally authenticity here has a meaning quite other than it has in the historical disciplines.[27]

[27]Origen, in his homilies on the Epistle to the Hebrews, after having expressed his views on the source of this epistle, of which the teaching is Pauline but the style and composition denote an author other than St. Paul, adds this: "If, then, some church considers this epistle as written by St. Paul, let it be honored also for that. For it is not by chance that the ancients have transmitted it under the name of Paul. But who wrote the epistle? God knows the truth." Fragment quoted by Eusebius, *Historia Ecclesiastica* VI, 25; P.G. 20, col. 584C.

Not only the Scriptures, but also the oral traditions received from the apostles have been conserved only by virtue of the Tradition—the Light which reveals their true meaning and their significance, essential for the Church. Here more than elsewhere Tradition exercises its critical action, showing above all its negative and exclusive aspect: it rejects the "godless and silly myths" (I Tim. 4:7) piously received by all those whose "traditionalism" consists in accepting with unlimited credulity all that is insinuated into the life of the Church to remain there by force of habit.[28] In the epoch in which the oral traditions coming from the apostles began to be fixed in writing, the true and the false traditions crystalized together in numerous apocrypha, several of which circulate under the names of the apostles or other saints. "We are not ignorant" says Origen,[29] "that many of these secret writings have been composed by impious men, from among those who make their iniquity sound loudest, and that some of these fictions are used by the Hypythiani, others by the disciples of Basilides. We must therefore pay attention, in order not to receive all the apocrypha which circulate under the names of saints, for some have been composed by the Jews, perhaps to destroy the truth of our Scriptures and to establish false teachings. But on the other hand we must not reject as a whole all that is useful for throwing light on our Scriptures. It is a mark of greatness of spirit to hear and to apply these words of the Scripture: 'test everything; hold fast what is good' (I Thess. 5:21)." Since the deeds and the words that the memory of the Church has kept since apostolic times "in silence free of disquiet and of curiosity"[30] have been divulged in writings of heterodox origin, these apocrypha, though separated from the scriptural canon, should nonetheless not be totally rejected. The Church knows how to extract from them some elements suitable for completing or for illustrating events on which

---

[28]In our days still, the literature of the *Synaxaria* and the *Leimonaria* offer similar examples, not to mention liturgical monstrosities which, for certain people, also receive a "traditional" and sacred character.

[29]*Commentary on Matthew* 28; P.G. 13, col. 1637.

[30]St. Basil, *De spiritu sancto* 27; P.G. 32, col. 188.

the Scriptures are silent but which Tradition recognizes as true. Further, amplifications having an apocryphal source serve to color the liturgical texts and the iconography of some feasts. Thus one uses apocryphal sources, with judgment and moderation, to the extent to which they may represent corrupted apostolic traditions. Recreated by the Tradition, these elements, purified and made legitimate, return to the Church as its own property. This judgment will be necessary each time that the Church has to deal with writings claiming to belong to the apostolic tradition. She will reject them, or she will receive them, without necessarily posing the question of their authenticity on the historical plane, but considering above all their content in the light of Tradition.

Sometimes a considerable labor of clarification and adaptation will be necessary, in order that a pseudepigraphic work finally may be utilized by the Church as a witness of her Tradition. Thus St. Maximus the Confessor had to make his commentary on the *Corpus Dionysiacum* in order to uncover the orthodox meaning of these theological writings, which were circulating in monophysite circles under the pseudonym of St. Dionysius the Areopagite, adopted by their author or compiler. Without belonging to the "apostolic tradition" properly so-called, the Dionysian corpus belongs to the "patristic tradition," which continues that of the apostles and of their disciples.[31] The same could be said of some other writings of this kind. As for the oral traditions claiming apostolic authority, above all in so far as concerns customs and institutions, the judgment of the Church will take into account not only their meaning but also the universality of their usage.

Let us note that the formal criterion of traditions which was expressed by St. Vincent of Lerins—*Quod semper, quod ubique, quod ab omnibus*—can only be applied in full to

---

[31]It would be as false to deny the traditional character of the work of "Dionysius," by basing oneself on the fact of its non-apostolic origin, as to wish to attribute it to the convert of St. Paul, on the pretext that these writings were received by the Church under the title of St. Dionysius the Areopagite. Both these attitudes would equally reveal a lack of true consciousness of the Tradition.

those apostolic traditions which were orally transmitted
during two or three centuries. The New Testament Scriptures already escape from this rule, for they were neither
"always," nor "everywhere," nor "received by all," before
the definitive establishment of the scriptural canon. Whatever
may be said by those who forget the primary significance
of Tradition, wishing to substitute for it a "rule of faith,"
the formula of St. Vincent is even less applicable to the
dogmatic definitions of the Church. It is enough to recall
that the term ὁμοούσιος was anything but "traditional."
With a few exceptions,[32] it was never used anywhere or by
anyone except by the Valentinian gnostics and the heretic
Paul of Samosata. The Church has transformed it into "words
that are pure, silver refined in a furnace on the ground,
purified seven times" in the crucible of the Holy Spirit and
of the free consciousness of those who judge within the
Tradition, allowing themselves to be seduced by no habitual
form, by no natural inclination of flesh and blood, which
often takes the form of an unconsidered and obscure devotion.

The dynamism of Tradition allows of no inertia either
in the habitual forms of piety or in the dogmatic expressions
that are repeated mechanically like magic recipes of Truth,
guaranteed by the authority of the Church. To preserve the
"dogmatic tradition" does not mean to be attached to doc-

[32]Before Nicaea, the term ὁμοούσιος is found in a fragment of the
commentary of Origen on the Epistle to the Hebrews, quoted by St.
Pamphilius the Martyr (P.G. 14, col. 1308), in the *Apology for Origen*
of the same Pamphilius, translated by Rufinus (P.G. 17, cols. 580-581), and
in the anonymous dialogue *On True Faith in God* falsely attributed to Origen
(ed. W. H. van de Sande Bakhuyzen [Leipzig, 1901]). According to St.
Athanasius, St. Dionysius of Alexandria was accused, about 259-261, of not
recognizing that Christ is consubstantial with God; Dionysius is said to have
replied that he avoided the word ὁμοούσιος, which is not in Scripture,
but recognized the orthodox meaning of this expression (St. Athanasius, *De
sententia Dionysii* 18; P.G. 25, col. 505). The treatise *On Faith* where one
finds the expression in the Nicene sense (P.G. 10, col. 1128) does not
belong to St. Gregory of Neocaesarea; it is a Post-Nicene writing, probably
of the end of the fourth century. Thus, the examples of the term among
orthodox writers before Nicaea are for the most part uncertain: one cannot
trust the translation of Rufinus. In any case the use of this term is very
restricted and has an accidental character.

trinal formulas: to be within the Tradition is to keep the
living Truth in the Light of the Holy Spirit; or rather, it is
to be kept in the Truth by the vivifying power of Tradition.
But this power, like all that comes from the Spirit, preserves
by a ceaseless renewing.

3

"To renew" does not mean to replace ancient expressions
of the Truth by new ones, more explicit and theologically
better elaborated. If that were so, we should have to recognize
that the erudite Christianity of theology professors represents
a considerable progress in relation to the "primitive" faith
of the disciples and the apostles. In our days there is much
talk of "theological development," often without taking
account of the extent to which this expression (which has
become almost a commonplace) can be ambiguous. In fact,
it implies, among some modern authors, an evolutionary
conception of the history of Christian dogma. Attempts are
made to interpret in the sense of "dogmatic progress" this
passage of St. Gregory of Nazianzus: "The Old Testament
manifested clearly the Father and obscurely the Son. The
New Testament manifested the Son, but gave only indications
of the divinity of the Holy Spirit. Nowadays, the Spirit is
among us and shows Himself in all His splendor. It would
not have been prudent, before recognizing the divinity of
the Father, openly to preach the divinity of the Son, and as
long as that of the Son had not been accepted, to impose
the Holy Spirit, if I dare so express myself."[33] But "the
Spirit is among us" since the day of Pentecost and, with
Him, the light of Tradition, *i.e.,* not only what has been
transmitted (as a sacred and inert "deposit" would have
been) but also the very force of transmission conferred on
the Church and accompanying all that is transmitted, as the
unique mode of receiving and possessing the Revelation.
However, the unique mode of having the Revelation in the

---

[33]*Or.* 31 (*Theologica* 5), 26; P.G. 36, col. 161C.

Holy Spirit is to have it in fulness, and it is thus that the Church knows the Truth in the Tradition. If there was an increase in knowledge of the divine mysteries, a progressive revelation, "light coming little by little," before the coming of the Holy Spirit, it is otherwise for the Church. If one can still speak of development, it is not knowledge of Revelation in the Church which progresses or is developed with each dogmatic definition. If one were to embrace the whole account of doctrinal history from its beginnings down to our own day, by reading the *Enchiridion* of Denzinger or the fifty in-folio volumes of Mansi, the knowledge that one would thus have of the mystery of the Trinity would be no more perfect than was that of a Father of the fourth century who speaks of the ὁμοούσιος, nor than that of an Ante-Nicene Father who does not yet speak of it, nor than that of a St. Paul, to whom even the term "Trinity" remains as yet foreign. At every moment of its history the Church gives to its members the faculty of knowing the Truth in a fulness that the world cannot contain. It is this mode of knowing the living Truth in the Tradition that the Church defends in creating new dogmatic definitions.

"To know in fulness" does not mean "to have the fulness of knowledge"; this belongs only to the world to come. If St. Paul says that he now knows "in part" (I Cor. 13:12) this ἐκ μέρους does not exclude the fulness *in which* he knows. It is not later dogmatic development that will suppress the "knowledge in part" of St. Paul, but the eschatological actualization of the fulness in which, confusedly but surely, Christians here below know the mysteries of Revelation. The knowledge ἐκ μέρους will not be suppressed because it was false, but because its role was merely to make us adhere to the fulness which surpasses every human faculty of knowledge. Hence it is in the light of the fulness that one knows "in part," and it is always through this fulness that the Church judges whether or not the partial knowledge expressed in this or that doctrine belongs to Tradition. Any theological doctrine which pretends to be a perfect explanation of the revealed mystery will inevitably appeal to be false: by the very fact of pretending to the fulness of knowledge it will set itself in opposition to the fulness in which the Truth is known in part. A doctrine is traitor to Tradition when it seeks to take its place: gnosticism offers a striking example of an attempt to substitute for dynamic fulness, given to the Church as the condition of true knowledge, a kind of static fulness of a "revealed doctrine." On the other hand, a dogma defined by the Church, in the form of partial knowledge, each time opens anew an access towards the fulness outside of which the revealed Truth can be neither known nor confessed. As an expression of truth, a dogma of faith belongs to Tradition, without all the same constituting one of its "parts." It is a means, an intelligible instrument, which makes for adherence to the Tradition of the Church: it is a witness of Tradition, its external limit or, rather, the narrow door which leads to knowledge of Truth in the Tradition.

Within the circle of dogma, the knowledge of the revealed mystery that a member of the Church will be able to attain—the degree of Christian "gnosis"—will vary in proportion to the spiritual measure of each. This knowledge of the Truth in the Tradition thus will be able to increase in a person, in company with his increase in sanctification (Col. 1:10): a Christian will be more perfect in knowledge at the age of his spiritual maturity. But would one dare to speak, against all the evidence, of a collective progress in the knowledge of the Christian mystery, a progress which would be due to a "dogmatic development" of the Church? Would this development have started in "gospel infancy" to end to-day—after a "patristic youth" and a "scholastic maturity"—in the sad senility of the manuals of theology? Or indeed should this metaphor (false, like so many others) give place to a vision of the Church like that which is to be found in the Shepherd of Hermas, where the Church appears in the features of a woman young and old at the same time, bringing together all ages in the "measure of the stature of the fulness of Christ" (Eph. 4:13)?

Returning to the text of St. Gregory of Nazianzus, so often misinterpreted, we shall see that the dogmatic development in question is in no way determined by an inner necessity, which would effect a progressive increase in the Church of the knowledge of revealed Truth. Far from being a kind of organic evolution, the history of dogma depends above all on the conscious attitude of the Church in face of historical reality, in which she has to work for the salvation of men. If Gregory spoke of a progressive revelation of the Trinity before Pentecost, it is in order to insist on the fact that the Church, in her economy in relation to the external world, must follow the example of the divine pedagogy. In formulating these dogmas (cf. κήρυγμα in St. Basil, see page 145 above), it must conform to the necessities of a given moment, "not unveiling all things without delay and without discernment, and nonetheless keeping nothing hidden until the end. For the one would be imprudent and the other impious. The one would risk wounding those without, and the other separating us from our own brothers."[34]

In replying to the lack of understanding of the external world, incapable of receiving Revelation—in resisting the attempts of the "debater of this age" (I Cor. 1:20) who, in the womb of the Church itself, seeks to understand the Truth "according to human tradition, according to the elemental spirits of the universe, and not according to Christ" (Col. 2:8)—the Church finds herself obliged to express her faith in the form of dogmatic definitions, in order to defend it against the thrust of heresies. Imposed by the necessity of the struggle, dogmas once formulated by the Church become for the faithful a "rule of faith" which remains firm forever, setting the boundary between orthodoxy and heresy, between knowledge within the Tradition and knowledge determined by natural factors. Always confronted with new difficulties to overcome, with new obstacles of thought to remove, the Church will always have to defend her dogmas. Her theologians will have the constant task of expounding and inter-

---

[34]*Ibid.* c. 27; P.G. 36, col. 164B. It is known that Gregory of Nazianzus reproached his friend St. Basil for excess of prudence with regard to the open proclamation of the Divinity of the Holy Spirit, a truth which had the character of traditional evidence for members of the Church, but which exacted a moderation in economy with regard to the *pneumatomachoi,* whom it was necessary to bring into the unity of the faith.

preting them anew according to the intellectual demands of the milieu or of the epoch. In critical moments of the struggle for the integrity of the faith, the Church will have to proclaim new dogmatic definitions, which will mark new stages in this struggle, which will last until all arrive at "the unity of the faith, and of the knowledge of the Son of God" (Eph. 4:13). Having to struggle against new heresies, the Church never abandons her ancient dogmatic positions in order to replace them by new definitions. These stages are never surpassed by an evolution; and, far from being relegated to the archives of history, they preserve the quality of an ever actual present, in the living light of the Tradition. Thus one can speak of dogmatic development only in a very limited sense: in formulating a new dogma the Church takes as her point of departure already existing dogmas, which constitute a rule of faith that she has in common with her adversaries. Thus, the dogma of Chalcedon makes use of that of Nicaea and speaks of the Son consubstantial with the Father in His divinity, to say afterwards that He is also consubstantial with us in His humanity; against the monothelites, who in principle admitted the dogma of Chalcedon, the Fathers of the Sixth Council will again take up its formulae on the two natures, in order to affirm the two wills and the two energies of Christ; the Byzantine councils of the fourteenth century, in proclaiming the dogma on the divine Energies, will refer, among other things, to the definitions of the Sixth Council, *etc.* In each case one can speak of a "dogmatic development" to the extent that the Church extends the rule of faith while remaining, in her new definitions, in conformity with the dogmas already received by all.

If the rule of faith develops as the teaching authority of the Church adds to it new acts having dogmatic authority, this development, which is subject to an "economy" and presupposes a knowledge of Truth in the Tradition, is not an augmentation of Tradition. This is clear if one is willing to take into account all that has been said concerning the primordial notion of Tradition. It is the abuse of the term "tradition" (in the singular and without an adjective to qualify it and determine it) by authors who see only its projection on the horizontal plane of the Church—the plane of the "traditions" (in the plural or with a qualification which defines them)—and above all a vexatious habit of designating by this term the Church's ordinary teaching authority which have allowed such frequent talk to be heard about a "development" or an "enriching" of tradition. The theologians of the Seventh Council distinguish clearly between the "Tradition of the Holy Spirit" and the divinely inspired "teaching (διδασκαλία) of our Holy Fathers."[35] They were able to define the new dogma "with all rigour and justice" because they considered themselves to be in the same Tradition which allowed the Fathers of past centuries to produce new expressions of the Truth whenever they had to reply to the necessities of the moment.

There exists an interdependence between the "Tradition of the Catholic Church" (= the faculty of knowing the Truth in the Holy Spirit) and the "teaching of the Fathers" (= the rule of faith kept by the Church). One cannot belong to the Tradition while contradicting the dogmas, just as one cannot make use of the dogmatic formulas received in order to oppose a formal "orthodoxy" to every new expression of the Truth that the life of the Church may produce. The first attitude is that of revolutionary innovators, of false prophets who sin against the expressed Truth, against the Incarnate Word, in the name of the Spirit to which they lay claim. The second is that of the conservative formalists, pharisees of the Church who, in the name of the habitual expressions of Truth, run the risk of sinning against the Spirit of Truth.

In distinguishing the Tradition in which the Church knows the Truth from the "dogmatic tradition" which she

---

[35]H. Denzinger, *Enchiridion symbolorum* no. 302: Τὴν βασιλικὴν ὥσπερ ἐρχόμενοι τρίβον, ἐπακολουθοῦντες τῇ Θεηγόρῳ διδασκαλίᾳ τῶν ἁγίων πατέρων ἡμῶν, καὶ τῇ παραδόσει τῆς καθολικῆς ἐκκλησίας. Τοῦ γὰρ ἐν αὐτῇ ἀκήσαντος ἁγίου πνεύματος εἶναι ταύτην γινώσκομεν. Ὁρίζομεν σὺν ἀκριβείᾳ πάσῃ καὶ ἐμμελείᾳ... "walking, so to speak, on the royal road, following the divinely inspired teaching of our Holy Fathers as well as the Tradition of the catholic Church (for we know that it belongs to the Holy Spirit, who dwells in the Church), we define in all rigor and justice..."

establishes by her teaching authority and which she preserves, we find again the same relationship as we have been able to establish between Tradition and Scripture: one can neither confound them nor separate them without depriving them of the character of fulness that they possess together. Like Scripture, dogmas *live* in the Tradition, with this difference that the scriptural canon forms a determinate body which excludes all possibility of further increase, while the "dogmatic tradition," though keeping its stability as the "rule of faith" from which nothing can be cut off, can be increased by receiving, to the extent that may be necessary, new expressions of revealed Truth, formulated by the Church. The ensemble of the dogmas which the Church possesses and transmits is not a body constituted once and for all, but neither has it the incomplete character of a doctrine "in process of becoming." At every moment of its historical existence, the Church formulates the Truth of the faith in its dogmas, which always express a fulness to which one adheres intellectually in the light of the Tradition, while never being able to make it definitively explicit. A truth which would allow itself to be made fully explicit would not have the quality of living fulness which belongs to Revelation: "fulness" and "rational explicitness" mutually exclude one another. However, if the mystery revealed by Christ and known in the Holy Spirit cannot be made explicit, it does not remain inexpressible. Since "the whole fulness of deity dwells bodily" in Christ (Col. 2:9), this fulness of the divine Word Incarnate will be expressed as much in the Scriptures as in the "abridged word" of the symbols of faith[36] or of other dogmatic definitions. This fulness of the Truth that they express without making explicit, allows the dogmas of the Church to be akin to the Holy Scriptures. It is for this reason that the Pope St. Gregory the Great brought together in the same veneration the dogmas of the first four Councils and the four Gospels.[37]

All that we have said of the "dogmatic tradition" can be applied to other expressions of the Christian mystery that

---

[36]See above at n. 20.
[37]*Epistolarum liber* I, *ep.* 25; P.L. 77, col. 613.

the Church produces in the Tradition, conferring on them equally the presence of the "fulness of him who fills all in all" (Eph. 1:23). Just like the "divinely inspired didascalia" of the Church, the iconographic tradition also receives its full meaning and its intimate coherence with other documents of the faith (Scripture, dogmas, liturgy) in the Tradition of the Holy Spirit. Just as much as dogmatic definitions, it has been possible for the icons of Christ to be compared to Holy Scriptures, to receive the same veneration, since iconography sets forth in colors what the word announces in written letters.[38] Dogmas are addressed to the intelligence, they are intelligible expressions of the reality which surpasses our mode of understanding. Icons impinge on our consciousness by means of the outer senses, presenting to us the same suprasensible reality in "esthetic" expressions (in the proper sense of the word αἰσθητικός: that which can be perceived by the senses). But the intelligible element does not remain foreign to iconography: in looking at an icon one discovers in it a "logical" structure, a dogmatic content which has determined its composition. This does not mean that icons are a kind of hieroglyph or sacred rebus, translating dogmas into a language òf conventional signs. If the intelligibility which penetrates these sensible images is identical with that of the dogmas of the Church, it is that the two "traditions" —dogmatic and iconographic—coincide in so far as they express, each by its proper means, the same revealed reality.

---

[38]"We prescribe the veneration of the holy icon of Our Lord Jesus Christ, rendering to it the same honor as to the Books of the Holy Gospels. For just as by the letters of these latter we all come to salvation, so by the action of the colors in images, all—learned as well as ignorant—equally find their profit in what is within reach of all. In effect, just as the word is set forth by letters, painting sets forth and represents the same things by colors. Hence, it someone does not venerate the icon of Christ the Savior, may be he unable to see His face at the second coming..." (Denzinger, no. 337). If we cite here the third canon of the anti-Photian Synod (869-870), whose acts have been rejected by the Church (not only in the East but also in the West, as shown by F. Dvornik, *The Photian Schism* [London, 1948], pp. 176-177 *et passim*), it is because this text gives a beautiful example of the rapprochement current between the Holy Scriptures and iconography, united in the same Tradition of the Church. Cf. the sequel to the text quoted, on icons of the Mother of God, of angels, and of the saints (Denzinger, *loc. cit.*).

Although it transcends the intelligence and the senses, Christian Revelation does not exclude them: on the contrary, it assumes them and transforms them by the light of the Holy Spirit, in the Tradition which is the unique mode of receiving the revealed Truth, of recognizing it in its scriptural, dogmatic, iconographic and other expressions and also of expressing it anew.

9

Concerning the Third Mark of the Church: Catholicity

We believe in one, holy, catholic and apostolic Church. Such is the Christian tradition concerning the Church, taught by the Fathers, declared by the Councils, preserved by Christendom throughout the ages.

No faithful Christian will ever hesitate to confess these four attributes of the Church, which he believes to be true in virtue of that instinct for the truth, that faculty which one may call "innate," that belongs to all children of the Church—the instinct or faculty which we call faith. It is understood (or at least it is felt, dimly but firmly) that the Church no longer would be the Church were she deprived of one of these attributes, that only the consensus of these four qualities professed in the Creed expresses the fulness of her being. But when we are concerned with formulating, with distinguishing attributes, with finding out wherein lies the characteristic proper to each one of them, we often fall into the haziness of overly general definitions, equivocal in meaning, tending to confusion, confounding the attributes which we see so precisely and clearly expressed in the Creed. This happens especially when attempts are made to define the third attribute of the Church, that of catholicity.[1] Here, one feels, is the tangled knot of all our difficulties. As long as catholicity remains ill-defined, we are involved inevitably in those confusions which obscure logical distinction of the marks of the Church. Otherwise, if we are going to safeguard the rights of logic by avoiding every difficulty, distinction of the marks of the Church remains superficial, accidental, and artificial. There is nothing more dangerous, more contrary to true theology, than a superficial clarity at the expense of profound analysis.

Every logical distinction presupposes not only differences between the terms that are to be distinguished, but also some degree of concordance with one another, which springs from a common ground, in virtue of which the distinction is possible. It is clear that the harmony of the four marks of the Church is of such a kind that to suppress or change the character of one member of this fourfold distinction would suppress the very concept of the Church, or at least would transform it profoundly, changing in their turn the characteristics of the other marks.

---

[1] We are thinking particularly of the unwarranted use of the word *sobornost'* by certain Russian authors who fail to translate the word by its French correlative "catholicité" [Eng.: "catholicity"]. Attempts even are made to translate it by other terms, such as "conciliarity," "conciliar spirit," "symphony," *etc.* All this is done to confront the Western reader with unfamiliar ideas, to manufacture an "Orthodoxy for export" which will appear exotic and queer and only for the initiate. Confronted with this preciousness one is tempted to say with Molière, "You must speak like a Christian if you want to be understood." This is what we wish to do in this short study of the concept of catholicity as it is presented by Orthodox thought.

An etymological note on the word *sobornost'* seems to us necessary. The Slavonic text of the Creed translates the adjective "catholic" of the original Greek very happily by the word *soborny*. From this Khomiakov produced the Russian neologism *sobornost'*, which corresponds exactly to the idea of catholicity which he developed in his writings on the Church; further, since the Slav root *sobor* means assembly and more particularly a council or synod, the derived words *soborny* and *sobornost'* thereby take on a fresh shade of meaning for the Russian ear, without losing their direct meaning of "catholic" and "catholicity."

For example, it would be impossible to imagine the Church without the mark of unity. St. Paul said so to the Corinthians, who had divisions among themselves: " 'I belong to Paul,' or 'I belong to Apollos,' or 'I belong to Christ.' Is Christ divided? Was Paul crucified for you? Or were you baptized in the name of Paul?" (I Cor. 1:12-13). Outside the unity of the Body of Christ, who cannot be divided, the other marks—holiness, catholicity, apostolicity—themselves cannot subsist. There is no longer the Church but a divided humanity, that of the confusion of Babel.

The Church also cannot be thought of without the mark of holiness. "We have never even heard that there is a Holy Spirit," said to St. Paul certain disciples of Ephesus, who had been baptized with the baptism of John, the baptism of repentance (Acts 19:2-7). Deprived of that which is both the source and the end of her existence, she would be no longer the Church, but a mystical body other than that of Christ—a body deprived of spirit and yet existing, a body left to the shadows of death and yet still awaiting its final destiny: like the body of Israel, which has misunderstood the realization of the promise of the Spirit.

In the same way, the mark of apostolicity could not be taken away from the Church without at the same time abolishing the other marks of the Church and even the Church herself, in that she is a concrete, historical reality. Without the divine power conferred on the apostles by the risen God-Man (John 20:22-23) and transmitted down to our own days by their successors, what would the Church be? On the one hand, a ghost of the "heavenly Church," disincarnate, useless and abstract; on the other, a multitude of sects endeavouring to reproduce "the spirit of the Gospel" outside the bounds of any objectivity, prey to the arbitrariness of their "free thought" and to the unbridled ragings of their disturbed spiritualities.

If the unity of the Church is based on the fact that she is a Body which has Christ as Head (Eph. 1:22-23); if her holiness—"the fulness of Him who fills all in all" (Eph. 1:23)—is of the Holy Spirit who came down in the tongues of fire of the day of Pentecost; if her apostolicity dwells in the power of the same Spirit infused into the apostles by the breath of Christ and transmitted to their successors (Acts 20:28): then not one of these three qualities can be either underestimated or modified without negating or transforming the very essence of what we call the Church. It is the same with catholicity—the mark which will be the principal object of this study.

To grasp better the meaning of catholicity, let us begin by making use of the same way of negation. Let us try to imagine what the Church would be without catholicity—an impossible task indeed, for, as we already have said, the four marks of the Church mutually support one another and cannot exist independently. Nevertheless, by eliminating in turn the part played by the other three marks, we have already attempted to obtain three different modes of what the Church would have been, were she not fully what she actually is. We are now concerned with seeing in what sense the Church would not be the Church, what would be her "mode of non-existence," were we to imagine her as one, holy—apostolic, but not catholic.

We see already, as soon as the question is posed, the yawning gap that it makes: the Church without Truth, without the assured knowledge of the data of revelation, without conscious and infallible experience of the divine mysteries. If she keeps her unity, it will be a unity of many opinions, products of diverse human mentalities and cultures, a unity having as its basis administrative constraint or relativistic indifference. If she—this Church deprived of assurance of the Truth—keeps her holiness, it will be an unconscious holiness, a lightless path towards sanctification, in the darkness of not knowing what grace is. If she keeps her apostolicity, it will be only a blind fidelity to an abstract principle, void of meaning.

Catholicity then shows itself to us as an inalienable mark of the Church in virtue of her possession of the Truth. Indeed one may say that Catholicity is a quality of Christian Truth. Thus one says "catholic dogma," "catholic teaching," "catholic truth," often interchanging this term with "universal," which is very close to it in meaning. Nevertheless, it is legitimate to ask whether catholicity means simply the universality of the truth preached by the Church. In a certain measure it is permissible to say so: Externally "catholicity" and "universality" coincide. Nevertheless we must recognize that these two terms are not perfectly synonymous expressions, in spite of Greek antiquity's usage of the adjective καθολικός. Etymology is not always a reliable guide in the domain of speculation. A philosopher runs the risk of losing the true value of concepts when he attaches too much importance to their verbal expression: much more so the theologian, who must be free even of concepts when he finds himself confronted with realities that surpass all human thought. It seems to us incontestable that the word "catholic" received a new meaning, a Christian meaning, in the language of the Church, which made it a special term, evoking a reality different from that attached to the common notion of "universal." "Catholic" means something at once more concrete, more intimate—something inherent in the very being of the Church. In short, all truth may be said to be "universal," but all truth is not the Catholic Truth. This latter term specifically designates Christian Truth, the mode of knowledge of this Truth proper to the Church, the teaching which she formulates. Does "catholicity" then mean "universality" in a more restricted and specialized acceptation of this word, in the sense of "Christian universality"? This may be admitted, but once again with a certain reserve: "universality" has too abstract a character, catholicity is concrete.

Opinions or truths which are said to be "universal" are opinions or truths received as such by everybody, common to all without exception. It is clear that Christian catholicity-universality cannot be understood in this sense. Nevertheless there are at times attempts to identify "catholicity" with the spread of the Church throughout the whole world, among all the peoples of the earth. If such a definition is taken literally, it would be necessary to recognize that the Church of the disciples gathered in the Upper Room in Zion on the day of Pentecost was far from being catholic, that the Church only became catholic in modern times, and that she is not yet definitively so. But we know quite well that the Church was always catholic. Therefore we must distinguish between catholicity in fact (Christian universality) and virtual catholicity (Christian universalism), the universalism of the Church and her message, spoken to the whole world, to the sum of that humanity which will receive it and come into the Church. This is clear. Nevertheless one has a sense of uneasiness in coming to the conclusion that we can see in the catholicity of the Church only a quality that is merely virtual.

In fact, if we want to identify the catholicity of the Church with the universal character of the Christian mission, we shall find ourselves constrained to attribute the mark of catholicity to other religions besides Christianity. The remarkable spread of Buddhism over the face of Asia, the shattering conquests of Islam, have been due to a clear consciousness on the part of those who profess these religions that their mission is a universal one. It is possible to speak of a Buddhist or a Muslim universalism, but should we in any sense call them "Catholic religions"? Is not catholicity an exclusive property of the Church, her fundamental characteristic?

If this is so, one must give up altogether the identification pure and simple of "catholic" with "universal." "Christian universality"—universality in fact or virtual universalism—must be distinguished from catholicity. It is a corollary of catholicity, a quality that necessarily flows from it and which is inseparably bound up with the catholicity of the Church, being nothing less than its external and material expression. This quality, from the earliest ages of the Church, was called ecumenicity.

The οἰκουμένη meant for Greek antiquity "the inhabited world," the known world, in contrast to the unexplored desert and to the ocean which surrounded the *orbis terrarum* peopled by men, perhaps also in contrast to the unknown countries of the barbarians. The οἰκουμένη of the first centuries of the Christian era was thought of in particular as the ensemble of the countries of Greco-Latin civilization, the Mediterranean world, the territory of the Roman Empire. For this reason the adjective οἰκουμενικὸς became a designation of the Late Empire—"the ecumenical Empire." Because the limits of the Empire coincided more or less with the expansion of the Church about the Constantinian epoch, the Church often used the term οἰκουμενικός. It was given as an honorific title to the bishops of the two imperial capitals, Rome and later Constantinople, the "New Rome." It was applied above all to the general councils of the Church that gathered together the episcopate of the ecumenical empire. Thus "ecumenical" marked what covered the totality of ecclesiastical territory, in contradistinction to what only had local or provincial value (for example, a provincial council, a local cultus). It is here that we can easily grasp the difference between ecumenicity and catholicity: the Church as a whole is called ecumenical, a qualification which does not apply to any portion of her; but every smallest portion of the Church—even one single faithful—can be called catholic. When St. Maximus, to whom ecclesiastical tradition gives the title of Confessor, replied to those who desired to force him to be in communion with the mono-thelites "Even if the whole world (οἰκουμένη) should be in communion with you, I alone should not be," he was opposing his catholicity to an ecumenicity which he regarded as heretical. If Christian universality, designated by the term *ecumenicity,* could be in so radical an opposition to *catholicity,* what then is the latter?

2

We have said earlier that catholicity is a quality of the revealed Truth given to the Church. One might say more exactly that it is a mode of knowledge of the Truth proper to the Church, in virtue of which this Truth becomes clear to the whole Church, as much to each of her smallest parts as to her totality. It is for this reason that the obligation of defending the Truth is incumbent on every member of the Church, as much on a layman as on a bishop, although the bishops are primarily responsible on account of the power which they have at their disposal. A layman is even bound to resist a bishop who betrays the Truth and is not faithful to the Christian tradition. For catholicity is not the abstract universalism of a doctrine imposed by the hierarchy, but a living tradition always preserved everywhere and by all— *quod semper, quod ubique, quod ab omnibus.* To maintain the contrary would be to confuse catholicity with apostolicity, with the power of binding and loosing, judging and defining, proper to the successors of the apostles. In that case, however, internal evidence of the truth disappears, and the tradition carefully kept by each one is replaced by submission to an external principle. At the same time, we must not fall into the contrary error which occurs when, in giving catholicity a charismatic character, we confuse it with holiness, seeing in it the personal inspiration of the saints, the sole witnesses of the Truth, the only true catholics. This would be to profess an error similar to Montanism and to transform the Church into a mystical sect. One is not catholic because one is a saint, but one cannot be a saint without being catholic. Catholic truth, carefully guarded by all, has the quality of an internal evidence more or less developed for every one according to the measure in which he is truly a member of the Church and is not separated, whether as an individual or as the member of a particular group, from the unity of all in the Body of Christ. But then, one might say, catholicity is nothing other than a function of the unity of the Church, "the universal capacity of its principles of unity" as Fr. Congar would have it—along with the majority of those theologians who confuse these two marks of the Church, unity and catholicity.

It cannot be denied that there is a Christological element at the root of catholicity, without which catholicity itself could not exist. But this is far from affirming with Fr. Congar that the catholicity of her Head is the principle of the catholicity of the Church. The Christological element of catholicity has a negative character: The Church, redeemed by the blood of Christ, is pure of all spot, separated from the principles of this world, free of sin, of all exterior necessity, of all natural determinism. The unity of the Body of Christ is a sphere in which the truth can manifest itself fully, without any restriction, without any mixture with that which is foreign to it, with that which is not the truth. For the Church this Christological element—the unity of human nature recapitulated by Christ—cannot suffice. Another element, and that a positive one, is necessary in order for the Church to become not only "the body of Christ," but also (as the same text of St. Paul has it) "the fulness of Him who fills all in all" (Eph. 1:23). Christ Himself said "I came to cast fire upon the earth" (Luke 12:49), that the Holy Spirit might descend upon the Church. To desire to base ecclesiology solely on the Incarnation, to see in the Church solely "an extension of the Incarnation," a continuation of the work of Christ, as is so often stated, is to forget Pentecost and to reduce the work of the Holy Spirit to a subordinate role, that of an emissary of Christ, a liaison between the Head and the members of the Body. But the work of the Holy Spirit, although inseparable from the work of Christ, is distinct from it. This is why St. Irenaeus, speaking of the Son and of the Spirit, calls them "the two hands of the Father" at work in the world. The Pneumatological element of the Church must not be underestimated, but fully accepted on an equal footing with the Christological, if the true foundation of the catholicity of the Church is to be found.

The Church is the work of the Son and of the Holy Spirit, sent by the Father into the world. As surely as she is the new unity of human nature purified by Christ, the unique Body of Christ, so she is also the multiplicity of persons, each one of whom receives the gift of the Holy Spirit. The work of the Son has for its object the common nature: this is what is redeemed, purified, and recapitulated by Christ. The work of the Holy Spirit is directed to persons, communicating the virtual fulness of grace to each human hypostasis in the Church, making each member of the Body of Christ a conscious collaborator (συνεργὸς) with God, a personal witness of the Truth. For this reason the Holy Spirit appeared on the day of Pentecost in the multiplicity of flames: a distinct tongue of fire came down and rested upon each one of those present; and down to this day a personal tongue of fire is invisibly communicated in the sacrament of the holy chrism to each one of those who enter into the unity of the Body of Christ by baptism. The relation of the work of Christ to that of the Holy Spirit in the Church would appear to have the character of an antinomy: the Holy Spirit diversifies what Christ unifies. Nevertheless a perfect concord is supreme in this diversity, and an infinite richness manifests itself in this unity. But there is more: without this personal diversity, the natural unity could not be realized and would be replaced by an external unity, abstract, administrative, blindly submitted to by the members of a collective body. So also, were it not for the unity of nature, there would be no place for development of the diversity of persons —a diversity which would be transformed into its opposite: the mutual oppression of individual and limited beings. There can be no unity of nature without diversity of persons, and no persons fully realized outside natural unity. Catholicity consists in the perfect harmony of these two terms: unity and diversity, nature and persons.

3

Here we touch the very source of catholicity, the mysterious identity of the whole and of the parts, the distinction between nature and persons, absolute identity which is at the same time absolute diversity—the initial mystery of the Christian revelation, the dogma of the Holy Trinity. If catholicity is, as we have already said, a quality of Christian Truth, it is possible now to define this quality. It is concrete, in that it is the very content of Christian Truth, which is the revelation of the Holy Trinity. This is the catholic dogma par excellence, for from it the Church receives her catholicity. God-Trinity can only be known in the unity-diversity of the catholic Church; and, on the other hand, if the Church possesses catholicity it is because the Son and the Holy Spirit, sent by the Father, have revealed the Trinity to her, not in an abstract way, as intellectual knowledge, but as the very rule of her life. Catholicity is a bond attaching the Church to God, who reveals Himself to her as Trinity, bestowing upon her the mode of existence proper to the divine unity-diversity, an ordering of life "in the image of the Trinity." For this reason every dogmatic error touching the Trinity must necessarily find its expression in the conception of the catholicity of the Church, must translate itself into a profound change in the ecclesiastical organism. And vice versa: when a person, or a group, or an entire local church falsifies in its historical development the perfect harmony between unity and diversity, this straying from the path of true catholicity will be a sure indication of an obscuring of knowledge of the Holy Trinity.

When, as often happens in the treatment of catholicity, the emphasis is placed on unity, when catholicity is above all other considerations based upon the dogma of the Body of Christ, the result is Christocentrism in ecclesiology. The catholicity of the Church becomes a function of her unity, becomes a universal doctrine that absorbs in imposing itself, instead of being a tradition evident to everyone, affirmed by all, at all times and in all places, in an infinite richness of living witness. On the other hand, when the emphasis is placed on diversity at the expense of unity, there is a tendency to base catholicity exclusively on Pentecost, forgetting that the Holy Spirit was communicated in the unity of the Body of Christ. The result is the disaggregation of the Church: the truth that is attributed to individual inspirations becomes multiple and therefore relative; catholicity is replaced by "ecumenism."

Based upon these two elements—Christological unity and Pneumatological diversity—as inseparable from one another as the Word and the Spirit, the Church faithfully preserves her catholicity, which realizes in her the dogma of the Trinity. We know the Holy Trinity through the Church, and the Church through the revelation of the Trinity. In the light of the dogma of the Trinity, catholicity appears as the mysterious identity of the one and the many—unity which is diversified and diversity which remains one. As in God there is not one nature apart from the three persons, so in the Church there is no abstract universality but a complete harmony of catholic diversity. As in God each one of the three persons, Father, Son and Holy Spirit, is not a part of the Trinity but is fully God in virtue of His ineffable identity with the one nature, so the Church is not a federation of parts: she is catholic in each one of her parts, since each part in her is identified with the whole, expresses the whole, has the value which the whole has, does not exist outside the whole. For this reason catholicity finds various expressions in the history of the Church. Local synods as well as councils called ecumenical are able to preface their acts with the formula used since the first council of all, the council of the apostles: "It has seemed good to the Holy Spirit and to us." So St. Basil, at a particularly grave juncture in the fight over dogma, was able to cry with catholic daring: "Whosoever is not with me is not with the Truth."

Catholicity knows no "private opinion," no local or individual truth. A catholic is one who surpasses the individual, who finds himself freed of his own nature, who mysteriously identifies himself with the whole and constitutes himself a witness of the Truth in the name of the Church. Herein is the invincible force of the Fathers, of confessors and martyrs, and also the tranquil assurance of the councils. Even if an assembly should be divided, even if a duly convoked council, yielding to pressure from without and to particular interests, should become through the sins of men "a meeting of robbers" as was the concilabulum of Ephesus, the catholicity of the Church will find its expression elsewhere and will manifest itself to all as tradition preserved always and everywhere. For the Church always recognizes her own, those who bear the seal of catholicity.

If the council, above all a general council, is the most perfect expression of the catholicity of the Church, of her symphonic structure, we are not bound to believe that the infallibility of its judgment is assured solely by the canons which define its legitimate character as a council. This is a necessary condition but not a sufficient one: the canons are not a magical recipe that forces catholic truth to express itself. To look for a criterion of Christian Truth in canonical formulas, without the Truth itself, is tantamount to depriving the Truth of its internal evidence. It would make of catholicity an external function, exercised by the hierarchy; *i.e.,* it would confuse the mark of catholicity with that of the apostolicity of the Church. Nor must we believe that catholic truth is made subservient in its expression to something resembling universal suffrage, to the affirmation of the majority: all the history of the Church witnesses to the contrary. Democracy in this sense is foreign to the Church, a caricature of catholicity. "The Church," Khomiakov has said, "does not consist in the greater or lesser quantity of her members, but in the spiritual bond that unites them." The internal evidence of the Truth has no place if constraint exercised by a majority on a minority is involved. Catholicity has nothing to do with "common opinion." There is no other criterion of truth than the Truth itself. And this Truth is the revelation of the Holy Trinity, who gives the Church her catholicity: an ineffable identity of unity and diversity, in the image of the Father, of the Son, and of the Holy Spirit, consubstantial and indivisible.

10

Catholic Consciousness: Anthropological Implications of the Dogma of the Church

Catholicity is not a spatial term indicating the extension of the Church over all the face of the earth. It is an intrinsic quality which was from the very beginning and always will be proper to the Church, independent of the historical conditions in which its space and number may be more or less limited. Among the Fathers of the first centuries the term Καθολική or *Catholica,* used as a noun, often becomes a synonym for *Ecclesia,* in order to denote a new reality that is not a part of the cosmos but a totality of a more absolute order. The Church exists in the world but the world cannot contain her. "The place is too narrow for me; make room for me to dwell in." St. Gregory of Nyssa teaches that in this prophecy of Isaiah (49:20) it is the Church who speaks.[1] For St. Ambrose the Church is greater than heaven and earth—a new universe having Christ as its sun. She encompasses in herself the entire *orbis terrarum* because all are summoned to become one in Christ, and the Church is even now this new totality.[2]

No differences of created nature—sex, race, social class, language, or culture—can affect the unity of the Church; no divisive reality can enter into the bosom of the *Catholica*. Therefore it is necessary to regard the expression "national Church"—so often used in our day—as erroneous and even heretical, according to the terms of the condemnation of phyletism pronounced by the Council of Constantinople in 1872. There is no Church of the Jews or of the Greeks, of the Barbarians or of the Scythians, just as there is no Church of slaves or of free men, of men or of women. There is only the one and total Christ, the celestial Head of the new creation which is being realized here below, the Head to which the members of the one Body are intimately linked. At this point any private consciousness which could link us with any ethnic or political, social or cultural group must disappear, in order to make way for consciousness "as a whole" (καθ' ὅλον), a consciousness greater than the consciousness which links us to humanity at large. In fact, our unity in Christ is not only the primordial unity of the human race, which has only one origin, but the final realization of this unity of human nature, which is "recapitulated" by the last Adam—ὁ ἔσχατος Ἀδάμ. This eschatological reality is not some kind of ideal "beyond" but the very condition of the existence of the Church, without which the Church would not be a sacramental organism: her sacraments would have only a figurative sense, instead of being a real participation in the incorruptible life of the Body of Christ.

In the complex but at times deceiving reality of Church life, where the decrepitude of the old Adam too often hides from our eyes the incorruptibility of the new Adam, one must be able to discern in the historical reality of the Church

---

[1] *In diem luminum sive in baptismum Christi*, P.G. 46, col. 577.
[2] On Ps. 118, 12, 25; P.L. 15, col. 1369.

—without going off into "metahistory"—the theological and imperishable structure of the *Catholica.* This structure—which is that of the new creation in the process of becoming—is not something totally alien to humanity. Therefore it presupposes several anthropological elements which one must take into account when one wishes to speak of the catholicity of the Church. But it is precisely these anthropological notions —which are always employed in speaking of the Church— which usually escape the control of theological thought.

In general Christian anthropology has not received sufficient theological elaboration. It is a field known above all from the point of view of Christology. But when the problem arises of recovering in ecclesiology such notions as "person," "created hypostasis," "human nature," "will" *etc.,* these expressions lose their pure character as theological terms and find themselves loaded with a philosophical content "according to the elemental spirits of the universe, and not according to Christ" (Col. 2:8). "Person" thus becomes a synonym for individual, "nature" for a concrete substance or a logical species, "will" for a phenomenon of the psychological order. Confusions are inevitable, and horizons find themselves obscured. This is the vengeance of the "old Adam" upon the theologian who wishes to speak of the Church in terms proper to his own language, without having taken care to purify his concepts, *i.e.* who approaches ecclesiological realities on the basis of secularized anthropology instead of approaching them from the top. Indeed, scientific anthropology, based upon observation of concrete facts, can have only an accidental value for theology. Theological anthropology must be constructed from the top down, beginning from Trinitarian and Christological dogma, in order to discover in human reality the unity of nature and the multiplicity of created hypostases, the will which is a function of the common nature, the possession of divine grace by created persons, *etc.* Then one will understand the extent to which the anthropological realities of our everyday experience are deformed by sin and correspond little to the pure norms of the new creation which is being realized in the Church. Actually, the individual who possesses a part of nature and

reserves it for himself, the subject who defines himself by
opposition to all that which is not "I," is not the person or
hypostasis who shares nature in common with others and
who exists as person in a positive relationship to other
persons. Self-will (combatted by all Christian asceticism)
is not identical to the will of the new creation—to the will
which one finds in renouncing oneself, in the unity of the
Body of Christ, wherein the canons of the Church make us
recognize a common and undivided will. Not the properties
of an individual nature, but the unique relationship of each
being with God—a relationship confirmed by the Holy Spirit
and realized in grace—is what constitutes the uniqueness
of a human person.

This brief introduction will suffice to establish that the
anthropologies of the old and new Adam, which are entangled
within the complex reality of the Church, cannot be equated.
We shall pause at only one anthropological notion, that of
consciousness, asking ourselves: to whom does the Catholic
consciousness of the Church belong?

It is clear that we are not speaking here of the consciousness of an individual or of any group whatever that might
be distinguished from the whole of the Body of Christ. This
would not be consciousness "as a whole"—καθ᾽ ὅλον—but
a particular consciousness—κατὰ μέρος—and, as such, void
of objectivity. But on the other hand, if one must attribute
this consciousness to pure ecclesiality in its totality, what
will become of the particular consciousness of a member of
the Church? Will it not be reduced practically to unconscious-
ness? Will not the life of the Church become depersonalized,
transformed into a supra-personal process in a sacramental
organism? How can this suffering consciousness, rent between
an anti-catholic subjectivism and an impersonal objectivism,
be healed?

The question is not easy to solve. I will even go so far
as to say that it is an insoluble question if one remains confined to the notion of consciousness which we find among
philosophers (especially in German Idealism), where consciousness inevitably means "self-awareness" (*Selbstbewusstsein*), a function of the subject, of an empirical or transcen-

dental "I," that knows and affirms itself in knowing its object. We constantly use the term "consciousness" when speaking of the Church, knowing that it corresponds to a reality that we wish to indicate by this word. But is this what human philosophies are speaking of? Is there an univocity between "consciousness" and "self-consciousness"? Or is it necessary to purify this concept and to transform it completely, as was the case with the notion of "person" or "hypostasis," identical with the notion of "individual" in everyday language but not in theological language, where it was transformed and charged with a new meaning? In order to answer this question, one should examine "consciousness" in its Christological or Trinitarian implications, before approaching the question on the level of theological anthropology. This we do not have time to do. Such an examination would take us away from our subject, which is the Church. Let us try to define the place which consciousness ought to occupy in our understanding of the Church.

In its Christological aspect, the Church is presented as the complement of the glorified humanity of Christ, as a continuation of the Incarnation, as one often says. But can we affirm of the Church everything that we affirm of the God-Man? We see here two wills, divine and human, two operations, and even two natures—created nature and divine grace, united without blending. If we pushed further this parallelism or, more accurately, this Christological identification, we would say that there is only one consciousness in the Church, a divine-human consciousness ("the-andric," as one loves to say today), a consciousness belonging to the Son, the Head of the Church, and which is communicated to men, who thus participate in this one consciousness inasmuch as they are members of the one Christ.

If this were so, it would be necessary to see in the Church one sole person, the person of Christ, and to affirm that He is the Church's person, in whom human hypostases are contained as particles of His unique Person. The consciousness of the Church would then be only a consciousness of the unity of the person of the Son or, more accurately, merely the consciousness of the one and only Son, in which human consciousnesses as well as human persons, distinct from one another and from the person of Christ, would fade away. It must be recognized that this representation of Christ—Head-of-the-Church recalls rather the image of Uranus devouring his children.

Two reasons oppose our recognizing as true such an understanding of our unity in Christ. First of all, since the theological notion of hypostasis or person implies an absolute difference, an ontological irreducibility, it is impossible to admit that a person or persons—divine or created—might be contained in a kind of supra-person, as its parts. Christian theology can conceive of a person containing different natures (Christ the God-Man) or of a common nature in distinct persons (the Holy Trinity). One can speak of a common nature which contains in itself a series of particular natures, which are divided among several individuals (the aggregate of humanity and human individuals). But as for a person or hypostasis containing other persons as parts of a whole, such a notion would be contradictory.

One will say: Christ, the Head of His Body, of this new humanity which is being realized in the Church, contains in Himself this renewed nature, but human persons also enter into this whole because they belong to this whole. Doubtless it would be so if persons were the same as individuals, truly parts of a common nature, divided or parceled out. If, in human reality as we know it, personal multiplicity is confused with individualistic, "egotistic" parceling out of the unity of nature, is this not the result of sin, which hides from us the true meaning of personal existence? The pure notion of person that we are able to perceive in the Trinity does not allow one to consider the divine hypostases as three *parts* of a one nature. So also, a created person as person means something other than an "individual being." He is not a part of the whole but in some way virtually contains the whole. In this sense each human person can be considered an hypostasis of the common nature, an hypostasis of the whole of the created cosmos or, more accurately, of earthly creation. (We set aside here the question of angelic hypostases and of the celestial cosmos; this constitutes a separate problem.) If we are one in Christ, then our unity in Him, while suppressing the partition of individual natures, in no way affects personal plurality.

The new unity of our nature in Christ does not exclude human "polyhypostasity." The ecclesiological text of Matthew 18:20 points simultaneously to the unity of our nature in Christ and to the personal relationship between the divine hypostasis and created hypostases. "For where two or three (personal multiplicity) are gathered in my name (unity of nature realized in the Church which bears the name of the Son), there am I *in the midst of them*." The Lord did not say "I contain them in Me" or "They are in Me," as He was able to do elsewhere in speaking of the unity of our nature recapitulated by Him, but precisely "I am in the midst of them," as a person who is *with other* persons who surround him.

Another reason opposed to a uniquely Christological solution to the problem of the consciousness of the Church is implied in the very image of the Church as the Body of Christ, where Christ, the Head of the one nature, is represented as the Bridegroom. If the two are united in order to form "one flesh"—εἰς σάρκα μίαν—and if the Bridegroom is the Head of this natural unity of His Body or unified nature, nonetheless He has beside Him another hypostasis of this one nature, of this unique body: the Bride. If this is so—if in the Body of Christ there is one or, more correctly, there are many hypostases of this created nature which are not the hypostasis of Christ, which are not contained in His hypostasis inasmuch as they are persons distinct from His person—then the members of the Body of Christ are at the same time persons who cannot be reduced to unity. Therefore the Church simultaneously displays natural unity and personal diversity, in the image of the Trinity. And if this is so, there is the need in the Church for another dispensation than that of the Son, who recapitulates the unity of nature—for a dispensation which is directed to each human person in particular, consecrating personal multiplicity in the unity of the Body of Christ. This is the dispensation of the Holy Spirit, the Pentecostal aspect of the Church.

Both dispensations—of the Son and of the Spirit—are inseparable; they mutually condition one another since one without the other is unthinkable. One cannot receive the Holy Spirit without being a member of the Body of Christ; one cannot call Christ "Lord," *i.e.* have a consciousness of His divinity, other than by the Holy Spirit. Personal multiplicity is crowned by the Holy Spirit only in the unity of the Body of Christ; but it acquires participation in this divinity through the grace conferred virtually upon each one in the gift of the Holy Spirit. This is why the two sacraments of Christian initiation, baptism and chrismation, are so intimately linked.

St. John the Evangelist says, "The anointing (χρῖσμα) which you received from Him abides in you, and you have no need that any one should teach you; as His anointing teaches you about everything" (I John 2:27). This text can give a new direction to our investigation of the consciousness of the Church. In fact, if it is necessary to discard the thesis according to which the consciousness of the Church is the consciousness of the person of Christ, ought we not attribute this consciousness rather to the third divine Hypostasis and make of the Holy Spirit the very consciousness of the Church? At the outset this thesis could appear very attractive: to know Revelation in the Holy Spirit, who would substitute Himself in some way for us, who would become our consciousness, the consciousness of the Church; to confess the divinity of Christ by the testimony that the Holy Spirit Himself renders. . . . This solution could appear conformed to the spirit of Orthodox theology by virtue of its patently pneumatological character. In fact, this aspect was able to attract Khomiakov, whose ecclesiology differs from that of Moehler and other German Catholic theologians of his time precisely by its pneumatological accent. For German Catholicism of the Romantic period, the consciousness of the Church was presented rather with a Christological emphasis, as a sacramental organism. Nevertheless, despite this difference of stress, both of these ecclesiologies are very close to one another. Both of them see and express very well the organic aspect of the Church; but the other aspect, that of the multiplicity of human hypostases, of the Church as the *communio sanctorum*, remains in both cases rather blurred. In fact, neither ecclesiology takes sufficiently into account anthropological realities which make of the consciousness of the Church a function of the Second or Third Person of the Trinity. And in both cases the conclusion is analogous: the persons are in each instance absorbed in a supra-Person, that of Christ or that of the Spirit. This objective supra-consciousness, which in the organic catholicism of Tübingen belongs to Christ or in the democratic *sobornost'* of the Slavophiles to the Holy Spirit, allows us to perceive a common source or, more correctly, a common philosophical background, tinted by German Idealism. And this is so despite the critical position which a Khomiakov could take toward the philosophy of Hegel, "the debater of this age" (I Cor. 1:20), as he labelled him. In replying to "the debater," we fall into dependence not only on his problematics, but often also on his manner of thought.

If the theological notion of human persons or hypostases cannot be reconciled with either the first or second of these theses, each of them is still valuable in its way. The first presents the Church to us as a Christological organism. The second emphasizes the role of the Holy Spirit, who bears witness to the Truth within the Church. In order to make more precise the character of this witness, let us turn to the text of Scripture: "But when the Counselor comes, whom I shall send to you from the Father, even the Spirit of truth, who proceeds from the Father, he will bear witness to me; and you also are witnesses, because you have been with me from the beginning" (John 15:26-27). The distinction between these two testimonies is clear: "He will bear witness to me" and "You also are witnesses, because you have been with me from the beginning."

If one has been with Christ from the beginning, why this witness of the Spirit, indispensable for enabling human persons, in their turn, to bear witness to Christ? In what consists this witness of the Holy Spirit, addressed to human persons? "He will teach you all things, and bring to your remembrance all that I have said to you" (John 14:26).

This "He will bring to your remembrance all" (ὑπομνήσει ὑμᾶς πάντα) is addressed not only to the apostles who accompanied Jesus Christ from the very beginning, but also to all Christians, to all the members of the Church, who have a common memory of the words of Christ, of what was "from the beginning": a memory which is called Tradition. This memory is common to all; it belongs to the unity of the Body of Christ, the Church; it is its memory or tradition, but it is actualized in each particular person upon whom the Holy Spirit confers His grace.

If this opening of consciousness on the interior evidence of the Truth is brought about by the Holy Spirit in each Christian person, it is nevertheless not uniform, for there is no measure common to all where persons are concerned. The evidence of Truth, the memory or tradition of the Church, that which constitutes the content of consciousness, is one and the same for all; but that does not mean that there is one single consciousness of the Church, which is imposed uniformly on all, as a "supra-consciousness" belonging to a "collective person." If one must recognize in ecclesial reality not only unity of nature but also multiplicity of hypostases, there necessarily will be a multiplicity of consciousnesses, with different degrees of actualization in different persons, more intensive in some, practically absent in others. Persons who are more deeply rooted in the Church, conscious of the unity of all in the Body of Christ, thus are more free of their own individual limitations, and their personal consciousness is more open to the Truth. Here is the paradox of catholicity: consciousness here is not a "self-consciousness" but a liberty concerning oneself. He is conscious of the Truth who ceases to be the subject of his own consciousness. Thus the Truth which one confesses is presented in all its objectivity: not as "one's own" opinion, not as "my own theology," but as the possession of the Church, καθ᾽ ὅλον, as catholic Truth. The mystery of the catholicity of the Church is realized in the plurality of personal consciousnesses as an accord of unity and multiplicity, in the image of the Holy Trinity which the Church realizes in her life: three consciousnesses but a single Subject, a single "Divine Council" or "Council of the Saints," a divine catholicity, if we dare apply this ecclesiological term to the Holy Trinity. In ecclesial reality, in the becoming of the new creation, the many personal consciousnesses are consciousnesses of the Church only insofar as they cease to be "self-consciousnesses" and put in the place of their own "self" the single subject of the multiple consciousnesses of the Church.

Since the catholicity of the Church is expressed in many consciousnesses of the same truth, of the same memory of the Church, actualized by the Holy Spirit in those who seek to define, to express in dogmas, and to defend the truths of Revelation, a Council (local or general), in which the voice of the Church must normally make itself heard, will have nothing in common with a democratic institution. It is not preponderant opinion which determines catholicity, nor collective consciousness which forms it: The Church does not know impersonal collectives any more than she knows individuals in revolt. The champions of catholicity are those who possess the consciousness of the unity of the Body of Christ, of the apostolic tradition common to all, those who struggle unremittingly that catholic Truth triumph in all consciousnesses. There are times when one is obliged to oppose a crushing majority: let us remember that after the Council of Nicaea dogmatic struggles continued for sixty years until the definitive triumph of ὁμοούσιος. "For there must be factions among you in order that those who are genuine among you may be recognized" (I Cor. 11:19). These champions who must be recognized so that all may be conscious of the Truth, so that catholic evidence may be actualized in all consciousnesses, are in the first place all those whom we venerate as Fathers of the Church. It is very significant that in the course of its liturgical year, the Orthodox Church, on the anniversaries of the great councils, celebrates the memory of the Fathers of the Councils rather than honoring this or that council as a collective group.

It is the consciousness of some, free from all subjectivity, which makes Truth triumph in the Church at large—the consciousness of those who speak not in their own name, but in the name of the Church, positing the Church as the unique subject of multiple personal consciousnesses. If we wish to apply the notion of consciousness to ecclesial reality, we must understand that in this reality there are many personal consciousnesses but only one subject of consciousness, only one "self-consciousness" (*Selbstbewusstsein*), which is the Church. In this sense the Fathers of the Church—and all those who, freed from their individual limitations, follow in their steps—are the fathers of the consciousness of the Church, those by whom Truth could be expressed in the councils in the form of dogmas, not as the "supra-conscious" constraint of a *deus ex machina,* but in full personal consciousness, engaging human responsibility. It is precisely this which permits us to make judgments in questions of faith and to say with catholic audacity: "It has seemed good to the Holy Spirit and to us" (Acts 15:28).

11

Panagia

The Orthodox Church has not made Mariology into an independent dogmatic theme: it remains integral to the whole of Christian teaching, as an anthropological *Leitmotif.* Based on Christology, the dogma of the Mother of God has a strong Pneumatological accent; and through the double economy of the Son and the Holy Spirit, it is inextricably bound up with ecclesiological reality.

In truth, if we were to limit ourselves to dogmatic data in the strict sense of the word and were dealing only with dogmas affirmed by the Councils, we should find nothing except the term Θεοτόκος, whereby the Church has solemnly confirmed the divine maternity of the Holy Virgin.[1] The dogmatic emphasis of the term Θεοτόκος, as affirmed against the Nestorians, is above all Christological: what is defended against gainsayers of the divine maternity is the hypostatic unity of the Son of God become the Son of Man.

---

[1]The term "Ever-virgin" (ἀειπάρθενος), found in conciliar acts from the Fifth Council on, has never been made particularly explicit by the councils which have employed it.

It is Christology which is directly envisaged here; but at the same time, indirectly, there is a dogmatic confirmation of the Church's devotion to her who bore God according to the flesh. It is said that all those who rise up against the appelation Θεοτόκος—all who refuse to admit that Mary has this quality which piety ascribes to her—are not truly Christians, for they oppose the true doctrine of the Incarnation of the Word. This should demonstrate the close connection between dogma and devotion, which are inseparable in the consciousness of the Church. However we know instances of Christians who, while recognizing for purely Christological reasons the divine maternity of the Virgin, abstain from all special devotion to the Mother of God for the same reasons, desiring to know no other mediator between God and man than the God-Man, Jesus Christ. This suffices to demonstrate that the Christological dogma of the Θεοτόκος taken *in abstracto,* apart from the vital connection between it and the devotion paid by the Church to the Mother of God, would not be enough to justify the unique position, above all created beings, assigned to the Queen of Heaven, to whom the Orthodox liturgy ascribes "the glory which is appropriate to God" (ἡ θεοπρεπὴς δόξα). It is therefore impossible to separate dogmatic data, in the strict sense, from the data of the Church's cultus, in a theological exposition of the doctrine about the Mother of God. Here dogma should throw light on devotion, bringing it into contact with the fundamental truths of our faith; whereas devotion should enrich dogma with the Church's living experience.

2

We are in the same position in relation to scriptural data. If we desired to consider scriptural evidence apart from the Church's devotion to the Mother of God, we should be obliged to limit ourselves to the few New Testament passages relating to Mary, the Mother of Jesus, and to only one direct reference in the Old Testament, the prophecy of the Virgin Birth of the Messiah in Isaiah. But if we look at the Bible through the eyes of the Church's devotion, or—to use the proper term at last—in the Tradition of the Church, then the sacred books of the Old and New Testaments will supply us with innumerable texts used by the Church to glorify the Mother of God.

Some passages in the gospels, if viewed externally, from a point of view outside the Church's Tradition, seem to contradict quite flagrantly this extreme glorification and unlimited veneration. Let us take two examples: Christ, when bearing witness to St. John the Baptist, calls him the greatest of those born of women (Matthew 11:11; Luke 7:28). It is therefore to him, and not to Mary, that the highest position among human beings should belong. In fact, in the practice of the Church, we find the Baptist with the Mother of God on either side of the Lord in the δέησις icons. But the Church has never exalted St. John the Forerunner above the Seraphim, nor has she ever placed his icon on a footing of equality with the icon of Christ, on one side of the entrance into the sanctuary, as is the case with the icon of the Mother of God.

Another passage in the gospels shows us Christ publicly opposing the glorification of his Mother. He answers the exclamation of the woman in the crowd who cries out "Blessed is the womb that bore you, and the breasts that you sucked," by saying "Blessed rather are those who hear the Word of God and keep it" (Luke 11:27-28). But it is precisely this passage in St. Luke, which seems to depreciate the fact of the divine maternity in comparison to the quality of those who receive and keep the divine revelation, which is the Gospel text read solemnly on feasts of the Mother of God, as if under its seemingly negative form it hid an even greater act of praise.

Again we face the impossibility of separating dogma from the life of the Church and Scripture from Tradition. Christological dogma obliges us to recognize the divine maternity of the Virgin. Scriptural evidence teaches us that the glory of the Mother of God does not reside merely in her corporeal maternity, in the fact that she carried and fed the Incarnate Word. In fact, the Church's Tradition, the holy memory of those who "hear and keep" the words of the revelation, gives to the Church the assurance with which she exalts the Mother of God, ascribing to her an unlimited glory. Apart from Church Tradition, theology would be dumb on this subject and unable to justify this astounding glorification. That is why Christian communities which reject any idea of Tradition are also alien to the veneration of the Mother of God.

The close connection between Tradition and all that concerns the Mother of God is not simply due to the fact that events of her earthly life—such as her Nativity, her Presentation in the Temple, and her Assumption—are celebrated by the Church without being mentioned in the Bible. If the Gospel is silent about these facts, and if their poetical amplification is due to apocryphal books of late date, still the fundamental theme which they signify belongs to the mystery of our faith and is not to be taken away from the Church's consciousness. In fact, the notion of Tradition is richer than we habitually think. Tradition does not merely consist of an oral transmission of facts capable of supplementing the Scriptural narrative. It is the *complement* of the Bible and, above all, it is the *fulfilment* of the Old Testament in the New, as the Church becomes aware of it. It is Tradition which confers comprehension of the meaning of revealed truth (Luke 24). Tradition tells us not only *what* we must hear but, still more importantly, *how* we must keep what we hear. In this general sense, Tradition implies an incessant operation of the Holy Spirit, who could have his full outpouring and bear his fruits only in the Church, after the Day of Pentecost. It is only in the Church that we find ourselves capable of tracing the inner connections between the sacred texts which make the Old Testament and the New Testament into a single living body of truth, wherein Christ is present in each word. It is only in the Church that the seed sown by the word is not barren, but brings forth fruit; and this fruition of Truth, as well as the power to make it bear fruit, is called Tradition. The Church's unlimited veneration of the Mother of God which, viewed externally, might seem to be in contradiction with the scriptural data, is spread far and wide in the Tradition of the Church and is the most precious fruit of Tradition.

But it is not only the fruit of Tradition; it is also the germ and the stem of Tradition. We can find a definite relationship between the person of the Mother of God and what we call the Tradition of the Church. Let us try, in setting forth this relationship, to see the glory of the Mother of God beneath the veil of silence of the Scriptures. We shall be led to this by an examination of the inner connection between the texts.

St. Luke, in a passage which is parallel to the one we have already quoted, shows us Christ refusing to see His Mother and His brethren, declaring that "My mother and my brothers are those who hear the word of God and do it" (Luke 8:19-21). The context is significant: in St. Luke, at the moment when the Mother of God desires to see her Son, he has just finished the parable of the Sower.[2] "And as for that in the good soil they are those who, hearing the word, hold it fast in an honest and good heart, and bring forth fruit with patience.... He who has ears to hear, let him hear.... Take heed then how you hear; for to him who has will more be given, and from him who has not, even what he thinks that he has will be taken away" (Luke 8:8, 15, 18). Now, it is precisely this faculty of keeping the words heard concerning Christ in an honest and good heart—the faculty which elsewhere Christ exalts above the fact of corporeal maternity (Luke 11:28)—which the Gospel attributes to no individual except the Mother of the Lord. St. Luke insists upon it, as he mentions it twice in his Infancy narrative: "But Mary kept all these things pondering them in her heart" (Luke 2:19, 51). She who gave birth to God in the flesh kept in her memory all the testimonies to the divinity of her Son. We could say that we have here a personification of the Church's Tradition before the Church was, were it not that St. Luke is careful to tell us that Mary and Joseph

---

[2]In St. Matthew (13:23) and St. Mark (4:1-20) the parable of the sower immediately follows the episode with the Lord's Mother and brothers. Here also the connection is evident.

did not understand the saying of the Child, that he must be about his Father's business (Luke 2:49-50). Therefore the meaning of the sayings kept faithfully in her heart by the Mother of God had not been fully realized in her consciousness. Before the consummation of the work of Christ, before the Day of Pentecost, before the Church, even she upon whom the Holy Spirit had come down to fit her for her part in the Incarnation of the Word had not yet attained the fulness which her person was called to realize. Nevertheless, it is already possible to see the connection between the Mother of God, as she keeps and collects the prophetic sayings, and the Church, the guardian of Tradition. One is the seed of the other. Only the Church, the complement of Christ's humanity, will be able to keep the fulness of revelation which, if it were entirely committed to writing, could not be contained within the space of the whole world. Only the Mother of God, she who was chosen to carry God in her womb, could fully realize in her consciousness all the import of the Incarnation of the Word, including the fact of her own divine maternity.

Those sayings of Christ which seem so harsh to his Mother are sayings which exalt the quality which she has in common with the sons of the Church. But while they, as guardians of Tradition, can only become conscious of the Truth and make it fruitful in themselves to a greater or lesser degree, the Mother of God, by virtue of the unique relationship between her person and God, whom she can call her Son, alone can rise from here below to a complete consciousness of all that the Holy Spirit says to the Church, realizing this plenitude in her own person. But this complete consciousness of God, this acquisition of the fulness of grace appropriate to the age to come, could only happen to a deified being. This places before us a new question, which we shall try to answer so that the special character of the Orthodox Church's devotion to the Sovereign Queen of Heaven can be better understood.

3

Christ, when bearing witness to St. John the Baptist, called him "the greatest of them that are born of women" (Matthew 11:11; Luke 7:28), but he added, "He who is least in the Kingdom of Heaven is greater than he." Here Old Testament holiness is contrasted with the holiness that could be realized when the redemptive work of Christ was accomplished and when "the promise of the Father" (Acts 1:4), the descent of the Holy Spirit, had filled the Church with the fulness of deifying grace. St. John, although "more than a prophet" because he baptized the Lord and saw the heavens open and the Spirit like a dove descending on the Son of Man, died without having received the promise, like all the others "well-attested by their faith," "of whom the world was not worthy," who according to the divine plan "apart from us should not be made perfect" (Hebrews 11:38-40), *i.e.* apart from the Church of Christ. It is only through the Church that the holiness of the Old Testament can receive its fulfilment in the age to come, in a perfection which was inaccessible to humanity before Christ.

It is beyond any question that she who was chosen to be the Mother of God represents the summit of Old Testament holiness. If St. John the Baptist is called "the greatest" of those before Christ, that is because the greatness of the All-Holy Mother of God belongs not only to the Old Testament, where she was hidden and does not appear, but also to the Church, in which she realized her fulness and became manifest, to be glorified by all generations (Luke 1:48). The person of St. John remains in the Old Testament dispensation; the most holy Virgin passes from the Old to the New; and this transition, in the person of the Mother of God, shows us how the New Covenant is the fulfilment of the Old.

The Old Testament is not only a series of prefigurations of Christ, which become decipherable after the Good News has come. It is above all the history of the preparation of humanity for the coming of Christ, a story in which human liberty is constantly put to the test by the will of God. The obedience of Noah, the sacrifice of Abraham, the Exodus of God's people through the desert under the leadership of Moses, the Law and the Prophets, is a series of divine elections, in which human beings sometimes remain faithful to the promise made to them and at other times fail and suffer punishments (the captivity and the destruction of the first temple). All the sacred tradition of the Jews is a history of the slow and laborious journey of fallen humanity towards the "fulness of time," when the angel was to be sent to announce to the chosen Virgin the Incarnation of God and to hear from her lips human consent, so that the divine plan of salvation could be accomplished. Thus, according to St. John of Damascus, "The name of the Mother of God contains all the history of the divine economy in this world."[3]

This divine economy, preparing human conditions for the Incarnation of the Son of God, is not a unilateral one: it is not a matter of the divine will making a *tabula rasa* of the history of humanity. In this saving economy, the Wisdom of God is adapted to the fluctuations of human wills, to the different responses of men to the divine challenge. It is thus that, through the generations of the Old Testament righteous men, Wisdom "has built her house": the all-pure nature of the Holy Virgin, whereby the Word of God will become connatural with us. The answer of Mary to the archangel's annunciation, "Behold, I am the handmaid of the Lord; let it be to me according to your word" (Luke 1:38), resolves the tragedy of fallen humanity. All that God required of human liberty since the Fall is accomplished. And now the work of redemption, which only the Incarnate Word can effect, may take place. Nicholas Cabasilas said, in his homily on the Annunciation, "The Incarnation was not only the work of the Father and of His Virtue and His Spirit; it was also the work of the will and faith of the Virgin. Without the consent of the All-Pure One and the cooperation of her faith, this design would have been as unrealizable as it would have been without the intervention

---

[3]*De fide orthodoxa* III, 12; P.G. 94, cols. 1029-32.

of the three Divine Persons themselves. Only after teaching
and persuading her does God take her for His Mother and
receive from her the flesh which she wills to offer Him.
Just as He voluntarily became incarnate, so He willed that
His mother should bear Him freely, with her own full and
free consent."[4]

From St. Justin and St. Irenaeus onwards, the Fathers
often have drawn attention to the contrast between the "two
virgins," Eve and Mary. By the disobedience of the first,
death entered into humanity. By the obedience of the "second
Eve," the author of life became man and entered into the
family of Adam. But between the two Eves lies all the
history of the Old Testament, the past from which she
who has become the Mother of God cannot be divided. If
she was chosen to take a unique part in the work of the
Incarnation, that choice followed and concluded a whole
series of other chosen ones who prepared the way for it.
It is not for nothing that the Orthodox Church, in her
liturgical texts, calls David "the ancestor of God" and
gives the same name of "holy and righteous ancestors of
God" to Joachim and Anna. The Roman Catholic dogma
of the Immaculate Conception seems to break up this un-
interrupted succession of Old Testament holiness, which
reaches its fulfilment at the moment of the Annunciation,
when the Holy Spirit came down upon the Virgin to make
her fit to receive the Word of the Father in her womb.
The Orthodox Church does not admit the idea that the Holy
Virgin was thus exempted from the lot of the rest of fallen
humanity—the idea of a "privilege" which makes her into
a being ransomed before the redemptive work, by virtue of
the future merits of her Son. It is not by virtue of a privilege
received at the moment of her conception by her parents
that we venerate the Mother of God more than any other
created being. She was holy and pure from all sin from her
mother's womb, but still this holiness does not place her
outside the rest of humanity before Christ. She was not, at
the moment of the Annunciation, in a state analogous to

---

[4]Ed. M. Jugie, *Patrologia orientalis* 19.2.

that of Eve before the Fall. The first Eve, "the mother of all living," lent her ear to the words of the seducer in the state of paradise, in the state of innocent humanity. The second Eve—she who was chosen to become the Mother of God—heard and understood the angelic word in the state of fallen humanity. That is why this unique election does not separate her from the rest of humanity, from all her fathers, mothers, brothers, and sisters, whether saints or sinners, whose best part she represents.

Like other human beings, such as St. John the Baptist, whose conception and birth are also feasts of the Church, the Holy Virgin was born under the law of original sin, sharing with all the same common responsibility for the Fall. But sin never could become actual in her person; the sinful heritage of the Fall had no mastery over her right will. Here was the highest point of holiness that could be attained before Christ, in the conditions of the Old Covenant, by one of Adam's seed. She was without sin under the universal sovereignty of sin, pure from every seduction in the midst of a humanity enslaved by the prince of this world. She was not placed above history in order to serve a special divine decree but realized her unique vocation while in the chains of history, sharing the common destiny of all men awaiting salvation. And yet, if in the person of the Mother of God we see the summit of Old Testament holiness, her own holiness is not limited thereby, for she equally surpassed the highest summits of the New Covenant, realizing the greatest holiness which the Church can attain.

The first Eve was taken out of Adam: she was a person who, at the moment of her creation by God, took unto herself the nature of Adam, to be his complement. We find an inverse relationship in the case of the New Eve: through her the Son of God became the "Last Adam," by taking unto Himself human nature. Adam was before Eve; the Last Adam was after the New Eve. However we cannot say that the humanity assumed by Christ in the womb of the Holy Virgin was a complement of the humanity of his Mother. It is, in fact, the humanity of a divine Person, that of the "man of heaven" (1 Corinthians 15:47, 48). The human nature of the Mother of God belongs to a created person, who is the offspring of the "man of earth." It is not the Mother of God, but her Son, who is the head of the new humanity, "the head over all things for the Church, which is his body" (Ephesians 1:22-23). Thus the Church is the complement of his humanity. Therefore it is through her Son, and in His Church, that the Mother of God could attain the perfection reserved for those who bear the image of the "man of heaven."

We have already indicated a close connection between the person of the Mother of God and the Church, when speaking of the Tradition which she personified, as it were, before the Church existed. She who bore God according to the flesh also kept in her heart all the sayings that revealed the divinity of her Son. This is a testimony concerning the spiritual life of the Mother of God. St. Luke shows us that she was not simply an instrument, who willingly let herself be used in the Incarnation, but rather a person who sought to realize, in her own consciousness, the meaning of the fact of her divine maternity. After having offered her human nature to the Son of God, she sought to receive through Him that which she did not yet have in common with Him: participation in the divine nature. It is in her Son that the fulness of the Godhead dwells bodily (Colossians 2:9). The natural connection which linked her to the God-Man did not yet confer upon the person of the Mother of God the state of a deified creature, although the descent of the Holy Spirit on the day of the Annunciation made her fit to accomplish her unique task. In this sense, the Mother of God, before the day of Pentecost, before the Church, still belonged to the humanity of the Old Testament, to those who waited for "the promise of the Father," expecting to be baptized with the Holy Spirit (Acts 1:4-5).

Tradition shows us the Mother of God in the midst of the disciples on the day of Pentecost, receiving with them the Holy Spirit, who was communicated to each of them as a distinct tongue of fire. This agrees with the testimony of Acts: after the Ascension, the apostles "with one accord devoted themselves to prayer, together with the women and

Mary the Mother of Jesus, and with his brothers" (1:14). "When the day of Pentecost had come, they were all together in one place" (2:1). The Mother of God received with the Church the last and only thing she lacked, so that she might grow "to mature manhood, to the measure of the stature of the fulness of Christ" (Ephesians 4:13).

4

She who by the power of the Holy Spirit received the divine Person of the Son of God into her womb, now receives the Holy Spirit, sent by the Son. The two descents of the Holy Spirit upon the Holy Virgin may be compared, in a certain sense, to the two communications of the Spirit to the apostles, one on the evening of the day of Resurrection and the other on the day of Pentecost. The first of these conferred on the apostles the power to bind and to loose. This is a function independent of their subjective qualities, due solely to a divine decree which selects them to play this particular role in the Church. The second communication of the Spirit, at Pentecost, gave to each of them the possibility of realizing his personal holiness—something which will always depend on subjective factors. But the two communications of the Spirit, the functional and the personal, are mutually complementary. One can see this in the apostles and their successors: no one can fulfill his function in the Church well unless he is striving to acquire holiness; on the other hand, it is hard for any one to attain holiness if he neglects the function in which God has placed him. The two should coincide more and more as life goes on; one's vocation normally becomes a way by which one acquires selflessness and personal sanctity. We can see something analogous in the otherwise unique case of the Mother of God: the objective function of her divine maternity, in which she was placed on the day of the Annunciation, will also be the subjective way of her sanctification. She will realize in her consciousness, and in all her personal life, the meaning of the fact of her having carried in her womb and having nourished at her breast the Son of God. It is thus that the words of Christ, which appear to abase his Mother in comparison with the Church, receive their meaning of supreme praise: blessed is she who not only was the Mother of God but also realized in her person the degree of holiness corresponding to that unique function. The person of the Mother of God is exalted more than her function, and the consumation of her holiness receives more praise than its beginnings.

The function of divine maternity is completed in the past; but the Holy Virgin, still on earth after the Ascension of her Son, remains as much as ever the Mother of Him who, in his glorious humanity, taken from the Virgin, is seated at the right hand of the Father, "far above all rule and authority and power and dominion, and above every name that is named, not only in this age but also in that which is to come" (Ephesians 1:21). What degree of holiness able to be realized her below could possibly correspond to the unique relationship of the Mother of God to her Son, the Head of the Church, who dwells in the heavens? Only the total holiness of the Church, the complement of the glorious humanity of Christ, containing the plenitude of deifying grace communicated ceaselessly to the Church since Pentecost by the Holy Spirit. The members of the Church can enter into a family relationship with Christ; they can be his "mother, brothers, and sisters" (Matthew 12:50) in the measure in which they accomplish their vocations. But only the Mother of God, through whom the Word was made flesh, will be able to receive the plenitude of grace and to attain an unlimited glory, by realizing in her person all the holiness of which the Church is capable.

5

The Son of God came down from heaven and was made man through the Holy Virgin, in order that men might rise to deification by the grace of the Holy Spirit. "To possess by grace what God has by nature": that is the supreme vocation of created beings and the final destiny to which the sons of the Church aspire here below, in the gradual development of the Church in history. This development is already consummated in the divine Person of Christ, the Head of the Church, risen and ascended. If the Mother of God could truly realize in her human and created person the sanctity which corresponds to her unique role, then she cannot have failed to attain here below by grace all that her Son has by His divine nature. But if this be so, then the historical development of the Church and the world has already been fulfilled, not only in the uncreated person of the Son of God but also in the created person of his Mother. This is why St. Gregory Palamas calls the Mother of God "the boundary between the created and the uncreated." Alongside the incarnate divine hypostasis there is a deified human hypostasis.

We have said above that in the person of the Mother of God it is possible to see the transition from the greatest holiness of the Old Testament to the holiness of the Church. But if the All-Holy Mother of God has consummated the holiness of the Church and all holiness which is possible for a created being, we are now dealing with yet another transition—the transition from the world of becoming to the eternity of the Eighth Day, the passage from the Church to the Kingdom of God. This last glory of the Mother of God, the ἔσχατον realized in a created person before the end of the world, henceforth places her beyond death, beyond the resurrection, and beyond the Last Judgment. She participates in the glory of her Son, reigns with Him, presides at His side over the destinies of the Church and of the world which unfold in time, and intercedes on behalf of all before Him who will come again to judge the living and the dead.

This supreme transition, by which the Mother of God rejoins her Son in His celestial glory, is celebrated by the Church on the day of the Feast of the Assumption. On that day the Church thinks of a death which, according to her inner conviction, could not but have been followed by the corporeal resurrection and ascension of the All-Holy. It is hard to speak and not less hard to think about the mysteries which the Church keeps in the hidden depths of her inner consciousness. Here every uttered word can seem crude, every attempt at formulation can seem sacrilegious. The authors of the apocryphal writings often alluded imprudently to mysteries about which the Church had maintained a prudent silence by economy towards those on the outside. The Mother of God was never a theme of the public preaching of the apostles. While Christ was preached on the housetops and proclaimed for all to know in a catechesis addressed to the whole universe, the mystery of the Mother of God was revealed only to those within the Church, to the faithful who had received the message and were pressing towards "the upward call of God in Christ Jesus" (Philippians 3:14). More than an object of faith, this mystery is a foundation of our hope, a fruit of faith, ripened in Tradition.

Let us therefore keep silence, and let us not try to dogmatize about the supreme glory of the Mother of God. Let us not be too loquacious, like the Gnostics who, wanting to say far more than was needful and indeed more than they were able, mingled their heretical tares with the pure wheat of Christian Tradition. Let us rather listen to St. Basil, who described that which pertains to Tradition as "an unpublishable and ineffable teaching, which was preserved by our fathers in silence, so as to be inaccessible to all curiosity and indiscretion, for they had been healthily instructed how to protect, by silence, the holiness of the mystery. It would not be proper to publish in writing the teaching given about things which ought not to be seen by the eyes of the uninitiated. Apart from that, the reason for an unwritten tradition is that many people who often inspect what is contained in these teachings are in danger of losing their veneration for the things concerned by becoming used to them. For teaching is one thing and preaching is yet another. Teachings are to be kept in silence; preaching is to be made manifest. A certain obscurity in the language which the Scriptures sometimes use is another way of keeping silence; thus the meaning of the teachings is made harder to understand, for the greater benefit of those who read them."[5]

If the teaching about the Mother of God belongs to Tradition, it is only through our experience of life in the Church that we can adhere to the unlimited devotion which the Church offers to the Mother of God; and the degree of our adherence to this devotion will be the measure of the extent to which we belong to the Body of Christ.

---

[5]*De spiritu sancto* 27; P.G. 32, col. 189.

12

Dominion And Kingship: An Eschatological Study

To speak about last things (or, as people express it nowadays, to deal with eschatological problems) is to enter a field where we constantly see our methods of theological research reduced to inadequacy by the multitude of aspects which must be grasped simultaneously—mobile intersecting planes which cannot be halted and held stationary in the mind without falsifying them. It must be remembered that even the sciences which deal with material reality, the so-called exact sciences, find themselves compelled in our days to have recourse to the idea of complementarity, and sometimes uphold two contrary theories without attempting to reconcile them, in order to do justice to all the complexity of such a phenomenon as light. How much more true this must be of the reality of which we are told "no eye has seen, nor ear heard, nor the heart of man conceived, what God has prepared for those who love him" (Isaiah 64:4; I Cor. 2:9). In order to avoid the twofold danger—of being too explicit, or of giving too great a share to the "inexpressible"

mystery—I shall permit myself to enter upon the eschatological theme itself only towards the end of my paper, at
the end of an indirect route which should show us in what
sense a Christian theologian may speak of the *"fulfilment* of
God's dominion."

2

We need first of all to examine the terms which we are
using here, in speaking of God's "dominion" and of its
"fulfilment." Dominion is a relative concept implying, as its
counterpart, submission to some dominant thing or person.
But to speak of submission means necessarily to admit a
possibility of "insubmissiveness" and rebellion against the
dominion which is exerted. Only that which offers or is
capable of offering resistance is dominated. The God of
Aristotle is not lord over his eternal world: he is only the
unconditioned first condition for the necessary operation of
the machine of the universe, from which all contingency is
excluded. Aristotle would have been astounded indeed if
anyone had sought to give his God—the first unmoved
Mover, the Thought which thinks itself—the name of
Κύριος, Lord.

Now, the God of the Bible is the Lord, the Lord of the
celestial hosts, of all spirits and of all flesh. His dominion
is "from generation to generation"; it is exerted "in every
place." Although it is impossible to escape from this universal
dominion (which is made all the more absolute by the fact
that the God of the Jews and Christians is the *Creator* of all
things), one can, nevertheless, *resist* it; and the uttered curses
of a man seeking to reach God in order to contend with
Him face to face are not, in the Bible, what they are in
ancient tragedy: the desperate outcry of a liberty falling back
on itself and recognizing its absurd and illusory quality
in face of a Destiny equally inexorable for gods and mortals.
We see, indeed, that God justifies Job, who contended
with him, while his wrath is kindled against Eliphaz and his
friends, who have spoken in favor of the irresistible and

necessary absolutism of his dominion: "You have not spoken of me what is right, as my servant Job has" (Job 42:7). For Job's protest, his refusal to accept a dominion which allowed of no dialogue between God and man, was a negative witness to the true nature of God's dominion. Job's complaint is a praise which exalts God higher, which enters more profoundly into His mystery, by refusing to halt at the abstract idea of His dominion which others make for themselves. This is a theology which aims higher than all clumsy theodicies, of which the speeches of Job's comforters are the prototype. While it is true that the absolute dominion of God is attested by many passages of the Old Testament, yet the Book of Job compels us to see in it something more than the anthropomorphic expression of a divine determinism.

It is true that in extension the dominion of the Creator includes all that exists, and even, according to St. Paul, reaches beyond existence, as a necessity to exist because of the creative word by which everything is maintained in being and can no more return into non-existence. Nevertheless this dominion, in its intensive aspect, is never uniform and invariable, but changing and dynamic. God the Lord who governs the world which he has created out of nothing is not a faceless Necessity: contingency is implied in the very act of creation; for what is *creation* in the absolute sense, creation out of nothing, but the production of new being, unconstrained by any external condition or internal necessity? God *willed* to be the Creator, and the contingency of his will confers a contingent aspect on his work, which cannot be reduced to the categories of a deterministic cosmology of perpetual recurrence. This contingent aspect, which excludes universal necessitarianism, culminates in the creation of angelic and human persons, endowed with self-determining freedom, with the αὐτεξούσιον in which the Fathers of the Church saw the primordial characteristic of a being created in the image of God. Hence the theo-cosmic relationship, God's dominion over the totality of his creation, presupposes the establishment of a personal bond between the Lord of heaven and earth and the created persons of the heavenly and earthly cosmos, angels and men, whose free submission to the will of God will be an everlasting praise of the Creator's almighty power.

If the God of the philosophers and the learned is only a First Necessity who ordains the chain of cause and effect and corrects automatically every chance deviation which introduces itself, taking no more notice of human freedom than of a grinding noise in the machinery, the God of the Bible reveals Himself by His very wrath as He who undertook the risk of creating a universe whose perfection is continually jeopardized by the freedom of those in whom that perfection ought to reach its highest level. This divine risk, inherent in the decision to create beings in the image and likeness of God, is the summit of almighty power, or rather a surpassing of that summit in voluntarily undertaken powerlessness. For "the weakness of God is stronger than men" (I Cor. 1:25): it surpasses to an infinite degree all the attributes of majesty and dominion which the theologians enumerate in their treatises *De deo uno.* This category of divine risk, which is proper to a personal God freely creating personal beings endowed with freedom, is foreign to all abstract conceptions of the divine dominion—to the rationalist theology which thinks it exalts the omnipotence of the living God in attributing to him the perfections of a lifeless God who is *incapable* of being subject to risk. But he who takes no risks does not love: the God of the theology manuals can love only himself, and it is his own perfection which he loves even in his creatures. He does not love any *person:* for personal love is love for another than oneself. Now the jealous God of the Bible is not "the cruel God of the Jews," greedy of His own glory, but a God whose love for His elect is "strong as death," whose jealousy against everything which separates His creature from Him is "cruel as the grave." God's dominion must be thought of in these terms of God's personal love which exacts from the freedom of His creatures a total conversion towards Him, a freely accomplished union. But a claim as absolute as this, addressed to the liberty of the person loved, would not be the claim of perfect love if it were not a desire for the realization in the beloved of absolute fulfilment, wished for by the beloved and accomplished with the cooperation of his own will.

3

If this is so, the dominion of God over the world which He has created is all the greater, inasmuch as it is less like dominion in the sense which we habitually give to the word— the sense of external constraint exerted upon the will of another. Hence the final fulfilment of the dominion of God (at its never-attained, but infinitely approachable limit) will be equivalent to the swallowing-up of all dominion in union between him who governs and his subjects. "God shall be all in all," or (looking at it the other way around) created beings will become by grace what God is by nature, to cite the bold saying of St. Maximus. This is the dialectic of the dominion of God in Trinity of Persons, transcendent in His unknowable nature, immanent in His love. He willed to create a world whose supreme perfection could not be attained without involving the will of the Creator in a gamble of love, going even to the "foolishness of the Cross." "For God so loved the world that he gave his only Son" (John 3:16).

Since the fulfilment of God's dominion coincides with the final deification of created being, and since this ultimate vocation of the creation cannot be realized automatically, without the free cooperation of the person, both in angels and men, it is necessary for each stage of the way which leads to this end to include an agreement of the two wills: the will of God and the will of creatures. From the time of the First Adam's sin, which rendered man (and through him the whole of the earthly cosmos) incapable of progress in the way of his vocation, until the moment when Christ "the last Adam" (ὁ ἔσχατος Ἀδάμ, I Cor. 15:45) "will recapitulate" (according to St. Irenaeus) fallen humanity— the harmony of the two wills can be only external. The successive covenants of the Old Testament are precisely of this

kind: that made with Noah, with Abraham, and finally with
Moses, imposing God's dominion as *Law* on the people whom
He had chosen for Himself to realize the redemptive work
which He alone could accomplish. The Law which con-
victed man of sin, making sin "exceeding sinful" according
to St. Paul, manifested the slavery of man to a dominion
other than that of God. This is a "third will," to which the
First Adam submitted himself freely, seduced by the promise
of a false deification outside the love of God. Along with this
perverse will of a spiritual power at enmity with God, the
dominion of sin and death entered the world, through man's
sin. The Law of Moses, given by the mediation of angels
(Gal. 3:19) showed to those who received it the helplessness
of man in face of the "law of sin" through which is exerted
the dominion of the angels of Satan, now prince of this
world. Harmony with the will of God is henceforth expressed
by confession of sin, by recognition that it is impossible to
be saved from the present situation except by God's own
intervention, and finally by faith in the Promise which
accompanies the Law, the Promise without which the Law
could not be an expression of the divine economy, a "school-
master to bring us unto Christ" (Gal. 3:24).

                                4

   "Why then the law? It was added because of transgres-
sions, till the offspring should come to whom the promise
had been made: and it was ordained (διαταγείς) by angels"
(Gal. 3:19). There is a close connection between the dominion of the Law and the law of sin and death, between the
revealed Law and the law of sin which it makes manifest,
between the legal order imposed by the agency of the angels
of the Lord and the power exerted over the world since
the Fall by the angels of Satan. There is no difficulty at all
in recognizing that the divine Law is proper to the catas-
trophic state of created being in subjection to the law of sin
and death. But we must also distinguish, in this miserable
state imposed on the earthly creation by the sin of man, in

that very law which St. Paul calls the "law of sin and death," the existence of an infallible order by means of which the dominion of God rules amid the disorders of the fallen world, preserving it from total destruction, setting bounds to the dominion of the powers of darkness. And there is more: even the dominion of the rebellious Angel over the fallen creature is not outside the scope of the will of God, who gives this captivity a certain legal character. God is sole Lord, and the spirits in revolt against him could not exercise their usurped dominion if in the last resort they did not remain subject, despite themselves, to his unique dominion. Though wishing to frustrate God's plan, the evil one finds himself finally compelled to serve it. Here the prophetic analogies about the captivity of Israel receive their full meaning: they are not concerned only with Babylon and all the Satanic powers which have ever persecuted the Church of God in the course of her history, but, at a deeper, metahistorical level, with Satan himself and the power which he has been able to wield over man and the terrestrial cosmos since the sin of Adam.

5

Here again the Book of Job shows us the problem of evil in true perspective—or, rather, the part played by the Evil One in the history of the struggle for universal sanctification. St. Gregory the Great, commenting on the "heavenly prologue" of the Book of Job which Goethe was to imitate twelve centuries later in *Faust,* remarks that Satan the Accuser, wishing to tempt the just man, has to apply to the Lord to "stretch forth his hand." "It is noteworthy," says St. Gregory, "that he does not claim for himself the power to strike, he who never fails to proclaim his presumption against the Author of all things. The devil knows that by himself he is able to do nothing, for he does not even exist by himself as a spirit. *Sciendum vero est, quia Satanae voluntas semper iniqua est, sed numquam potestas iniusta: quia a semetipso voluntaltem habet, sed a Domino potestatem*—It must be known that the will of Satan is always evil, but his power is never unrighteous: for his will comes from himself, but his power from God. That which he wills to do in his malice, God in His righteousness allows him to accomplish." The holy pope concludes: "We must not fear him who can do nothing without permission. That Power alone is to be feared who, by allowing the Enemy to be unleashed, makes his unrighteous will serve for the execution of righteous judgments" (*Moralia* II, 16-17).

The divine economy makes use of the rebel will to fulfil the design of the Creator, in spite of all the obstacles set up by human or angelic free will. If this is so, God's design, which is fixed as to the end in view (the deification of all created beings), must be likened, as to its execution, to a strategy of ever-changing tactics, infinitely rich in possibilities, to a multiform (πολυποίκιλος) Wisdom of God in action. But it is not so for the rationalist theologians. The devitalized theology of the Christian descendants of Job's comforters has accustomed us to think of the divine plan *sub specie aeternitatis,* lending to the eternal Will of God the only characteristic of eternity which they know: that of necessary and immutable preordinations, in the likeness of the miserable fixed eternity which is usually attributed to the truths of mathematics.

This is to falsify Biblical anthropomorphism, with its wealth of teaching, and replace it by what I might dare to call the poor abstract anthropomorphism of a reasonable animal turned theologian. For this class of theologians the phrases of St. Gregory the Great (not to mention, of course, those of the Scriptures, which are always scandalous) may appear too daring, and the thought of the dominion of God being exerted upon the fallen creation through the dominion of the prince of this world—blasphemous. In order to save the reputation of a Father of the Church, efforts will be made to include the devil's part within the predetermined divine plan, avoiding in this way the difficulties which "contingent futures" might introduce into a program fixed once and for all. Certainly, this safeguards the tranquil existence of God and the intellectual comfort of the theologian, but "the seriousness of God's love" on which Romano Guardini has insisted of late, has no meaning in relation to this God of the theologians, made in the image of the God of the philosophers and learned men of this world. This God is perhaps very close to him whom the young Augustine thought he found in the books of the Neoplatonists: an almighty God, who cannot, however, be really involved in the history and salvation of his creation—to the point of becoming man to undergo death—without losing his right to the perfections proper to the Deity. This is certainly not the God of the Scriptures, the Church Fathers, and St. Augustine himself. It is the God of Job's friends, weighing down his creation with a dominion which has the deathly character of necessary, inexorable law, administered by a judge from whom there is no appeal. Job protested against this false image of the true God, against the caricature of His royal person, distorted by the dominion of the prince of this world —a caricature in which the just man refused to recognize the face of the Lord whom he sought.

It is remarkable that God's reply to the "words without knowledge," spoken by Job, ends with the description of Behemoth, who is called "the first of the works of God" (40:19) and of Leviathan, "king over all the sons of pride" (41:34). These monstrous animals, whose mighty strength can only be controlled by Him who created them, are not merely zoological curiosities from the Hebrew bestiaries. For a Christian who wishes to see in the sacred texts something more than a record of Jewish folklore, and who refuses to reduce theological knowledge to the level of a positivist science of "de-mythologizing" (*Entmythologisierung*), these monstrous beings which God shows to Job represent the "sub-celestial" (ἐπουράνιος) power of the Angels (κοσμο-κράτορες—Eph. 6:12) which have become spirits of darkness by their rebellion against God. Denouncing their dominion,' to which man has voluntarily subjected himself, God suggests that Job might break Satan's pride, binding Leviathan to be a plaything for his maidens (41:5). Only then will God recognize that man can accomplish his salvation in his own power (40:14). The magnitude of Satan's spiritual power, shown to Job, demonstrates the vastness of the cosmic catastrophe brought about by man's sin, the blindness and helplessness of his perverted freedom. All this is to show the beneficent character of the law of mortal existence, which rules by necessity over the new state established by God's will for His creation, enslaved by sin. The repentance of Job (whose "words without knowledge" had "darkened counsel") consists in recognizing, besides the necessary and ineluctable character of the dominion which he had refused to accept, the contingency of the divine economy, which always directs the terrestrial world towards the realization of its supreme vocation, that realization in which fallen man has become incapable of cooperating.

Job's attitude in accusing God is opposite to that of his friends, who, in assuming the hypocritical role of defenders of God, defended, without knowing it, Satan's right to an unlimited dominion. Like most defenders of the *status quo,* in wishing to justify the legitimate character of the present condition of humanity, they gave an absolute value to the legal situation, projecting it on to the very nature of God. In this wrong perspective, the different levels of human, demonic, angelic, and divine reality, bound up in the complex and shifting economy of salvation, are telescoped together, welded together and crystallized in a single vision of a God-Necessity, comparable to the inexorable and impersonal Fate ('Aνάγκη) of Greek paganism. They speak solely of the God of the Law, but not of the God of the Promise; God dominates their creation but does not become involved in it, does not run the risk of being frustrated in His love. This God is only a dictator, not a King. But Job aimed higher than his friends, for he believed the Promise, without which the Law would have been a monstrous absurdity and the God of the Old Testament could not have been the God of Christians. That is why the Book of Job is the first of the books of the Old Testament, in the traditional order, to open up the eschatological horizon, by placing the dominion of God and the condition of man in their true perspective—something which we must take into account in speaking of the fulfilment of the dominion.

6

The New Testament speaks much of the Kingdom (Βα-σιλεία), but scarcely ever uses the terms "dominion" (κυ-ριότης) or "to dominate or govern" (κυριεύειν) in connection with God. This corresponds to the radical change in the condition of man after the messianic Promise, after the enthronement of Christ. Those who have acknowledged their King know him otherwise than by the actions of a dominion imposed from outside. Satraps govern, the King reigns. His royal character does not depend on the acts of government which he does or does not perform; even when he mounts the scaffold to be put to death by his subjects, he remains King. The divine Kingship is revealed in an unexpected manner, equally astonishing both to men and angels, in the person of the Son of God, come to earth to undergo death upon the cross. "I call him King," says St. John Chrysostom, "because I see him crucified; it is proper to a king to die for his subjects." But Christ rises again, ascends to heaven and sits at the right hand of the Father, exalting the human nature which he has taken "far above all rule and authority and power and dominion" (Eph. 1:21). These four names of the celestial hierarchies, chosen by St. Paul to make clear the overthrow of the cosmic order, all express the idea of dominion. The exterior aspect of the Kingship of God is thus transcended; the relation established between the heavenly Head of the Church and His earthly members transcends the category of dominion. This new situation is seen in the cosmic order in the "spoiling of the Powers" by Christ, the God-Man. "He disarmed the principalities and powers and made a public example of them, triumphing over them in him" (Col. 2:15). Not only are the powers of darkness dispossessed by Redemption (Col. 1:13), Satan no longer having power over the sons of the Kingdom, but also the angels, establishers and guardians of the legal order, no longer have the same role to play after the abolition of the law and the change in the condition of man. Indeed, all that is dominion halts at the threshold of the Church, the new reality which appears in the world after the Ascension of Christ and the Descent of the Holy Spirit. The sons of the Church are out of reach of the flaming sword of the Angel who closes the gate of paradise to the descendants of the First Adam.

But to the eyes of the outside world nothing has changed, and those whom St. Peter calls "scoffers" can still ask, "Where is the promise of his coming? For ever since the fathers fell asleep all things continue as they were from the beginning of the creation" (II Peter 3:3-4). We still keep the "coats of skins" with which God clothed Adam and Eve when they were driven out of paradise—this biological condition, subject to the necessity of death, which has become a new law of the existence of the earthly creation, through the sin of man. The demonic will continues to be active in the world, not only in the children of this age who persecute and seek to dominate the Church, but also in the children of the Kingdom, creating discord in the heart of the Church itself, where some wish to dominate, and others oppose to them a revolutionary will to schism. What the irreligious and cynical pagan poet Lucian said of the pagan priests, what Lucretius said of the Roman augurs, often unhappily applies to the Christian clergy. Nothing changes; and the eternal recurrence, the wearisome repetition which the Preacher calls "vanity," continues to govern us, as a necessary and all-powerful law of existence. "Where is the promise of his coming?"

It is not at all surprising that the Jews who still await the promise, not having recognized the Messiah in the "Man of Sorrows," should reason thus. It is only too natural that the new pagans, who expect nothing from beyond this life, should want the history of the world to be subject to the law of a rigorous dialectic. But when this way of looking at the universe, the only one accessible to "those outside," whether religious or atheistic, affects Christians also, and even determines their theological concepts, this proves that the realization of the Promise has not been recognized by all believers. For some, the Christ of the Gospel remains Jesus of Nazareth, and cannot be seen by our faith as Son of the living God except "on the eschatological plane."

I cite this one extreme example of the false type of eschatology, the enemy of all theological thought, to show just how far defeatism can go among Christians. But abstract eschatology can take many forms; it is to be met to some extent everywhere, if not in theory at least in practice. We must notice that the eschatology fashionable today in no way resembles the waiting for the immanent return of Christ which impelled the apostles and their disciples to proclaim to Jews and Gentiles the overthrow of the cosmic order, brought about by Christ in his victory over death and sin. Neither does it resemble that theology oriented towards the End with which the Fathers of the Church took triumphant possession of all the seeds of truth scattered through human thought, in order to make them all grow up into the fulness of Christ (Eph. 4:15). On the contrary, this false eschatology has nothing dynamic about it; it consists of erecting eschatology into an epistemological category, which allows us quietly to continue our earthly activities without concerning ourselves about what belongs to "another plane." Theological difficulties? Heresies? Divisions among Christians? All will be resolved in the eschatological order; or, rather, all has already been resolved in the Kantian other-world of an eschatology which is—and never will be—Parousia, that is to say Presence.

7

We are here faced with the same error of telescoping together different levels which we observed in Job's friends. There it was a question of many planes of legal dominion being fused together and projected on to God. Here it is the eschatological Promise—realized and still being realized on different levels—which is telescoped by a false vision, without any perspectives. Job's comforters failed to perceive the risk involved in the love of a God who engages Himself fully in the economy of the salvation of His creatures. The Christian descendants of these reasonable theologians have aggravated the error of their fathers, for they have misunderstood the eschatological involvement of man, replacing it by an abstract faith, which is unable to move the mountains of demonic domination, because the devils also know this kind of faith.

Eschatology becomes present at the moment when man becomes capable of cooperating in the divine plan. The realization of the eschatological Promise begins at the point at which the economy of salvation is fulfilled—after the death, resurrection, and ascension of Christ. In the historical order, human fulfilment follows upon divine fulfilment. The eschatologies of the Prophets took in at a single glance the messianic promise of redemption, the outpouring of the Holy Spirit, the Last Judgment, and the transfiguration of the cosmos. It was only ten days after the Ascension of the Lord that the eschatological era began with the descent of the Holy Spirit, "the Promise of the Father" (Acts 1:4-5), the fire which Christ had come to throw upon the earth (Luke 12:49). Eschatology can only "begin" at the end. But this end is not a static terminus, a limit; it is the continually renewed beginning of an infinite way of deifying union, in which the dominion of God and the vocation of creation is fulfilled. This realization of the last end, by the grace of the Holy Spirit and by human freedom, is the inner mystery of the Church, a mystery which is accomplished with the angels as wondering witnesses, but which remains impenetrable to those outside—to the devils, to the children of this age, and to ourselves when we philosophize "according to the elemental spirits of the universe, and not according to Christ" (Col. 2:8). This mystery of the final vocation is already realized in one human person—Mary the Mother of God: She who gave human life to the Son of God has received from her Son the fulness of the Divine Life. The mystery of deification which is being fulfilled in the Church is eschatology at work, the hidden but entirely new center which is shaping the whole history of the world.

But we ought to speak of many centers, for the final vocation is worked out, in differing measure, in each Christian person—in each created hypostasis of the terrestrial universe which works its way with effort towards its deification by grace. St. Paul tells us that the creation awaits with impatience the revelation of the sons of God, which will set it free from the bondage of corruption, from the fixed law of birth and death, from the round of seasons, and the repeated cycles of existence. For the whole of terrestrial nature, of creation dependent on man, did not submit voluntarily to this universal necessity which Ecclesiastes and St. Paul call "vanity." The terrestrial universe, which was corrupted by man's sin, must also participate in the liberty of the glory of the sons of God (Rom. 8:19-22). When the cyclical law of repetition suddenly stops its rotating movement, creation, freed from vanity, will not be absorbed into the impersonal Absolute of a Nirvana but will see the beginning of an eternal springtime, in which all the forces of life, triumphant over death, will come to the fulness of their unfolding, since God will be the only principle of life in all things. Then the deified will shine like stars around the only Star, Christ, with whom they will reign in the same glory of the Holy Trinity, communicated to each without measure by the Holy Spirit.

But we still groan with the whole of earthly creation, awaiting "the resurrection of the dead and the life of the age to come." The victory of Christ and the changing of the cosmic order is not a reestablishment of the primordial condition before Adam's sin. For the final end is not the earthly paradise, but a new heaven and a new earth. The eschatological condition is a new departure, beginning with the New Adam, towards an end which is always new; but this new way opens in the conditions of the old world which is falling into decay, in the flesh of the "Old Adam" which is frail and subject to death, in spite of the uncreated grace which dwells in it. We have received the royal unction of the Holy Spirit, but we do not yet reign with Christ. Like the young David, who after his anointing by Samuel had to endure Saul's hatred before he obtained his kingdom, we must resist the armies of Satan, who like Saul is dispossessed but still remains "the prince of this world."

Christ, the Head of the Church, is enthroned on the right hand of his Father until his enemies are put under his feet (Ps. 109:1). The war which we must wage here below

under his command for the Kingdom which is not of this
world, cannot be undertaken except with the arms of Christ;
for "we are not contending against flesh and blood" but
against the "spiritual hosts of wickedness in the heavenly
places" (Eph. 6:12). This struggle which began in the
spiritual spheres of the angelic heavens is continued in the
earthly cosmos, and in the struggle human freedom is at
stake. The spiritual level where this war for the inheritance
of the sons of God is waged is more profound than any
of the superficial layers of reality which are accessible to
analysis by the human sciences. None of the sciences—not
psychology, nor sociology, nor economics, nor the political
sciences—can detect the true origin of the different evils
which they observe and attempt to define, in their efforts to
exorcise them or at least to restrict the damage they do.
Even philosophy, though it speaks of the human spirit and
uses the terms "person" and "nature," cannot reach the level
at which the problem of human destiny is posed. The terms
which it uses are, for the most part, the result of the
decadence and secularization of theological ideas. Philosophy
is never eschatological: its speculation never goes to the
furthest extremes, it inevitably transposes into ontology
truths which are metaontological. Its field of vision remains
on this side of the two abysses which theology alone can
name, with fear and trembling: the uncreated abyss of the
Life of the Trinity and the abyss of hell which opens within
the freedom of created persons.

8

We know that the gates of hell shall never prevail against
the Church, and that hell's power, shattered by Christ,
remains unreal so long as our will does not make common
cause with that of the enemy of our final vocation. The
Church strives only for the realization of this final goal set
before all creation. All other conflicts in which we are obliged
to take part in this world are restricted to the interests of a
group, a party, a country, a human ideology: they inevitably

exclude and sacrifice our enemies. Here, however, no one is excluded or sacrificed: even when the Church takes action against men, it is still for the salvation of these men that she continues to strive.

This is the guiding principle of her struggle, and its field extends ever wider as our eschatological involvement becomes more intense. But what is this intense involvement if not sanctity realized? It is said that St. Isaac the Syrian prayed not only for the enemies of Truth but also for the devils. This is only possible at a spiritual height where man already participates in the secret of the divine Counsel. In spite of some allusions in St. Paul, the question of angelic eschatology remains inaccessible to our theology, in proportion to the degree of our spiritual elevation. To raise the question of the salvation of the angels is to enter a field where inevitably in one direction or another we should produce heresies by wanting to make hasty theological syntheses. We must not forget, however, that the fulfilment of God's dominion, which is also the final sanctification of the whole creation, is realized on several planes which we can only partly apprehend. The fulfilment of our final vocation is related first of all to the destiny of the terrestrial cosmos of which men are the created hypostases, created in the image of God. On this level, which is the level of the Church's theology, Satan is the sole enemy, against whom the Church will have to struggle until the end of time. We know that this conflict will be ended by the Advent of Christ, when all his enemies will be put under his feet, and that the final Judgment will take place before "the kingdom of the world has become the Kingdom of our Lord and of his Christ" (Rev. 11:15). But let us not forget, in the presence of the awesome countenance of Christ the Judge, that the supreme prerogative of a King is mercy.

Bibliography of Writings of Vladimir N. Lossky (1903-1958)

BOOKS

Spor o Sofii [The Controversy about Sophia] (in Russian), Paris: Confrèrie de Saint Photios, 1936

Essai sur la Théologie mystique de l'Eglise d'Orient, Paris: Aubier, 1944. English translation by members of the Fellowship of St. Alban and St. Sergius: *The Mystical Theology of the Eastern Church*, Naperville, Illinois: Alec R. Allenson, Inc., 1957, and London: James Clark and Co., Ltd., 1957. German translation by Mirjam Prager: *Die mystische Theologie der morgenländischen Kirche*, Graz: Verlag Styria, 1961. Russian translation in *Bogoslovskie Trudy* 8 (1972), 7-128.

Der Sinn der Ikonen (in collaboration with L. Ouspensky), Bern und Olten: Urs Graf-Verlag, 1952. English translation by G. E. H. Palmer and E. Kadloubovsky: *The Meaning of Icons*, Boston: Boston Book & Art Shop, Inc., 1952. [Individual essays from this monumental work have been reprinted in a great number of periodicals, especially in French in *Messager* and in Russian and English in *Zhurnal Moskovskoy Patriarkhii* (hereafter cited as *ZhMP*) and *Journal of the Moscow Patriarchate* (hereafter *JMP*). No attempt has been made to trace and identify each reprinting.]

Théologie négative et connaissance de Dieu chez Maitre Eckhart, Paris: J. Vrin, 1960.

Vision de Dieu, Paris: Editions Delachaux et Niestle, 1962. English translation by Asheleigh Moorhouse, with a preface by John Meyendorff: *The Vision of God*, Clayton, Wisconsin: American Orthodox Press, 1963, and London: The Faith Press, 1963. German translation by Brigitte Hirsch: *Schau Gottes*, Zurich: EVS Verlag, 1964. Russian translation of chapter 8 in *Messager de l'Exarchat du Patriarche russe en Europe occidentale* 61 (1968), 57-68; chapter 9 in *Messager* 62-63 (1968), 151-163; both reprinted in *Bogoslovskie Trudy* 8 (1972), 187-203.

A l'Image et à la Ressemblance de Dieu, Paris: Aubier-Montaigne, 1967. English translation, this volume.

Sept Jours sur les Routes de France, unedited manuscript.

Cours d'Histoire du Dogme, unedited manuscript.

ESSAYS

"Otritsatel'noe bogoslovie v uchenii Dionisiya Areopagita" [Negative Theology in the Teaching of Dionysius the Areopagite], *Seminarium Kondakovianum* 3 (1929), 133-144.

"La Notion des 'Analogies' chez Denys le pseudo-Aréopagite," *Archives d'histoire doctrinale et littéraire du Moyen-Age* 5 (1931), 279-309.

"Les dogmes et les conditions de la vraie connaissance," *Bulletin de la Confrérie de St. Photius le Confesseur* 1 (1934), 2-9.

'Pis'mo V. Losskago N. A. Berdyaevu" [An Open Letter to Nicolas A. Berdyaev], *Put'* 50 (1936), 27-32.

"La théologie négative dans la doctrine de Denys l'Aréopagite," *Revue des sciences philosophiques et théologiques* 28 (1939), 204-221.

"Etude sur la terminologie de saint Bernard," *Archivum Latinitatis Medii Aevi (Bulletin du Cange)* 17 (1942), 79-96.

"La Théologie de la Lumière chez saint Grégoire de Thessalonique," *Dieu Vivant* 1 (1945), 94-118. Reprinted in *A l'Image...*pp. 39-65. Russian translation (I) *ZhMP* 3 (1967), 76-77; (II-VII) *ZhMP* (1967), 49-62. English translation by T. E. Bird in this volume.

"Otkrytoe pis'mo Sobraniyu predstaviteley russkikh tserkvey v Zapadnoy Evrope" [An Open Letter to the Meeting of Representatives of the Russian Churches in Western Europe], *Sovetsky Patriot* 103 (Oct. 11, 1946), 3 [Signed by Vladimir Lossky and F. T. P'yanov].

"Redemption and Deification," English translation by E. Every in *Sobornost* 12 (Winter 1947), 47-56, and in this volume. Russian translation in *ZhMP* 9 (1967), 65-72. French translation in *Messager* 15 (1953), 161-170. Reprinted in *A l'Image...*pp. 95-108.

"Lichnost' i mysl' svyateyshego patriarkha Sergiya" [The Personality and Thought of His Holiness Patriarch Sergius], *Dukhovnoe nasledstvo Patriarkha Sergiya,* Moscow: The Moscow Patriarchate, 1947, pp. 263-270. English translation by T. E. Bird in *Diakonia* 5 (1971), 163-171.

"La Procession du Saint-Esprit dans la doctrine trinitaire orthodoxe," Paris: Editions Setor, 1948. English translation by E. Every in *The Eastern Churches Quarterly* 7 [supplementary issue] (1948), 31-53, and in this volume. French version reprinted in *A l'Image...*pp. 67-93 and in *JMP* 9 (1973), 54-58, and 10 (1973), 70-78. Russian translation in *Messager* 25 (1957), 54-62.

'The Byzantine Patriarchate," *Sobornost* 3 (Summer 1948), 108-112.

"Du troisième Attribut de l'Eglise," *Dieu Vivant* 10 (1948), 78-89. Reprinted in *Messager* 2-3 (1950), 58-67, and in *A l'Image*...pp. 167-179. English translation by Austin Oakley, "Concerning the Third Mark of the Church: Catholicity," in *The Christian East* 1 [New Series] (1951), 142-149, and in this volume. Reprinted in *One Church* 19 (1965), 181-197.

"Panagia," English translation by E. Every in *The Mother of God: A Symposium*, ed. E. L. Mascall, London: Dacre Press, 1949, pp. 24-36, and in this volume. French translation in *A l'Image*...pp. 193-207. Russian translation in *ZhMP* 1 (1968), 65-73; reprinted in *Cerkiewny Wiestnik* [Warsaw] 11 (1973), 8-12.

"Soblazni tserkovnogo soznaniya" [The Temptations of Ecclesial Awareness], *Messager* 1 (1950), 16-21. French translation in *Messager* 1 (1950), 21-28. English translation by T. E. Bird in a forthcoming issue of *Sobornost*.

"Existence and Analogy," *Sobornost* 7 (Summer 1950), 295-297.

"Tradition and Traditions," English translation by G. E. H. Palmer and E. Kadloubovsky in *The Meaning of Icons*, Boston: Boston Book & Art Shop, Inc., 1952, pp. 13-24, and in this volume. German translation in *Der Sinn der Ikonen*, 1952. French translation in *Messager* 30-31 (1959), 101-121, and in *A l'Image*...pp. 139-166. Rumanian translation in *Studii Teologice* 7-8 (1970), 585-598.

"Explanation of the Main Types of Icons," English translation by G. E. H. Palmer and E. Kadloubovsky: *The Meaning of Icons*, pp. 69-216, *passim*.

"'Ténèbre' et 'Lumière' dans la connaissance de Dieu," *Ordre, Désordre, Lumière*, Paris: J. Vrin, 1952, pp. 133-143. English translation by E. Every: "Darkness and Light in the Knowledge of God," in *The Eastern Churches Quarterly* 8 (Winter 1950), 460-471, and in this volume. French translation in *A l'Image*...pp. 25-37. Russian translation in *ZhMP* 9 (1968), 61-67.

"Dominion and Kingship: An Eschatological Study," English translation by A. M. Allchin in *Sobornost* 14 (Winter 1953), 67-69, and in this volume. French translation in *Messager* 17 (1954), 43-55, and in *A l'Image*... pp. 209-225. Russian translation in *Bogoslovskie Trudy* 8 (1972), 205-214.

"L'Apophase et la théologie trinitaire," Collège philosophique. Paris: Centre de Documentation Universitaire, n.d. [1953]. Reprinted in *A l'Image*... English translation by T. E. Bird, in this volume.

"Les éléments de 'Théologie négative' dans la pensée de saint Augustin," *Augustinus Magister* I, Paris: Editions des Etudes Augustiniennes, 1954, pp. 575-581. English translation by T. E. Bird in a forthcoming issue of *St. Vladimir's Theological Quarterly*.

"La dogme de l'Immaculée Conception," and "Lourdes," *Messager* 20 (1954), 246-251. Russian summary *ZhMP* 5 (1955) 78-79. English translation by T. E. Bird in *One Church* 6 (Nov.-Dec. 1971), 277-281.

"La notion théologique de la personne humaine," *Messager* 24 (1955), 227-235. Reprinted in *A l'Image*...pp. 109-121. English translation by T. E. Bird in this volume.

"Le Problème de la 'Vision face a face' et la Tradition patristique de

Byzance," *Studia Patristica,* ed. Kurt Aland and F. L. Cross, Berlin: Akademie Verlag, 1957, 2, Band 64, pp. 512-537. English translation by T. E. Bird in *Greek Orthodox Theological Review* 2 (Fall 1972), 231-254.

The Theology of the Image," English translation by Joan Ford in *Sobornost* 22 (Winter 1957-1958), 510-520, and in this volume. French translation in *Messager* 30-31 (1959), 123-133, and in *A l'Image...*pp. 123-137.

"Obraz i podobie" [Image and Likeness], *ZhMP* 3 (1958), 53-64.

"Foi et théologie," *Contacts* 13 (1961), 163-176.

"Les Startsy d'Optino," *Contacts* 33 (1961), 4-14.

"Le Starets Leonide," *Contacts* 34 (1961), 99-107.

"Le Starets Macaire," *Contacts* 37 (1962), 9-19.

"Notes sur le 'Credo' de la Messe," *Contacts* 38-39 (1962), 84-86, 88-90.

"Le Starets Ambroise," *Contacts* 40 (1962), 219-236.

"La conscience catholique: Implications anthropologiques du dogme de l'Eglise," *Contacts* 42 (1963), 76-88. Reprinted in *A l'Image...*pp. 181-192. Russian translation in *ZhMP* 10 (1969), 74-80. English translation by T. E. Bird in *St. Vladimir's Theological Quarterly* 14 (1970), 187-195, and in this volume.

"Théologie dogmatique," *Messager* 46-47 (1964), 85-108; 48 (1964), 218-233; 49 (1965), 24-35; 50 (1965), 83-101. Russian translation in *Bogoslovskie Trudy* 8 (1972), 131-183.